Religion, Gender, and Industry
Exploring Church and Methodism in a Local Setting

Edited by
Geordan Hammond
Peter S. Forsaith

Foreword by
D. Bruce Hindmarsh

©

James Clarke & Co.

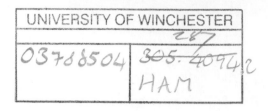
James Clarke & Co.

P.O. Box 60

Cambridge

CB1 2NT

www.jamesclarke.co

publishing@jamesclarke.co

ISBN: 978 0 227 17387 9

British Library Cataloguing in Publication Data
A record is available from the British Library

Copyright © Wipf & Stock 2011

First Published, 2011

This edition is published by arrangement with
Pickwick Publications

Contents

Foreword

IN THE EIGHTEENTH CENTURY, as today, people did not live their lives in disciplinary silos, with their religious lives nicely separated from their workaday experience of getting and spending or their experience of relationships as men and women. Then, as now, they lived their lives for the most part in a local milieu where the factors that shaped their lives, day by day, were interconnected and very particular. Even large forces of cultural, demographic, and economic change were encountered not in the abstract but in the names and things of one's own familiar place. Since the rise of the new social history and since the anthropologist Clifford Geertz first coined the term *thick description* in the 1970s, it has been common for many historians to aspire to an integrated depiction of the lives of those they study in their local context. Like a Peter Breughel painting of village life, the historian's account aspires to somehow capture the interrelatedness of all aspects of life in its local setting with as much detail as possible crowded into the picture frame. This attention to the local is not, however, mere antiquarianism. Several British historians have used this sort of careful local history to good effect to test, refine, or question general models of historical change such as secularization theory, or broad claims about the relationship of church and politics, or the tacit assumption of a trickle-down influence of the ideas of intellectual elites.

The genius of this present volume is not only its awareness that the interconnectedness of life on the ground requires an interdisciplinary framework for investigation, but also the particular locale chosen for study. In the eighteenth century, the parish of Madeley in Shropshire was, at one and the same time, the cradle of the Industrial Revolution, a heartland for Methodism, and the setting for the public ministry of several remarkable women and men—and all of this remains richly documented in a vast archive of well-preserved manuscripts. Between 1760 and 1840, the parish was notable for the evangelical ministries of the Reverend John Fletcher and his wife, Mary, both of whom were Methodist associates of the Wesleys, as well as for the ministry of Mary's assistant and successor, Mary Tooth. The parish also included Coalbrookdale in the Ironbridge Gorge, where the Quaker Abraham Darby pioneered the smelting of iron ore using coke, a process central to the rise of industrial society. Historians of gender, religion, and industry all have a stake, therefore, in understanding the life of Madeley during the last half of the eighteenth century through the early decades of the nineteenth century. This is the right place to shine the spotlight during these years, since the issues illuminated in Madeley are issues that remain of great concern to scholars today.

The essays presented here originated at a conference held on location, June 16–18, 2009, at the Telford (Priorslee) campus of the University of Wolverhampton, with sessions nearby at Madeley and Ironbridge. The conference attracted more than fifty scholars from around the world. Uniquely, in my experience, it put theologians and industrial historians in the same room with specialists in women's studies and church historians and others. As I listened to the various papers, and thought about the vastly different training and academic discourses represented by the presenters, I was not left with the feeling one so often has at academic conferences, namely, of an incommensurable unlikeness papered over by the clever rhetoric of a creative chairperson. No, these papers genuinely illuminated each other and helped to build up a larger picture of life in Madeley and its environs as a case study of larger issues important in the formation of the modern world. On the same day, I was listening to dream narratives from the archive of Mary Fletcher and Abiah Darby, viewing an exhibition of haunting landscape paintings of blast furnaces at night in Coalbrookdale, and thinking about the sophisticated theology of Trinitarian dispensations of John Fletcher and its influence upon later Methodism. But it all fit together, and when I got back home, I found myself revising one of my class lectures on early modern Christian spirituality in a way that drew on all of this.

It is a real service that Peter Forsaith and Geordan Hammond have edited these essays together for publication so that a wider audience can benefit from the Breughel-like picture of life in Madeley that emerges from its pages, and so that we can all revise our understanding of the late eighteenth century accordingly.

D. Bruce Hindmarsh
James M. Houston Professor of Spiritual Theology
Regent College, Vancouver

Introduction

Geordan Hammond and Peter S. Forsaith

THE THEMES AND CONTEXTS

THE NAME OF COALBROOKDALE is synonymous with the dawn of the industrial age, where in 1709 Abraham Darby I pioneered new technologies of smelting iron. This came to be symbolized by the world's first iron bridge, constructed nearby over the River Severn in 1779, and recognized in the 1986 award of "World Heritage Site" status to the Ironbridge Gorge, among the first in the United Kingdom.

Less well known are the religious aspects of the area and the people, as well as the part played by women. The Darby family, and some of their associates, were Quakers, and John Wilkinson, another leading ironmaster, was brother-in-law to the Unitarian (and scientist) Joseph Priestley. Coalbrookdale was situated in the Church of England parish of Madeley, which had been a stronghold of old Catholicism: Charles II took refuge here after his defeat at the Battle of Worcester in 1651. It was to this parish, with its potential religious tensions and social significance and demands, that the evangelical clergyman John Fletcher (1729–1785) was appointed as vicar in 1760, where he ministered "with uncommon zeal and ability" for the remainder of his life.[1]

His wife, Mary (née Bosanquet, 1739–1815), continued to have effective, though wholly unofficial, dominance over the parish, followed after her death by her protégé, Mary Tooth (1777–1843). Their reputation meant that other evangelical women looked to them for support.

---

1. Inscription on the Reverend John Fletcher's tomb, Madeley churchyard.

Abiah Darby (1716–1793), widow of Abraham Darby II, was also celebrated as a leading and influential Quaker. Thus the area can be seen as paradigmatic for positive readings of the place of women in eighteenth-century society and religion.

John Fletcher[2] was a Swiss migrant, born Jean de la Fléchère, who came to England aged about twenty. He came under the influence of the Methodists, and was associated with the Wesleys, Lady Huntingdon, and George Whitefield. His persona and his ministry in Madeley became renowned; he was noted for his personal godliness and as a leader among the Methodists, a potential successor to John Wesley and formulator of "Arminian" dogma.

Mary Bosanquet[3] was the daughter of a wealthy Huguenot businessman in London. She too underwent a Methodist religious experience and started a school for poor girls which relocated to Yorkshire in 1768, where it developed into a more extensive Christian community. She also preached in the neighborhood and led Methodist class meetings. She married John Fletcher in 1781.

Both John and Mary Fletcher became subjects for Methodist hagiography in the nineteenth century, a process which brought the accretions and inaccuracies of legend. Through the same period, the Severn Gorge, "the most extraordinary district in the world,"[4] with its iron bridge which had been the wonder of the age in its time, and which visitors from across Europe came to see, slowly fell into neglect.

However, over recent decades, a number of emerging themes in academic studies have led to growth of interest in aspects of religious history and biography, gender studies and industrial archaeology, disciplines which converge in this volume. The place of religion, often dismissed by a previous generation of historians, has become reintegrated in the general picture, and a pessimistic view of the eighteenth-century church as moribund and corrupt has been challenged. The emergence of

---

2. For recent brief treatments, see Patrick Streiff, "Fletcher, John William (*bap.* 1729, *d.* 1785)," *Oxford Dictionary of National Biography* (Oxford University Press, 2004) and Peter S. Forsaith, "Fletcher, John William," *Dictionary of Methodism in Britain and Ireland*, available online: http://www.wesleyhistoricalsociety.org.uk.

3. John A. Hargreaves, "Fletcher, Mary (1739–1815)," *Oxford Dictionary of National Biography* and E. Dorothy Graham, "Bosanquet, Mary (Mrs Fletcher)," *Dictionary of Methodism in Britain and Ireland*.

4. Joseph Plymley, *A General View of the Agriculture of Shropshire* (London: Phillips, 1803).

disciplines such as Women's Studies has brought new interest to Mary Fletcher and her context.

Industrial archaeology has been another discipline to emerge, and it was Barrie Trinder's pioneering work in tracing the growth of early industry in Shropshire which drew attention to the huge significance of the area.[5] A key factor of his studies was to recognize the importance of the religious life of the area, for much of the new industry was centered in or around what then comprised Madeley parish (it was subdivided into three in the nineteenth century).

By that time some significant archive sources were also becoming more readily accessible. Around the late 1950s, a number of Madeley parish records associated with the Fletchers were deposited in the Shropshire County Records Office. The 1960 publication of George Lawton's *Shropshire Saint* at one and the same time presented (for the first time) a critical study of John Fletcher, and by an Anglican (yet published by the Methodists).[6]

The relocation to the John Rylands Library, Manchester, of the Methodist Church's historic papers has arguably been a major stimulant for new research. The greater accessibility of this archive, as well as others, has led scholars to start to challenge the dominant place of John Wesley in early Methodist historiography, and to question the narrative of Methodism's past from the centre. Stories from elsewhere—as this volume indicates—sometimes give a different account and legitimize alternative viewpoints. The largest single collection of the Methodist Archives remains the "Fletcher-Tooth" papers.

So the juxtaposition of some of the leading figures at the start of the Evangelical Revival, arguably the most significant Protestant religious movement since the Reformation, including several influential women, in the area which has come to be known as the "cradle of industrial revolution" formed the rationale for the "Religion, Gender, and Industry" conference in 2009, at which the papers in this volume were presented.

5. Barrie Trinder, *The Industrial Revolution in Shropshire* (Chichester: Phillimore, 1973 [1st ed.]).

6. George Lawton, *Shropshire Saint* (London: Epworth, 1960).

THE CONFERENCE

It had its origins one summer's day in 2006 when ten people met in Manchester to discuss the progress and scope of their research into the lives and ministries of John and Mary Fletcher and their circle, and the religious life of Madeley parish. Some were established researchers in the area, others new hands, so there was a meeting of minds, both of long-held opinions against new approaches, and different disciplines— centrally theology, history and literature, but taking account of gendered readings in these areas. It became clearer that day that numbers of people were working in and around these strands—that it was a growing area of interest—and so the idea of a full conference was mooted.

If the germ of the idea was sown at the Nazarene Theological College that day, one immediate issue was where to hold such a conference. Manchester or Oxford, locations of the partner organizers, would have been straightforward, but it seemed much more appropriate to hold it in its geographical setting of east Shropshire. A suggestion of the Priorslee campus of the University of Wolverhampton was made and plans started to become realities.

No comparable conference to this one—specifically around the Fletchers and Madeley, and rooted in that locale—had been attempted before. It was an adventure, particularly as its aim was to contextualize the specific subjects, both against each other and against their larger background. It also became clear that certain partners were needed on board, centrally Madeley churches and the Ironbridge Institute, the academic face of the Ironbridge Gorge Museum. Respectively, the Reverend Henry Morris and David de Haan became willing supporters, offering advice and—most crucially—premises to hold conference sessions in St Michael's, Madeley (splendid after an internal re-ordering) and Coalbrookdale.

Perhaps one memorable highlight of the conference could not have been planned or predicted. At the end of the middle day, after a full schedule of papers and visits, it was planned to visit the historic 1779 iron bridge itself. But it had been the kind of damp and dreary weather that the British midsummer can so readily provide; yet, driving down the dale and into the Severn Gorge, the clouds cleared and by the time the bridge was reached the sun was shining. The bridge, which years ago was rusting and threatening collapse, was rarely more spectacular than on that evening, with the sun on the raindrops in the trees sparkling like diamonds.

The success of the conference depended on a number of factors, and most critically achieving a balance. The theme was "Religion, Gender, and Industry," to reflect the aspects of the field, but ensuring that different disciplines and varying interest groups were present was critical. Having conference participants from Europe, Australasia, Canada, and the United States helped make the event and perspectives truly international. Hopefully, this is reflected in the essays.

In retrospect, the scope and balance might have been improved had it been possible to include speakers on recusancy and Quakerism.[7] Perhaps there could have been more on the industrial background, although the "Feo9" conference, celebrating three hundred years since Abraham Darby's pioneering development in iron smelting, had taken place very shortly before. The exhibition of art of the Industrial Revolution, curated by David de Haan, at Coalbrookdale, was a significant contribution to the tercentenary.

Those who would have wanted to be present, and to have contributed, but who could not included Herbert McGonigle (John Fletcher's theology), who generously hosted the original 2006 meeting, Bishop Patrick Streiff, Rhonda Carrim, David Frudd, and Gareth Lloyd (on Mary Bosanquet/Fletcher).[8]

THE PAPERS

This volume presents an important contribution to discussions on the separate issues involved, but most significantly links them together and is thus especially a landmark addition to the literature on religion, gender, and industry in Madeley parish. Existing works range from the

7. For further reading, see Malcolm Wanklyn, "Catholics in the village community: Madeley, Shropshire 1630–1770," in Marie Rowlands, ed. *English Catholics of Parish and Town 1558–1758* (Wolverhampton: University and Catholic Record Society, 1999); Rachel Labouchere, *Abiah Darby* (York: Sessions, 1988).

8. Herbert Boyd McGonigle, *Sufficient Saving Grace: John Wesley's Evangelical Arminianism* (Carlisle: Paternoster, 2001) esp. chap. 11; Gareth Lloyd, *Catalogues of The Fletcher-Tooth Papers* (Manchester: John Rylands Library, from 1994) and with David Frudd, "Mary Bosanquet-Fletcher's Watchwords," *The Asbury Journal* 61:2 (Fall 2006) 5–94. See also the essays by Carrim, Frudd, and Lloyd in Norma Virgoe, ed. *Angels and Impudent Women in Methodism* (Wesley Historical Society, 2007).

largely biographical, such as John Wesley's 1786 *Short Account* of John Fletcher and Henry Moore's *Life of Mrs Mary Fletcher* (1817) through to recent broader studies including Patrick Streiff's *Reluctant Saint?* (2001) and Phyllis Mack's *Heart Religion in the British Enlightenment* (2008). As with many works of that age and genre, Luke Tyerman's comprehensive and heavily detailed *Wesley's Designated Successor* of 1882 has come to be challenged in its veracity and thesis. These papers bring a series of new insights and angles to the growing body of research and literature. It will hopefully come to be seen not simply as a fruit of new research, but as a stimulus to continuing studies.

There were four keynote papers at the conference. The opening and closing papers by Jeremy Gregory and Peter Forsaith, respectively, along with that by Barrie Trinder, are published in this volume. In lieu of Phyllis Mack's paper not appearing in this book, the editors selected David Wilson's important essay as an "honorary keynote," in that it is published in full here. The other nine essays in the volume are revised versions of shorter papers originally given in the conference sessions. The essays have been ordered in a roughly thematic and chronological sequence. The first four essays by Gregory, Trinder, Gibson, and Wilson help to set the historical framework for the rest of the volume. These are followed by two essays that look at John Fletcher's spirituality and theology (Lineham and Loyer), four essays on the contribution of women to the Evangelical Revival and life in Madeley (White, McInelly, Lenton, and Blessing), two essays that examine the impact of the Fletchers in early American Methodism (Raser and Wood), and the closing keynote by Forsaith.

The volume opens with a sweeping historiographical essay by Jeremy Gregory on the themes of religion, gender, and industry, which have all been major topics of research by historians of eighteenth-century Britain, but usually considered independently of one another. Providing a critical context for the rest of the volume, Gregory brings these topics together to demonstrate how recent research in these areas has questioned some long-held interpretations of these subjects.

The three essays that follow contribute further to the historical context for the volume, while advancing understanding of aspects of John Fletcher's context, life, and ministry. Barrie Trinder draws on decades of research into the early industrial history of Shropshire to point out a number of ways in which knowledge of Fletcher's early industrial context can challenge existing interpretations and encourage deeper investigation into his role in the community in which he served. Through a study of Lord James Beauclerk's work as bishop of Hereford from 1746 to 1787, William Gibson sheds light on some possible reasons why Fletcher's High Church diocesan declined to criticize his Methodist practices and Methodism more generally. David Wilson's essay deals directly with one of the central themes discussed at the conference: Madeley as the most notable instance of Methodism remaining within the Church of England. Wilson argues that John and Mary Fletcher's gradually expanding ministry, which included the building of new meeting rooms and setting up of religious society groups throughout the parish, effectively fused Anglican and "Methodist" means of providing pastoral care.

Essays by Peter Lineham and Kenneth Loyer advance knowledge of John Fletcher's spirituality and theology. Lineham gives a fascinating account of Fletcher's little known interest in the mystical theosophy of Emanuel Swedenborg. This essay helps advance understanding of the attraction of mystical writers and theology to Fletcher and other evangelicals. The doxological nature of Fletcher's Trinitarian theology is the theme of Loyer's study. He shows that Fletcher's doctrine of the Trinity is grounded in experimental religion in a way that set him apart from both English Unitarianism and English rational theology.

The following four essays explore the part played by women in the Evangelical Revival, which had a key focus in John and Mary Fletcher and their immediate circles. Eryn White's essay looks at their prominent role in the spiritual, social and economic life of the Trefeca community led by the Welsh evangelical leader Howel Harris, with which John Fletcher came into contact during his time as President of Lady Huntingdon's college at Trefeca. In "Mothers in Christ: Mary Fletcher and the Women of Early Methodism," Brett McInelly provides an alternative to the trend of an influential strand of scholarship that has focused on the social consequences of women's involvement in early Methodism. While he affirms that their actions did indeed have political ramifications, evidence from the writings of these women shows that their focus was first and foremost on their spiritual experiences. John Lenton and Carol Blessing offer studies of women in Madeley and Methodism more widely in the early nineteenth century. Lenton illustrates how women (and a few men) supported each other's ministry in the face of growing opposition to women's preaching in Methodism following a hostile declaration from the Methodist Conference in 1803. He outlines three regional clusters of women who provided such support for one another: one based in and around Madeley, another centered around Mary and Zechariah Taft, and a group in East Anglia. Through telling the story of Mary Tooth's ministry in Madeley, Blessing demonstrates the continuation of female ministry in the parish that was carried on by Tooth for nearly thirty years following Mary Fletcher's death in 1815. Along with Lenton, Blessing's essay highlights the fact that female preaching could survive in spite of official hostility from Methodist leadership.

The influence of the ministry and writings of the Fletchers extended beyond Britain and their own lifetime, particularly in the United States. This fact is insightfully expressed in essays by Laurence Wood and Harold Raser. Wood argues that John Fletcher was a dominant theologian of early American Methodism through the ongoing influence of his theological writings. His thinking profoundly shaped American Methodist doctrine and spirituality. This is clearly reflected in the life and ministry of Phoebe Palmer, the prominent American revivalist who is the subject of Raser's essay. Raser argues that Palmer's theological vision, which continues to shape the holiness movement, owes more to the writings of John and Mary Fletcher than any other source.

The final essay of the volume was the concluding keynote presentation from the conference by Peter Forsaith. He charts the development of research on the Fletchers and Madeley parish and offers incisive comments on how Fletcher can be used as a "case study" to enlighten central concerns for historians of the eighteenth-century church in England, such as the complex relationship between evangelicals, "Methodists," and the Church of England. What, then, he asks, is the way forward for continued research into the Fletchers and Madeley parish that retains the relevance of this subject in the wider area of religion, gender, and industry in eighteenth-century Britain and beyond? Based on his experience of studying John Fletcher's life for over thirty years, Forsaith concludes that the answer lies in fidelity to primary sources and attention to cross-disciplinary study.

Recent published work has included pieces around the women of Madeley, by two conference speakers: Phyllis Mack (keynote) and Joanna

Cruickshank. Neither is published here since they were already committed for publication elsewhere, and similarly, Jonathan Clark's paper was taken from his introductory chapter in the recent *Oxford Handbook of Methodist Studies*.[9]

ACKNOWLEDGMENTS

Thanks are due to many people, without whom neither the conference nor this volume could have come into being. First to Reverend Dr. Herbert McGonigle and Prof. William Gibson, respectively (now emeritus) director of the Manchester Wesley Research Centre and director of the Oxford Centre for Methodism and Church History (Oxford Brookes University), for their support and contributions, and also to Margaret Pye, who so efficiently acted as administrator for the conference and has formatted the essays for publication. David Wilson also generously gave editorial support to the volume.

In Shropshire itself, we should thank the Reverend Henry Morris and Geoff Pochin, as well as the congregation of St Michael's, Madeley; and the Reverend Peter Clarke and members of Fletcher Memorial Methodist Church (who bravely provided lunch for conference members). In Coalbrookdale, we are grateful for the support of David de Haan, Steve Miller and colleagues at the Ironbridge Institute. The staff of the University of Wolverhampton (Priorslee campus) worked hard to make the conference arrangements a success.

Lastly, to the contributors, whose work on the themes of religion, gender, and industry as they interacted in the fascinating parish of Madeley in Shropshire is offered as a contribution to these areas of research. We hope this international group of scholars and their multi-disciplinary perspectives will spur on further research into the subjects of this volume and lead to future conferences and writings on its themes.

9. Phyllis Mack, "Religion and Popular Beliefs: Visionary Women in the Age of Enlightenment," in Ellen Pollak, ed. *A Cultural History of Women in the Age of Enlightenment*, vol. 4 of A Cultural History of Women (forthcoming, Berg). Joanna Cruickshank, "'If God . . . see fit to call you out': 'Public' and 'Private' in the Writings of Methodist Women, 1760–1840," in *Religion in the Age of Enlightenment*, vol. 2 (New York: AMS Press, 2010) 55–76. See also Cruickshank, "'Friend of my Soul': Constructing Spiritual Friendship in the Autobiography of Mary Fletcher," *Journal of Eighteenth-Century Studies* 32:3 (2009) 373–87. J. C. D. Clark, "The Eighteenth-Century Context," in William J. Abraham and James E. Kirby, eds. *The Oxford Handbook of Methodist Studies* (Oxford: Oxford University Press, 2009) 3–29.

1

Religion, Gender, and Industry in the Eighteenth Century

Models and Approaches

Jeremy Gregory

TAKEN INDIVIDUALLY, THE THREE coordinates of this collection of essays—religion, gender, and industry in the eighteenth century—have been the subject of a great deal of research, although that research effort has not necessarily been split equally between the topics. Moreover, the bulk of this research has been carried out by historians working on one rather than two, let alone all three, of these themes, since they have most often been viewed not as a trinity of interconnected topics so much as three separate historical deities. By and large, these deities have only occasionally spoken to one another, although when they have done so, it has been with significant consequences. But in general, they have had their own tribes of votaries and acolytes, who have operated within their distinct intellectual and academic traditions, practices, and agendas, with scholars often working in completely different departments and faculties (such as theology, humanities, or social sciences), and publishing in different journals and meeting at different conferences.

Of the three, certainly until the early 1980s, the lion's share of the research effort was devoted to the goddess Industry (of which more later).[1] Until then, work on eighteenth-century religion tended to fall into some well-defined and predictable channels, and was generally pursued along denominational lines. In the shadow of Norman Sykes (a quondam Dean of Winchester Cathedral), who in a series of studies published between the 1920s and 1950s had offered a qualified rehabilitation of the Anglican Church against the then dominant view, shared by both Evangelicals and Tractarians in the nineteenth and twentieth centuries, that the eighteenth-century Church had been corrupt and pastorally stagnant,[2] there was what G. V. Bennett (a onetime chaplain of New College, Oxford, and himself a student of Sykes) referred to as "a minor industry"[3] of biographies of bishops and leading Churchmen, often published by the Society for the Promotion of Christian Knowledge (SPCK) and usually written by Anglican clerics.[4] There were also thematic studies of Anglican piety, liturgy, and worship, as well as some work on church parties.[5] In similar fashion, there were a number of studies of the Wesleys and early Methodism, almost without exception written by scholars who were themselves Methodists,[6] including of course that

1. Much of this research was conveniently summarized in Peter Mathias, *The First Industrial Nation: An Economic History of Britain, 1700–1914* (London: Methuen, 1969).

2. Norman Sykes, *Church and State in England in the Eighteenth Century* (Cambridge: Cambridge University Press, 1934).

3. G. V. Bennett, *The Tory Crisis in Church and State, 1688–1730: The Career of Francis Atterbury, Bishop of Rochester* (Oxford: Clarendon, 1975) vii.

4. G. V. Bennett, *White Kennet, 1660–1728, Bishop of Peterborough* (London: SPCK, 1957); E. Carpenter, *Thomas Sherlock, 1678–1761* (London: SPCK, 1936); Carpenter, *Thomas Tenison, Archbishop of Canterbury: His Life and Times* (London: SPCK, 1948); W. M. Marshall, *George Hooper, 1640–1727: Bishop of Bath and Wells* (Milbourne Port: Dorset, 1976); A. Tindal Hart, *The Life and Times of John Sharp, Archbishop of York* (London: SPCK, 1949); C. E. Whiting, *Nathaniel Lord Crewe, Bishop of Durham (1674–1721) and his diocese* (London: SPCK, 1940). Note also the biographies written by Sykes: *Edmund Gibson, Bishop of London, 1669–1748: A Study in Politics and Religion in the Eighteenth Century* (Oxford: Oxford University Press, 1926); and *William Wake: Archbishop of Canterbury, 1657–1737*, 2 vols. (Cambridge: Cambridge University Press, 1957).

5. W. Lowther Clarke, *Eighteenth Century Piety* (London: SPCK, 1944); G. W. O. Addleshaw and F. Etchells, *The Architectural Setting of Anglican Worship: An Enquiry into the Arrangements of Public Worship in the Church of England from the Reformation to the Present Day* (London: Faber, 1948); G. Every, *The High Church Party, 1688–1718* (London: SPCK, 1956).

6. Such as Maldwyn Edwards, *John Wesley and the Eighteenth Century: A Study of His Social and Political Influence* (London: Epworth, 1933); Edwards, *Family Circle. A Study of the Epworth Household in Relation to John and Charles Wesley* (London:

lapsed Methodist E. P. Thompson, whose provocative chapter eleven of his *Making of the English Working Class*, first published in 1963,[7] ensured that for a time in the 1960s, 1970s, and early 1980s, all social historians of the late eighteenth century had a take on Methodism, class, and industrialization without having to read any Wesleyan or Methodist primary documents. There were also studies of Quakers, Baptists, Presbyterians, and other religious denominations,[8] again almost always from an "insider" point of view, or what social scientists call "emic" perspectives. But there was very little on popular religion (apart from an article by John Walsh on "Methodism and the mob"),[9] and there was very little social history of religion (apart from R. F. Wearmouth's older studies of Methodism's contribution to working-class consciousness, and those whom he called, in a phrase which now seems to belong to a bygone era, "the common people").[10]

There was also very little of what might be termed "the history of religion in a local setting." In 1980, apart from editions of visitation returns which would provide the raw source material for future studies of this kind,[11] there were only a handful of articles,[12] a number of

Epworth, 1949); F. C. Gill, *Charles Wesley, the First Methodist* (London: Lutterworth, 1964).

7. E. P. Thompson, *The Making of the English Working Class* (London: Gollancz, 1963; rev. ed. 1968).

8. G. Bolam, R. Thomas et al., *The English Presbyterians* (London: Allen & Unwin, 1968); R. Tudor Jones, *Congregationalism in England* (London: Independent, 1962); W. T. Whitley, *A History of the British Baptists* (London: Kingsgate, 1932); William C. Braithwaite, *The Second Period of Quakerism*, 2nd ed. (Cambridge: Cambridge University Press, 1961).

9. John Walsh, "Methodism and the Mob in the Eighteenth Century," in G. J. Cuming and Derek Baker, eds., *Popular Belief and Practice*, Studies in Church History 8 (Cambridge: Cambridge University Press, 1972) 213–27.

10. R. F. Wearmouth, *Methodism and the Common People of the Eighteenth Century* (London: Epworth, 1945).

11. For example, *Archbishop Herring's Visitation Returns, 1743*, ed. S. L. Ollard and P. C. Walker, Yorkshire Archaeological Society Record Series 71, 72, 75, 79 (1928–35); *The State of the Bishopric of Worcester, 1782–1808*, ed. M. Ransome, Worcester Historical Society, n.s. 6 (1969); *Wiltshire's Returns to the Bishop's Visitations Queries, 1783*, Wiltshire Record Society 26 (1972).

12. J. Addy, "Bishop Porteus's Visitation of the Diocese of Chester, 1778," *Northern History* 13 (1977) 175–98; M. R. Austin, "Queen Anne's Bounty and the Poor Livings of Derbyshire, 1772–1832," *Derbyshire Archaeological Journal* 92 (1972) 78–89; N. Caplan, "Visitation of the diocese of Chichester in 1724," *Sussex Notes and Queries* 15

unpublished theses, and really no more than a couple of published monographs on the Church in a particular locality, namely those by Arthur Warne on Devon and Diana McClatchey on Oxfordshire,[13] most typically represented by a diocese, and for the purpose of this volume the most obviously relevant of these was William Marshall's 1978 PhD thesis,[14] half of which was devoted to the diocese of Hereford in which the parish of Madeley lay. In this, eighteenth-century Church historians lagged behind their colleagues working on the sixteenth and early seventeenth centuries, who had for the previous two decades and more been producing seminal case studies of the impact of the Reformation in particular localities and regions, and also behind colleagues working on the nineteenth century who had published on the churches in various localities, towns, and cities (in particular London).[15] And the research into religion in eighteenth-century localities which did exist was overwhelmingly focused on the study of the clergy, the services and functions they provided, and institutional and organizational structures, without giving us much sense of lay religion and lay piety, although in part this was because of the nature of the surviving source material where, in particular for the Church of England, institutional records predominated, and were bound to give a clergy's eye perspective.

Even more tellingly, perhaps, in 1980 religious concerns were seldom incorporated into the wider political and social studies of the period, which makes Thompson's inclusion of religion in his seminal work of social history stand out, although it was a rather backhanded compliment since his view of Methodism was that it went against the progressive story he was wanting to tell, and was, for him, a chillingly

---

(1962) 289–95; A. Whiteman, "The Church of England, 1542–1837," in *VCH Wiltshire* 3 (1956) 28–56.

13. A. Warne, *Church and Society in Eighteenth-Century Devon* (Newton Abbott: Daid & Charles, 1969); D. McClatchey, *Oxfordshire Clergy, 1777–1869: A Study of the Established Church and the Role of its Clergy in Local Society* (Oxford: Clarendon, 1960).

14. W. M. Marshall, "The Administration of the Dioceses of Hereford and Oxford, 1660–1760," PhD thesis, University of Bristol, 1978. This has recently been published as *Church Life in Hereford and Oxford: A Study of Two Sees, 1660–1760* (Lancaster: Carnegie, 2009).

15. For the earlier period, see A. L. Rowe, *Tudor Cornwall: Portrait of a Society* (London: Capo, 1941); P. Clark, *English Provincial Society from the Reformation to the Revolution: Religion, Politics and Society in Kent, 1500–1640* (Hassocks: Harvester, 1977); and for the nineteenth century, see H. McLeod, *Class and Religion in the Late Victorian City* (London: Croom Helm, 1974).

repressive force. Instead, religion was seen by political, social, economic, and intellectual historians as a discrete entity, viewed almost as of antiquarian interest only, with no real purchase on the wider history of the age, and so could be safely left to denominational insiders. Moreover, in overviews of the period, religion was either hardly mentioned, or was relegated to a separate chapter, often tagged on to the end of the volume almost as an afterthought which readers and students could study as an add-on, if they so wished, but only after they had covered the really important topics of mainstream political and social history.[16]

This neglect in 1980 by mainstream historians of religious topics could be explained by two separate but interrelated factors. First, the overarching model of the century was one of secularization (and even historians of religion tended to subscribe to this),[17] where religion and the churches played an increasingly marginal role in political, social, cultural, economic, and intellectual life, and thus those who studied religion were studying a topic which was apparently losing force—hardly a shrewd thing when entering the job market. Second, the Church of England (by far and away the dominant religious body, to which even in the 1790s perhaps over 90 percent of the population at least nominally belonged) was, despite the efforts of Norman Sykes, still often seen as lethargic, if not corrupt, and distanced from the bulk of its parishioners, or at best just worldly and lacking any "real" sense of religion.[18] Here, in most of the overviews of the period, Parson Woodforde's "Diary" was usually cited as evidence of the model of the this-worldly cleric, and reference was frequently made to the fact that the only matter that Woodforde seemed to be interested in recording was what he had to eat (which is in fact a gross misrepresentation of the unabridged source, and misjudges the nature of the text).[19] As late as 1982, a final examination paper in the School of Modern History at the University of Oxford asked

16. Textbooks written on the eighteenth century in the 1950s, 1960s, and 1970s are indicative in this regard: see J. H. Plumb, *England in the Eighteenth Century* (Harmondsworth: Penguin, 1950); Dorothy Marshall, *English People in the Eighteenth Century* (London: Longmans, 1956).

17. See A. D. Gilbert, *Religion and Society in Industrial England: Church, Chapel, and Social Change, 1740–1914* (London: Longman, 1976).

18. Roy Porter, *English Society in the Eighteenth Century* (Harmondsworth: Penguin, 1982) 184.

19. For the full version, see *The Diary of a Country Parson*, ed. James Beresford, 5 vols. (Oxford: Oxford University Press, 1924–1931).

candidates whether they agreed that the eighteenth-century Church was "a servile appendage of a semi-pagan aristocracy,"[20] a slight variant of R. H. Tawney's view (first articulated in 1926 in his *Religion and the Rise of Capitalism*). I answered that question and have in some ways been trying to respond to it ever since.

The eighteenth century was, after all, "the Age of Reason," and home to the Enlightenment, which for most historians working before the early 1980s was seen as a distinctly secularizing force, although ironically Roy Porter, who elsewhere, and in his *Enlightenment: Britain and the Creation of the Modern World* (published in 2000 in the United States and in 2001 in the United Kingdom), celebrated its secular nature, had, as early as 1981, in one of his brilliant synoptic essays, argued that, in England at least, piety and reason went hand in hand, and that the English enlightenment worked *with* rather than *against* religion.[21] The secularizing model of eighteenth-century society raised some complications (which were seldom thought through) for those interested in topics such as the rise of Methodism and the Evangelical revival. How should they be fitted into the supposedly increasingly secular period? One answer was that Methodism (and Evangelicalism more broadly) was a countercultural movement, reacting against the dominant secularizing forces of the day. But within this there was some debate about to what extent Methodism was in essence a reactionary and backward-looking movement, representing a kind of last gasp of religious fervor, or a sort of religious death rattle before secularization kicked in, or was it more of a forward-looking force, anticipating movements such as Romanticism, and forging new kinds of social and religious communities?[22]

20. The original phrase referred to bishops as "servile appendages to a semi-pagan aristocracy": R. H. Tawney, *Religion and the Rise of Capitalism*, new ed. (London: Murray, 1948) 193.

21. Roy Porter, "The Enlightenment in England," in R. Porter and M. Teich, eds., *The Enlightenment in National Context* (Cambridge: Cambridge University Press, 1981) 1–18. However, in some of Porter's later and more extended considerations of the themes, he tended to see the Enlightenment as a secularizing force: R. Porter, *The Enlightenment* (Basingstoke: Macmillan, 1990) and *Enlightenment: Britain and the Creation of the Modern World* (London: Penguin, 2001). See also Sheridan Gilley's pioneering article: "Christianity and the Enlightenment: An Historical Survey," *History of European Ideas* 1 (1981) 103–21.

22. For a discussion of the Wesleys and Methodism as countercultural and reactionary, see David Hempton, *Methodism: Empire of the Spirit* (New Haven: Yale University Press, 2005) 11, 32, 201, and, in a different way, Thompson, *Working Class*. For the for-

So much for the state of the study of eighteenth-century religion in about 1980. What about the study of gender in the eighteenth century at around that date? In the early 1980s, gender per se was still in its gestation period as a research topic for historians (remember, this was the world before Joan Scott had published her "Gender: A Useful Category of Historical Analysis" in 1986),[23] although work had, of course, been done on aspects of the history of women in the eighteenth century (but not necessarily within the feminist paradigms of "women's history"). There were some studies of royal and aristocratic women, although at that date biographies of people such as Queen Anne, and the duchesses of Marlborough and Devonshire, tended to focus on them as apart from mainstream political life (and the latter's canvassing for Whig votes in the 1784 election was seen as something of an oddity).[24] There was also work which could be fitted into a longer tradition of "women's history" by such pioneers as Ivy Pinchbeck, whose *Women Workers and the Industrial Revolution, 1750–1850*, first published in 1930, was an early exploration in what would be a highly influential model of describing the large-scale shift from a preindustrial family economy to an exploitative wage economy as a consequence of the development of capitalism, and with profound consequences for women (although historians differed over which century this happened in: was it the sixteenth, seventeenth, eighteenth, or in fact the nineteenth century?). For Pinchbeck, the transformation in women's work could be attributed to the period between 1750 and 1850 (the period of the "classic" Industrial Revolution), and the move from shared agricultural labor or domestic industry to factory work and work outside the home. In this model, then, historians have seen the changes in work patterns associated with the Industrial Revolution as having a profound effect on gender roles, replacing cottage industry with the factory system, and thereby removing women

---

ward-looking and "progressive" effects of the Wesleys' message, see R. F. Wearmouth's trilogy: *Methodism and the Working Class Movements of England, 1800–1850* (London: Epworth, 1937), *Methodism and the Common People of the Eighteenth Century* (London: Epworth, 1945), and *Some Working Class Movements of the Nineteenth Century* (London: Epworth, 1948). For the "proto-Romantic" nature of Methodism, see F. C. Gill, *The Romantic Movement and Methodism* (London: Epworth, 1937) 63–71.

23. Joan Scott, "Gender: A Useful Category of Historical Analysis," *The American Historical Review* 91 (1986) 1053–75.

24. For a corrective, see Amanda Foreman, *Georgiana, Duchess of Devonshire* (London: HarperCollins, 1997).

from "work." Although, in common with other studies in this tradition, Pinchbeck noted the negative effects this had on women economically in the short term, she actually argued that in the long term industrialization brought women more economic and social independence, and ultimately better education. Weighing up the positive and negative effects of the Industrial Revolution for women remains a debate within women's history.

In addition, by the late 1970s, some historians of Methodism, such as Thomas Morrow in his *Early Methodist Women* (1967), had explored the new opportunities for women as preachers and class leaders, and these studies could be seen as part of a line of interest in such issues starting with Zechariah Taft's *Biographical Sketches of the lives and public ministry of various holy women*, first published in 1828 and interesting for our purposes, since Mary Fletcher was one of the "holy women" he included, and when some of the women he mentioned (such as Mary Tooth) were in fact still alive. But there was in 1980 very little on "men's history," save for a couple of articles by Randolph Trumbach on London's homosexual subculture,[25] although some feminist historians had argued that most history was in fact men's history since women were by and large ignored. There was nothing on eighteenth-century "masculinity" per se, since this, along with "femininity," was not yet seen as an "historicized" issue.

Against the rather internally driven work on religion in 1980, and the rather scanty, if not nonexistent, work on gender, the large volume of publications on industry by that date (much of it emanating from what are tellingly now defunct departments of economic history) can be explained by the fact that up until the early 1980s the eighteenth century was unquestioningly seen as the period of "the Industrial Revolution." It was this, and its concomitant developments, such as urbanization (and secularization) which, so the argument went, thrust England into the modern world, and for the onset of global modernity the English Industrial Revolution was deemed to be as crucial as, if not more crucial than, the American and especially the French Revolutions.[26] The Industrial Revolution was regarded as eighteenth-century England's

25. Randolph Trumbach, "London's Sodomites: Homosexual Behaviour and Western Culture in the Eighteenth Century," *Journal of Social History* 11 (1977) 1–33.

26. See the discussion in Eric Hobsbawm, *The Age of Revolution: Europe, 1789–1848* (London: New English Library, 1962).

vital contribution to world history, and it put England, and indeed the world, on the road to capitalism. Historians were thus preoccupied with debating the causes of industrial takeoff: what precisely was it about England that made it the first industrial nation? Was it technological inventions, key natural resources, the existence of an entrepreneurial class, or a relative liberalization of trade, to name some of the most often cited explanations?[27] Historians were also concerned with the consequences of the Industrial Revolution (part of which was the "standard of living debate").[28] As such, the "Industrial Revolution" could be put alongside (and was often seen as the culmination of) other supposedly "modernizing" revolutions within eighteenth-century British history—some seemingly obviously related, such as "the Agricultural Revolution," and others where the connection was less clear-cut, such as "the Glorious Revolution," and where the precise relationship between that and the later economic revolutions were vague and ill-defined (with scholars positing necessary or contingent connections between constitutional democracy and the free market). In all these cases the very word *revolution* indicated a complete transformation and a break with the past, and the setting of a new paradigm. The revolutionary model in all these spheres of activity implied radical and usually sudden change.

What is interesting to note for our purposes is that alongside the Glorious, Agricultural, Industrial, and French Revolutions, other historians had discerned a religious revolution, commonly called the "Evangelical Revival," and indeed to spell out the comparison with all those other revolutions, Bernard Semmel wrote in 1973 of *The Methodist Revolution*, although long before his book of that name historians had viewed Methodism as a religious and spiritual revolution.[29] That "revolution" could be viewed in both senses of the word. The Methodist revolution—in the older meaning of the term—could be seen as going back full circle to "primitive Christianity," or conversely it could be seen as transforming the status quo. These historians (often Methodists themselves) stressed the novelty of Methodism (at least

27. R. M. Hartwell, ed., *The Causes of the Industrial Revolution in England* (London: Methuen, 1967); C. Wilson, *England's Apprenticeship, 1603–1763* (London: Longman, 1966).

28. Arthur J. Taylor, ed., *The Standard of Living in Britain in the Industrial Revolution* (London: Methuen, 1975) collected together the articles written by the leading participants in the debate during the 1950s and 1960s.

29. Bernard Semmel, *The Methodist Revolution* (London: Heinemann, 1973).

within its eighteenth-century context), and social and economic historians (many of whom had probably read little Wesley and had certainly never investigated how Methodists actually behaved) found it easy to assimilate and absorb this view into the "revolutionary agenda," and their cursory reading of Weber helped locate Wesley as one of the makers of the capitalist work ethic.[30] The Methodist Revolution, as the first part of an Evangelical Revival (or Evangelical Revolution), could be seen in a number of ways—the stress on the religion of the heart, the development of field preaching, the use of lay preachers and the class meetings and the new social communities Methodism engendered (explored for instance by Wearmouth)—and these changes made it adept at adapting to, and perhaps even helping to create and shape, the new socioeconomic contexts found within Industrial society. Those two landmark projects in the history of Methodism—Townsend, Workman, and Eayres' *A New History of Methodism* (published in 1909), and Davies and Rupp's first volume in *A History of the Methodist Church of Great Britain*, published in 1965—were both able to fit Wesley and Methodism into the overriding picture of eighteenth-century change and incipient modernity, with Methodism both creating and reflecting that change. If Methodism itself shaped new social relations, it was also dependent on new contexts. W. J. Townsend, for example, noted that without the new road and communications networks, the Methodist connexion would have been impossible, and, he argued, improvements in lighting provided the necessary conditions for the evening meetings which became such a staple of the new Methodist religiosity.[31] This view of the period as one dominated by modernizing change was implicitly shared by most historians writing in

---

30. See Max Weber, *The Protestant Ethic and the Spirit of Capitalism* (first published in 1905) where ch. 4 has a discussion of Methodism. See also Yuki Kishida, "John Wesley's Ethics and Max Weber," *Wesleyan Quarterly Review* 4 (1967) 43–58. On eighteenth-century Methodist and Wesleyan attitudes to work and property, see John Walsh, "John Wesley and the community of goods," in *Protestant Evangelicalism: Britain, Ireland, Germany and America, c. 1750–c. 1950*, ed. Keith Robbins, Studies in Church History Subsidia 7 (Oxford: Blackwell, 1990) 25–50, and Walsh, "'The Bane of Industry'? Popular Evangelicalism and Work in the Eighteenth Century," in *The Use and Abuse of Time in Church History*, ed. R. N. Swanson, Studies in Church History 37 (Woodbridge: Boydell, 2002) 223–41.

31. W. J. Townsend, "The Times and Conditions," in Townsend, Workman, and Eayres, *A New History of Methodism*, 2 vols. (London: Hodder & Stoughton, 1909) 1:77–133, and "English Life and Society, and the Condition of Methodism at the Death of Wesley," 1:335–78, at 82.

the nineteenth century and for much of the twentieth century, whatever their own political and religious standpoints. This interpretation owed much to Thomas Babington Macaulay's *History of England from the accession of James II* (1848), and in particular the famous third chapter which measured the social improvements in England by the early nineteenth century when compared with the situation in 1685. Townsend, for example, contrasted the period when Wesley was born, with that when he died, highlighting progress in economic, social, political, and cultural life from around 1760, which anticipated something like the modern world.[32] In a similar vein, Herbert Butterfield, writing in the Davies and Rupp volume, emphasized the changes in all aspects of eighteenth-century life as his context for the rise of Methodism, claiming that changes on all fronts after circa 1780 were like a "tidal wave."[33]

While, as I noted at the outset, the bulk of the research into the three areas of religion, gender, and industry has usually focused on one of these areas, nevertheless, within this paradigm of "revolutionary change," a number of powerful interpretations of the period have attempted to explore the interrelationships and connections between two, and even three, of the coordinates of this volume, although those interrelationships and connections have sometimes been assumed rather than actually researched, in part because of the logistical difficulties of being expert in all three fields. In some ways it was possible to make (or suppose) the seeming connections between the developments in all three of our fields of enquiry because they could all be understood within the "revolutionary paradigm." If there was an Industrial Revolution, a revolution in work practices which affected both men and women, and a revolution in religion, then it was easy enough to see them operating somehow in tandem. It has, for example, long been a commonplace to assert that the Church of England was "threatened" and "challenged" by both "the Evangelical Revival" and "the Industrial Revolution."[34] I say "assert" because in fact both these assumptions were not really based on research into the situation in any given locality. It was

32. Townsend, "English Life and Society," 342.

33. Herbert Butterfield, "England in the Eighteenth Century," in R. E. Davies and E. G. Rupp, eds., *A History of the Methodist Church in Great Britain*, vol. 1 (London: Epworth, 1965) 3–33.

34. See Gilbert, *Religion and Society*. For a similar framework, see A. Armstrong, *The Church of England, the Methodists and Society, 1700–1850* (London: University of London Press, 1973).

assumed, rather than necessarily proved, that the Church's stronghold was rural England, and that with its medieval parish structure it was simply overwhelmed by the new industrial towns and settlements. Both the Evangelical Revival and Industrial Revolution have often been seen as dramatically changing traditional patterns of behavior, thought, and feeling, and according to some interpretations they must be linked. For example, Wellman Warner's *The Wesleyan Movement in the Industrial Revolution* (1930) argued that Methodism must be understood as an *amalgamation* of social, economic, and religious change, arguing that the "affinity of the economic and religious movements was so close that the vitality of one injected itself into the other."[35] Warner not only saw connections between the Evangelical and Industrial revolutions, he further suggested that this affected Methodist women because they were accorded a "working equality" with men that reflected a working equality among the industrial workforce, and thus the relationship between Wesleyanism and the Industrial Revolution helped women gain religious and social recognition. A more modern take on the connections between Industrialization and Evangelicalism was made by Alan Gilbert, who, in *Religion and Society in Industrial England: Church, Chapel, and Social Change, 1740–1914* (1976), argued that, along with urbanization, the Industrial Revolution was one of the factors which not only weakened the position of the Church of England in favor of Evangelicalism and Methodism (creating the rigid cleavage between "Church" on the one hand and "chapel" on the other), but also marked a vital stage in the secularization of English society. In his *The Making of Post-Christian Britain; A History of the Secularization of Modern Society* (1980), Gilbert talks of "the great discontinuity" caused by the Industrial Revolution.[36] So the Industrial Revolution, for Gilbert and others, becomes responsible in this model both for creating a religious alternative to the Church in the form of the Methodist revival, and ultimately for causing secularization. (But I am not sure that the potential contradiction and tensions between the two developments in Gilbert's model were fully resolved: how does the Industrial Revolution help both a religious revival *and* secularization?) Another tension within Gilbert's analysis is that he seems

35. Wellman Warner, *The Wesleyan Movement in the Industrial Revolution* (London: Longmans, 1930) 166.

36. A. D. Gilbert, *The Making of Post-Christian Britain: A History of the Secularization of Modern Society* (London: Longman, 1980) 42.

to veer between seeing the Industrial Revolution as causing unstoppable structural damage to the Church, and blaming the Church itself for its poor showing.[37] Indeed, for Gilbert, the West Midlands, which I take it is where he would locate Madeley, was one of those areas of the country where "institutional decay and clerical negligence had seriously weakened whatever hold Christianity had managed to obtain over the hearts and minds of local communities."[38]

Another influential way of connecting the themes of religion, gender, and industry was Leonore Davidoff and Catherine Hall's *Family Fortunes: Men and Women of the English Middle Class, 1780–1850*, first published in 1987. This book, which has been hugely influential for women's history and gender history, saw changes in the economy (specifically the development of the capitalist enterprise in business) and changes in religion (specifically the rise of Evangelicalism) as the twin crucial factors in creating a shift in ideas about gender in the late eighteenth and nineteenth centuries, and in particular the emergence of a particular form of family organization among the middle class, one that stressed separate spheres for men and women, demarcating distinctions between "public" and "private." It offered an account of the economic, associational, religious, and domestic lives of middle-class families in Birmingham, Essex, and Suffolk, and argued that gender played a crucial role in structuring an emergent middle class culture, and that it was the ideology of domesticity and separate gender spheres which gave characteristic form to middle class identity.

This then was the state of play of research into religion, gender, and industry around 1980, and some of the models which attempted to see connections between them. But research over the last twenty-five years or so has challenged, or at least qualified, most of the statements I have made so far. What I want to do in what follows is to explore how some of this research has modified our understanding of eighteenth-century history as outlined above, and as such I hope to provide a vital context for the rest of this volume.

What has happened to the ways in which religion in the eighteenth century is now understood? The secularization thesis which used to be taken for granted even by historians of religion, and in which the eighteenth century was deemed to be the crucial step on the ladder, has now

37. Gilbert, *Religion and Society.*
38. Gilbert, *Post-Christian Britain,* 70.

been criticized from several directions: its start has been delayed until the nineteenth or even the twentieth century; some have argued that in England this only occurred in the 1960s (and according to Callum Brown, this can be dated precisely to 1963),[39] others have denied that it happened at all, and what was assumed to be the "inevitable" trajectory not only of Western European but of world history looks less convincing in the early twenty-first century when religion can be viewed as being at the center of world affairs.[40] On a related point, one of the most significant historiographical developments during the past twenty years has been to widen and to complicate what might be meant by "the Enlightenment." Traditional scholarship, based on a French model of "the Enlightenment," viewed it as an antireligious force and as an important marker in the birth of a secular society. More lately, scholars working on British history have argued that the Enlightenment was not necessarily antireligious at all, and the relationship between "religious" and "enlightenment" concerns is now one of the most fruitful areas of research. Jane Shaw's *Miracles in Enlightenment England*, for example, has demonstrated how a large range of commentators were able to balance "religious enthusiasm" with "reason," and her reading incorporates elements of the supernatural into an enlightenment worldview which clearly challenges older models of an enlightenment hostile to religious sensibilities.[41] Moreover, Phyllis Mack's stunning *Heart Religion in the British Enlightenment* sees interesting and complex links between the religion of the heart and the ideals of the enlightenment, which transcends older models which saw religion and enlightenment as polar opposites.[42] So, if religion itself is now understood to be more central to eighteenth-century life than it was in the 1970s, then it is not surprising to note that its role in mainstream history has been reemphasized. In many ways the most overt and revisionist statement which has helped to put religion

39. Hugh Mcleod, *The Religious Crisis of the 1960s* (Oxford: Oxford University Press, 2007); Callum Brown, *The Death of Christian Britain: Understanding Secularisation, 1800–2000* (London: Routledge, 2001).

40. David Nash, "Reconnecting Religion with Social and Cultural History: Secularisation's Failure as a Meta-Narrative," *Cultural and Social History* 1 (2004) 302–25.

41. Jane Shaw, *Miracles in Enlightenment England* (New Haven: Yale University Press, 2006).

42. Phyllis Mack, *Heart Religion in the British Enlightenment: Gender and Emotion in Early Methodism* (Cambridge: Cambridge University Press, 2008).

back into the center stage of political and social history continues to be Jonathan Clark's highly influential *English Society, 1688–1832: Ideology, Social Structure and Political Practice during the Ancient Regime* (1985, rev. ed. 2000). Clark applied the model of "the confessional state"—a term which was being used at around the same time by historians of early modern Europe, and in particular Germany, to denote the interplay of religion and state building, whereby a state had a single confession of faith to which the whole population conformed,[43] to England between the Restoration and the constitutional changes of 1828–1832. Although, as some of Clark's critics have emphasized, sections of the English population did not conform to the Church, nevertheless he is surely right to argue that the centrality of the Church's legal position had a profound impact on political and social life, given that the State, the English universities, the army and the civil service were Anglican strongholds, and in the localities clergy were often a justice of the peace and as such were responsible for the administration of local government. In this regard, perhaps a more accurate description of the Church's position is not Clark's "confessional state" but, as he himself has suggested, an Anglican hegemony,[44] which is indicative of the ways in which, although its position was contested, the Church effectively dominated and sought to marginalize those who challenged its social and political role. In similar ways, in a series of studies, David Hempton has integrated Methodism into the broader political and social history of the period.[45]

Furthermore, where traditionally the eighteenth century was seen as a nadir in the history of the Anglican Church, and a byword for lax standards and pastoral negligence, during the last twenty-five years or so there has emerged what might be called a revisionist school of historians whose detailed work, particularly on what the Church was doing at the local and diocesan level, has modified and in some cases reversed the more negative opinions of some of their predecessors.[46] Rather than

43. J. C. D. Clark, "England's Ancient Regime as a Confessional State," *Albion* 21 (1989) 450–74.

44. Clark, "Confessional State."

45. David Hempton, *Methodism and Politics in British Society 1750–1850* (London: Hutchinson, 1984); *Religion and Political Culture in Britain and Ireland: From the Glorious Revolution to the Decline of Empire* (Cambridge: Cambridge University Press, 1996); *The Religion of the People: Methodism and Popular Religion, c. 1750–1900* (London: Routledge, 1996); *Methodism: Empire of the Spirit*.

46. Contributions to this reassessment include: *The Church of England, c. 1689–c.*

dwelling on the failures and shortcomings of the established Church, they have highlighted instead its successes and strengths, and have argued that in many respects the Church was more effective than at any time since the Reformation. And, perhaps surprisingly for someone who is often seen as one of the Church's sternest critics, as late as 1787 Wesley could preach: "it must be allowed that ever since the Reformation, and particularly in the present century, the behavior of the Clergy in general is greatly altered for the better. In so much that the English and Irish Clergy are generally allowed to be not inferior to any in Europe, for piety, as well as for knowledge."[47] The Church is now seen as having been more pastorally dynamic than traditional interpretations allowed, which has raised questions about the relationship between Methodism, Evangelicalism, and "mainstream Anglicanism." Recent scholarship has emphasized the ways in which, long before Wesley's "conversion" in May 1738, Anglicanism had itself been undergoing a movement of renewal and reform. This was witnessed most obviously by the creation of the religious societies (from about 1678, first in London then elsewhere), the SPCK in 1698, and the Society for the Propagation of the Gospel in Foreign Parts (SPG) in 1701 (all of which John and Charles Wesley and the Methodists were influenced by, and drew on). It is thus possible to argue, as I have elsewhere, that the Wesleys and the Methodists can be seen as emerging from within an Anglican Church which was itself experimenting with developments in pastoral care.[48] I have also suggested

---

1833: From Toleration to Tractarianism, ed. J. Walsh, C. Haydon, and S. Taylor (Cambridge: Cambridge University Press, 1993); Mark Smith, *Religion in Industrial Society: Oldham and Saddleworth, 1740–1865* (Oxford: Oxford University Press, 1994); Judith Jago, *Aspects of the Georgian Church: Visitation Studies of the Diocese of York, 1761–1776* (Cranberry, NJ: Fairleigh Dickinson University Press, 1996); Jeremy Gregory, *Restoration, Reformation, and Reform, 1660–1828: Archbishops of Canterbury and Their Diocese* (Oxford: Oxford University Press, 2000); J. Gregory and J. S. Chamberlain, eds., *The National Church in Local Perspective: The Church of England and the Regions, 1660–1800* (Woodbridge: Boydell, 2003); W. M. Jacob, *The Clerical Profession in the Long Eighteenth Century, 1680–1840* (Oxford: Oxford University Press, 2007); Robert G. Ingram, *Religion, Reform and Modernity in the Eighteenth Century: Thomas Secker and the Church of England* (Woodbridge: Boydell, 2007).

47. *The Works of John Wesley, Sermons, III*, ed. Albert C. Outler (Nashville: Abingdon, 1986) "On Attending the Church Service," 470. This sermon is a defense of the efficacy of the Church, even when clergy might be deemed unworthy.

48. See my "'In the Church I will live and die': John Wesley, the Church of England and Methodism," in William Gibson and Robert Ingram, eds., *Religion and Identity in Eighteenth-Century Britain* (Aldershot: Ashgate, 2005) 147–78; and "Charles Wesley

that that Methodist "innovations" can be seen within a long tradition of providing spiritual extras and add-ons to the normal pastoral provision, rather than as something intended to rival or contradict it. The Wesleys' insistence that Methodist meetings should not be scheduled to clash with Church services is an obvious point, but what we need to know more about is what went on in the local setting.

Other work has examined in painstaking detail the relations between different religious denominations on the ground, particularly after the Toleration Act of 1689. Keith Snell and Paul Ell in *Rival Jerusalems* (2000), though ostensibly on Victorian religion, have provided a model (gleaned from religious censuses) of the fragile and often short-lived nature of dissenting and nonconformist meetings in the eighteenth century.[49] Their model is not one of hard-and-fast divides but one where dissenting meetings could fail as much as they could rise, and that moreover membership between them and that of the Church was far more porous and permeable than is sometimes supposed from imposing Victorian denominational models and practices back on to the eighteenth century. To complicate what used to be seen as a sharp divide between the Church and nonconformity, some social historians of religion have pointed to the fluidity with which parishioners moved between religious groups.[50] The vicar of St. Alphege's, Canterbury, reported in 1786 that "many go to the Cathedral in the morning, to the Presbyterian meeting in the afternoon, and to the Methodist meeting at night."[51] We need to work through what this might mean for people's allegiance to the Church, to dissent, and to Methodism. This statement is also a reminder that since 1980, we have begun to uncover the religious views of the laity, although there is much still to do here. William Jacob's study of lay piety (1996) was a landmark project,[52] as was in some ways the publication of the diary of the Sussex shopkeeper Thomas Turner

---

and the Eighteenth Century," in *Charles Wesley: Life, Literature, and Legacy*, ed. Kenneth G. C. Newport and Ted A. Campbell (Peterborough: Epworth, 2007) 18–39.

49. K. D. M. Snell and Paul S. Ell, *Rival Jerusalems: The Geography of Victorian Religion* (Cambridge: Cambridge University Press, 2000).

50. See Jacob, *Lay People and Religion in the Early Eighteenth Century* (Cambridge: Cambridge University Press, 1996) 6, 14, 45, 77.

51. Quoted in Gregory, *Restoration, Reformation and Reform*, 273.

52. See footnote 50.

(1984), which gave a vivid portrayal of how religion and the Church were central to his life.[53]

All this has greatly nuanced our understanding of eighteenth-century religion since about 1980. Yet it still strikes me that all this new work has not really yet made much of an impact on social historians in particular, and there is still the paradox that while many recent studies have emphasized the pastoral diligence of the eighteenth-century Church, few writing outside what might be deemed "Church history" are aware of it. In this respect, Carolyn Steedman's *Master and Servant: Love and Labor in the English Industrial Age* (2007) was groundbreaking and was arguably the first major study by a leading social historian to take seriously the revisionist approaches to the eighteenth-century Church, where the master of the title and the hero of the book is a late eighteenth-century Church of England cleric, whose charitable attitude to his unmarried pregnant servant, and then her daughter, makes him almost a model of the clerical professional. It will be interesting to see how far Steedman's book is to be a pattern for future social history.

How has our understanding of the Industrial Revolution fared? Downplaying the "revolutionary" character of industrial change for the eighteenth century, research on the Industrial Revolution since 1980 has instead stressed the persistence of "traditional" work practices well into the nineteenth century. A number of historians have argued that the social and economic developments of the time were less transformative than was once thought and that, in most regards, these changes were accommodated within long-established forms of organization and behavior. Despite undoubted advances in industry (and agriculture) and a marked population growth—which were, it is now often maintained, more *evolutionary* than *revolutionary* in character—the qualitative changes relating to quantitative growth, it is contended, happened in the nineteenth rather than in the eighteenth century.[54] But if much of the emphasis on industrialization proper now lies in the nineteenth century, the long lead-in of population growth, commercial development, and

53. *The Diary of Thomas Turner, 1754–1765*, ed. David Vaisey (Oxford: Oxford University Press, 1984).

54. Roderick Floud and Donald McCloskey, eds. *The Economic History of Britain since 1700*, 2 vols. (Cambridge: Cambridge University Press, 1981); N. F. C. Crafts, *British Economic Growth During the Industrial Revolution* (Oxford: Oxford University Press, 1985); Maxine Berg, *The Age of Manufactures, 1700–1820: Industry, Innovation, and Work in Britain* (London: Fontana, 1985).

urbanization in the eighteenth century has given rise to the concept of pre- or proto-industrialization (although it must be said that the very concept is fraught with issues and depends on a Whiggish reading of developments.)[55] In general, work on the Industrial Revolution has tended to create a growing awareness of the sheer complexity of the changes taking place. In addition, some of the presumed effects of industrialization, such as the breakdown of community and the development of "anomie," have been questioned. For example, Keith Snell, this time in his *Parish and Belonging: Community, Identity, and Welfare in England and Wales, 1700–1950* (2006), does not "believe that industrialization between c. 1750–1870 destroyed local attachments and community." Rather, he claims that "there was often more community in the epicentres of industrialisation than there ever was in those districts before. Across the country, the Industrial Revolution coincided with strong and often heightened senses of place and belonging, as well as with an intensification of regional cultures and local pride."[56] Instead, Snell feels that it is the process of deindustrialization that has most damaged the sense of community and place. In all this, where does Madeley fit into these models? On the one hand, Madeley might be a prime example of the red heat of the Industrial Revolution, and Philip de Loutherbourg's *Coalbrookdale by Night* (painted in 1801, but looking back to the 1770s and 80s) might be taken as a representation of the revolutionary nature of industrial change in this local setting. But, of course, industrial development in the parish can be seen as evolutionary and occurring over a longer timescale. Abraham Darby's 1709 furnace is itself evidence of the longer durée.

What about work on gender since 1980? Starting from its low base, it is clear that over the last twenty-five years, gender history has made a significant impact on the writing of eighteenth-century history, although only now are we really taking seriously Joan Scott's point that gender history requires us to look at men as well as women, and that we should be doing comparative investigations (and again, this is where Phyllis Mack's book has made such a contribution not just to the history

55. L. A. Clarkson, *Proto-Industrialisation: The First Phase of Industrialisation?* (Basingstoke: Macmillan, 1985); Berg, *Age of Manufactures;* D. C. Coleman, "Proto-industrialisation: A Concept Too Many," *Economic History Review* 36 (1983) 435–48.

56. K. D. M. Snell, *Parish and Belonging: Community, Identity and Welfare in England and Wales, 1700–1950* (Cambridge: Cambridge University Press, 2006) 499.

of religion, but to gender history by taking women and men together.) There has, of course, been a large increase of published research into eighteenth-century women, and at all sorts of social levels. Put simply, we know far more about women in the eighteenth century than we did in 1980. Edward Gregg's biography of Queen Anne,[57] which came out that year, has been followed by a number of studies of royal and aristocratic women, which have helped locate them within the wider political, social, and religious structures of the age, including a number of biographies of the Countess of Huntingdon,[58] and Elaine Chalus' *Elite Women in English Political Life* (2005) is the major text here.[59] One broad modification has been to challenge the creation of the separate spheres model for gendered behavior, and particularly in its influential reincarnation in Davidoff and Hall's *Family Fortunes*, which now looks in some ways as a continuation of an older thesis rather than a new model. Their work was indeed criticized in Amanda Vickery's spirited review article "From Golden Age to separate spheres?" in which Vickery pointed out the problems with their interpretation: there were restrictions long before the eighteenth century and, conversely, she argued that developments in the later eighteenth century opened up opportunities for women as much as confined them.[60] For our purposes, it is Hall and Davidoff's (and Vickery's) treatment of Evangelicalism that needs some comment. While they have opposing views on the effects of Evangelicalism on women's roles (Davidoff and Hall seeing it as narrowing women to the domestic sphere and Vickery as a factor which took them in to the public sphere), both interpretations are agreed that Evangelicalism was a new factor and represented a novel injection of religious ideology into thinking about gender. Davidoff and Hall, for instance, contrast "traditional" eighteenth-century views of masculinity—with its codes of "sport," "honor," and "drinking and wenching"—with the "new"

57. E. Gregg, *Queen Anne* (London: Routledge & Kegan Paul, 1980).

58. These include Edwin Welch, *Spiritual Pilgrim: A Reassessment of the Life of the Countess of Huntingdon* (Cardiff: University of Wales Press, 1995) and Boyd Schlenther, *Queen of the Methodists: The Countess of Huntingdon and the Eighteenth-Century Crisis of Faith and Society* (Bishop Auckland: Durham Academic Press, 1997).

59. E. Chalus, *Elite Women in English Political Life* (Oxford: Oxford University Press, 2005).

60. Amanda Vickery, "Golden Age to Separate Spheres: A Review of the Categories and Chronology of English Women's History," *Historical Journal* 36 (1993) 383–414.

Christian manliness associated with the Evangelical Revival.[61] But in many ways this is to take Evangelical rhetoric at face value, and to exaggerate the differences between pre-Evangelical and Evangelical views on gender (and on much else). A decade ago, I pointed to the religious elements behind eighteenth-century understandings of eighteenth-century masculinity, and more recently, William Van Reyk has explored ideals of Christian manliness throughout the long eighteenth century and has concluded that there was nothing new about the Christian manliness promoted by Evangelicalism.[62]

One of the ways in which research over the last twenty years or so into religion, gender, and industry has developed in tandem is that all three topics, to a greater or lesser extent, have been sensitive to issues of region and locality, which makes this volume all the more timely. A common research agenda, particularly with religion and industry, has been to question or modify our older assumptions and generalizations by detailed examination of a locality or a place. For the Church of England, in 2003, Jeff Chamberlain and I brought together some of the findings from several of the key diocesan and parish studies that had been produced in the 1980s and 90s,[63] and it is clear that there are probably enough new studies completed since then for a further volume to be published. As we noted in that volume, one of the dangers traditionally associated with "local studies" is that they can easily become antiquarian in nature, but one of the marks of local and regional research into both religion and industry is that they have kept the big questions to the fore, using the local picture to refine, modify, or confirm the general picture, and a key strength of local or regional work is that it allows for detailed investigation of a local community. One of the fruits of this has been to note the differences that could exist in different areas. Of course, one of the major questions is how far those differences overrode elements of similarity, and there is also the issue of how far those differences are "real ones" or how far they are the product of the use of differing sources,

61. Davidoff and Hall, *Family Fortunes*, 110.

62. Jeremy Gregory, "'Homo religiosus': Masculinity and Religion in the Long Eighteenth Century," in *English Masculinities, 1600–1800*, ed. Tim Hitchcock and Michèle Cohen (London: Longman, 1999) 85–110; William Van Reyk, "Christian Ideals of Manliness during the Period of the Evangelical Revival, c. 1730–c. 1840," DPhil thesis, Oxford University, 2007; and Van Reyk, "Christian Ideals of Manliness in the Eighteenth and Early Nineteenth Centuries," *Historical Journal* 52 (2009) 1053–1073.

63. *The National Church in Local Perspective*, ed. Gregory and Chamberlain.

or even the different mind-sets of the investigators. Take, for example, the case of the Church of England in Lancashire, the heartland of the Industrial Revolution, where the damp, mild weather conditions provided the ideal environment for the spinning of cotton, and thus a natural starting point for the birth of the textiles industry. During the 1980s and 1990s three studies appeared, all with rather different conclusions.[64] In particular, the differences between Mark Smith's interpretation of the fortunes of the Church in Oldham and Saddleworth (in his *Religion in Industrial Society* [1994]—a twist on Gilbert's title) and Mike Snape's investigation of Whalley (in his *The Church of England in Industrialising Society* [2003], a take on both Gilbert and Smith)—the two parishes being barely twenty miles away from each other as the crow flies—call for some comment. Was it really the case that the Church in Oldham and Saddleworth was doing so well, able to reach out to new areas of industrial growth with its chapels of ease, and by and large working with Methodism as part of a united evangelical front, when the Church in Whalley seemed to be losing out to Methodism, and seemingly increasingly detached from ordinary parishioners? While the first might present us with a fairly optimistic account of the state of the Church of England, the second is much more downbeat and pessimistic. In any case, it is not as if we need to try to iron out or ignore these differences. Although at first sight the differences between the selected localities may seem to be structural and organizational, they were also the result of human agency.

In a similar vein, research on the Industrial Revolution has developed a regional approach, such as Barrie Trinder's work on *The Industrial Revolution in Shropshire* (1973), which took a long view, from the late seventeenth to the mid-nineteenth century, and work of this kind almost predated the "revisionist" views of the Industrial Revolution. Interestingly, Trinder's study did include recognition of the role of John and Mary Fletcher in the locality, which, as reviewers noted on its publication, was rare in these kinds of economic histories.[65] Some of this work was brought together in a collection of essays edited by Pat Hudson and titled *Regions and Industries: A Perspective on the Industrial Revolution*

64. Jan Albers, "Seeds of Contention: Society, Politics, and the Church of England in Lancashire, 1689–1790," PhD thesis, Yale University, 1988; Smith, *Religion in Industrial Society*; M. F. Snape, *The Church of England and Industrialising Society: The Lancashire Parish of Whalley in the Eighteenth Century* (Woodbridge: Boydell, 2003).

65. B. Trinder, *The Industrial Revolution in Shropshire* (Chichester: Phillimore, 1973).

in Britain.[66] Taken together, these essays argued that industrialization in Britain (and elsewhere) occurred first and foremost within regions rather than in the nation as a whole, and that attempts to understand the "first industrial revolution" as a fundamentally important economic, social, and political process are best undertaken with the regional perspective at center stage. The volume emphasized the need to evaluate aggregate studies of "national" variables in the light of contrasting regional experiences.

Gender history, too, has developed a regional slant. Hannah Barker, in her study of businesswomen in northern towns after 1760, has recently argued for their involvement in the economic life of towns and, in particular, the manner in which they exploited and facilitated commercial development, and this forces us to reassess our understanding of both gender relations and urban culture in late Georgian England.[67] In contrast to the traditional historical consensus that the independent woman of business during this period—particularly those engaged in occupations deemed "unfeminine"—was insignificant and no more than an oddity, Barker presents businesswomen not as footnotes to the main narrative, but as central characters. She shows that factors traditionally thought to discriminate against women's commercial activity—particularly property laws and ideas about gender and respectability—did have significant impacts upon female enterprise. Yet it is also evident that women were not automatically economically or socially marginalized as a result. The woman of business might, according to Barker, be subject to various constraints, but at the same time, she could be blessed with a number of freedoms, and a degree of independence that set her apart from most other women—and many men—in late Georgian society.

Thus this volume, with its aim of exploring religion, gender, and industry in a local setting, intervenes at a pertinent juncture in the historiography. The essays that follow explore how far the lives and beliefs of the men and women of Madeley confirm, complicate, or challenge the models and approaches I have outlined here. What does Madeley tell us about religion in the eighteenth century, and in particular, what does it tell us about the relationship between the Church and Methodism?

66. P. Hudson, *Regions and Industries: A Perspective on the Industrial Revolution in Britain* (Cambridge: Cambridge University Press, 1989).

67. H. Barker, *The Business of Women: Female Enterprise and Urban Development in Northern England, 1760–1830* (Oxford: Oxford University Press, 2006).

What do the experiences of these Shropshire men and women tell us about gender relations, and how were they affected by the economic and industrial contexts in which they lived, worked, and worshipped?

2

John Fletcher's Parishioners

Reflections on Industrial Revolution and Evangelical Revival in the Severn Gorge

Barrie Trinder

HALF A CENTURY AGO John and Mary Fletcher could still be re-garded as "saints," which might have excused further examination of their roles in the history of the communities to which they minis-tered. Since that time the availability of probate records, the investiga-tion of the role of music in sacred and secular contexts, and the study of landscape history have increased our understanding of the nature of the early industrial communities in Madeley and adjacent parishes. At the same time the reinterpretation of the Fletchers' correspondence and the examination of their place in Methodist historiography have raised new questions about Madeley and about the Evangelical Revival nation-ally. This essay argues that the community to which Fletcher ministered was too complex to be aligned with the "unbelieving and impenitent" of theological discussion.

More than forty years ago I began to consider John Fletcher's in-fluence in Madeley. Since then my research has been concerned with other topics and other periods, but I have constantly reexamined the Severn Gorge in Fletcher's time and it has shaped my thinking about many aspects of history. It is a particular pleasure that so many scholars who have considered Fletcher's thinking, the nature of his ministry, and his role in the wider pattern of church history have gathered in Madeley in the summer of 2009.

First, I would like to reflect on the situation in 1965 when I first saw Fletcher's tomb, entered the church of St. Michael, and walked past the Wesleyan chapel of 1832 to view the Fletcher chapel that succeeded it in 1841. I had some experience of the history of Methodism in market towns, and one of my mentors had warned me that in undertaking a job that involved responsibility for local history in the Ironbridge Gorge, I was entering on "*Methodist* holy ground." It was difficult in the 1960s to escape the view that Fletcher was chiefly important as part of the movement that became the influential Wesleyan Connexion of the mid-Victorian years. The very title of the standard biography—*Wesley's Designated Successor*—placed him firmly in that pigeonhole. In 1877 the Connexion officially published an edition of Fletcher's writings, which we now know to have been severely edited.[1] George Lawton had recently published a biography encapsulating what were then traditional views about Fletcher, and Raymond Skinner had written *Nonconformity in Shropshire*, which portrayed Fletcher in the broad context of Evangelical religion and drew attention to new sources.[2] Part of my work was to tutor an adult education research class on the history of religion in the Shropshire Coalfield, which was about to be transformed by the development of the new town of Telford. It was hosted by Christopher Nankivell, then vicar of St. Leonard's, Malins Lee. Much of the work of the class concerned the chapel-based Methodism, once strong in the area, which was slowly coming to an end. As in the communities in County Durham analyzed by Robert Moore, chapels were essentially the concerns of particular families.[3] It was enlightening to hear from people then in their eighties of the intensity of church activity in the face of economic depression in the 1890s, but while such memories were interesting, they

1. Luke Tyerman, *Wesley's Designated Successor* (London: Hodder & Stoughton, 1882); John Fletcher, *The Works of the Reverend John Fletcher, Late Vicar of Madeley* (London: Wesleyan Methodist Conference Office, 1877) (hereafter cited as Fletcher, *Works*).

2. George Lawton, *Shropshire Saint* (London: Epworth, 1960); Raymond Skinner, *Nonconformity in Shropshire 1662–1816* (Shrewsbury: Wilding, 1964).

3. Robert Moore, *Pit-Men, Preachers and Politics: The Effects of Methodism in a Durham Mining Community* (Cambridge: Cambridge University Press, 1974) 126–32.

were not helpful in understanding the ministry of John Fletcher and the nature of the Coalfield at a time of economic expansion in the mid-eighteenth century. From contacts with Edward Thompson—whose *Making of the English Working Class* had recently been published—and John Walsh, I came to appreciate the differences between eighteenth-century religion and that of the late Victorian years.[4] I spent much of my research time in 1966–69 reading the Fletcher-Tooth Collection in the cellars in City Road, London that accommodated the Methodist Archives. Much of what I learned was incorporated in the first edition of *The Industrial Revolution in Shropshire* in 1973.[5] I tried in that book to present a holistic view of the history of the Shropshire Coalfield, concerned not with the minutiae of Arminianism, the puddling process or back-to-back houses, but with the broad social changes taking place in the area between 1700 and 1870.

Since the 1960s research by many people has enlarged our understanding of the Coalfield and its landscapes. Probate inventories for the period between 1660 and the beginning of Fletcher's ministry have been published, and the later probate documents for Madeley and neighboring parishes have been analyzed. Our interpretation of Fletcher's own thinking has been profoundly changed by the publication of an unexpurgated version of letters that were bowdlerized by his nineteenth-century biographers.[6]

My own research since 1973 has made me aware of the range of contexts in which the establishment of manufacturing enterprises or the

4. E. P. Thompson, *The Making of the English Working Class* (London: Gollancz, 1963); John Walsh, "Methodism at the End of the Eighteenth Century," in R. Davies and G. Rupp, eds., *A History of the Methodist Church in Great Britain*, vol. 1 (London: Epworth, 1965); Walsh, "The Origins of the Evangelical Revival," in G. V. Bennett and John Walsh, eds., *Essays in Modern English Church History in Memory of Norman Sykes* (London: Black, 1966).

5. Barrie Trinder, *The Industrial Revolution in Shropshire* (1st ed., Chichester: Phillimore, 1973; 3rd ed., Chichester: Phillimore, 2000).

6. Judith Alfrey and Kate Clark, *The Landscape of Industry: Patterns of Change in the Ironbridge Gorge* (London: Routledge, 1993); Barrie Trinder and Jeff Cox, eds., *Yeomen & Colliers in Telford: The Probate Inventories of Dawley, Little Wenlock, Wellington & Wrockwardine* (Chichester: Phillimore, 1980); Barrie Trinder and Nancy Cox, eds., *Miners & Mariners of the Severn Gorge: The Probate Inventories of Benthall, Broseley, Little Wenlock & Madeley, 1660–1764* (Chichester: Phillimore, 2000); Peter Forsaith, ed., *"Unexampled Labours": Letters of the Revd John Fletcher to Leaders in the Evangelical Revival* (Peterborough: Epworth, 2008).

ministries of Evangelical clergy in particular places have to be seen. Such contexts are illustrated by the subject matter of this conference. Fletcher's ministry took place in an England that was part of an Atlantic economy, in which people and goods moved ceaselessly between the British Isles, West Africa, the Caribbean, and the colonies that became the United States. The visits of John Wesley and George Whitefield to Georgia, the ordination of Thomas Coke, and the ministry of Francis Asbury are part of the framework of Methodist history. Abiah Darby entertained members of the Society of Friends from Pennsylvania and other states at her home in Coalbrookdale, where pig iron from Maryland was refined at the Lower Forge. Shropshire products were familiar in the United States. Elihu Burritt, who grew up in Bristol, Connecticut, wrote of his childhood: "All Americans who were boys forty years ago will remember three English centers of particular interest to them. These were Sheffield, Colebrook Dale and Paternoster Row. There was hardly a house or log cabin between the Penobscot and the Mississippi which could not show the imprint of these three places, on the iron tea-kettle, the youngest boy's Barlow knife and his younger sister's picture-book. To the juvenile imagination of these times, Sheffield was a huge jack-knife, Colebrook Dale a porridge pot, and Paternoster Row a psalm book."[7]

Through the nineteenth-century American evangelists influenced this area. Lorenzo Dow inspired the growth of Primitive Methodism which had a substantial presence in the Coalfield, Alexander Parker passed through Shropshire in June 1847, and we have learned that Phoebe and Walter Palmer visited Madeley in 1862.

There is similarly a European context. Eighteenth-century England had many links with the continent. Fletcher preached in a gruff Swiss accent, however fluent his English prose style. In his years in London he had Huguenot connections, preached in French at Spitalfields, and later married Mary Bosanquet, a member of a Huguenot family. The Moravian Brethren had a profound influence on British religion, evidenced by their settlements at Fulneck, Ockbrook, Fairfield, and Gracehill. The skills of workmen from this area were sought by con-tinental entrepreneurs and some found their way to Le Creusot, the Ruhrgebiet and Liège, while some navvies building the Severn Valley Railway in the 1860s had worked in Normandy and the Rhone Valley.

---

7. Elihu Burritt, *A Walk from London to John O'Groats* (London: Low & Marston, 1864) 3.

German musicians, chiefly from the western Palatinate, played throughout England in the nineteenth century, and in April 1861 a band of six players aged between sixteen and thirty-three was staying in a lodging house near the Bedlam furnaces. Jewish hawkers of jewelry from Prussia and Poland frequently passed through the area. John Fletcher's nationality and Mary Fletcher's descent from an immigrant family were parts of a pattern of interchange between England and continental countries.

Fletcher's arrival in Madeley coincided with the "takeoff" of the iron industry. In 1755 Abraham Darby II and Thomas Goldney III blew-in the first of the blast furnaces at Horsehay that produced pig iron that could readily be refined into wrought iron. Within less than five years, nine blast furnaces were built in the vicinity, and until the end of the century the Shropshire Coalfield was the most productive iron-making region in Britain.[8] The opening of the Iron Bridge on New Year's Day 1781 brought celebrity to the area. Fletcher knew Madeley before his induction into the parish and felt a particular call to minister to its poor. He wrote to Charles Wesley in December 1758: "The extent of ye Parish, containing near 2000 Souls which are as sheep scatter'd without a Shepherd, & mostly of those who enter first into the kingdom, poor laborers, & colliers."[9] Fletcher's determination to settle in Madeley was dictated by his wish to engage with the social consequences of the growth of mining and iron making, and not because he saw it as an island of tranquility, suitable for theological reflection.

Yet there may have been a sense in which Madeley was a retreat from bruising controversy. The parishioners included people whom Fletcher called "half-gentlemen," whose substantial houses can readily be recognized near the parish church and in Madeley Wood.[10] Fletcher encountered difficulties with some of them, but they were legalistic rather than theological. Some may have shown him disrespect, as when he went to survey the Birches land slip of 1773, but neither they nor the colliers seem to have indulged in the kind of fevered theological debate that characterized dissenting congregations in some market towns. In Leominster from 1739 when "some few inhabitants met together and read some good sermons of the old Puritans without knowing anything of Methodism," there was rivalry between different groups,

8. Trinder, *Revolution*, 29–35.

9. Forsaith, *Unexampled Labours*, 56.

10. Ibid., 142.

which became more intense after visits by George Whitefield in 1740, James Beaumont in 1741, and John Wesley in 1744, resulting in 1747 in "dreadful disputes and altercations."[11] Similarly, in Banbury "a few serious people in the town began to meet on a Thursday evening" in 1772–73, after which a congregation was formed whose allegiances varied between Selina, Countess of Huntingdon and William Huntington, the "converted collier." Members in the 1790s held very different beliefs, and strong convictions regularly disturbed the peace of an assembly that initially strove to accommodate differing views.[12] Nothing in the documentation of Fletcher's ministry suggests that this kind of theological rancor was present in Madeley.

Theologically legitimate views of Fletcher's parishioners may differ from those of social historians, anxious to avoid the dismissal of groups by such terms as *the mob* or *the lumpenproletariat*. We have learned at this conference how theologians of Fletcher's time were accustomed to categorize their congregations, that those unmindful of religious experience might be placed at the base of a pyramid as "sinners" or "unbelieving and impenitent." It may be legitimate to envisage a particular group in theological terms as the base of a hierarchy. It is less legitimate for a social historian to use such terms as "harlots, publicans and thieves," which can allow galloping rhetoric to displace analysis. In my work on nineteenth-century common lodging houses, institutions which, however insanitary, had particular functions relating to the working class and the socially distressed, I found that Evangelicals tended to use rhetorical language based on representations of Sodom, Gomorrah and Hell rather than detached observation.[13] It is easy to ratchet up a sense of revulsion, and some writers about Fletcher have used ever more exaggerated language about the depravity of his parishioners. According to Benson, "Madeley was remarkable for little else than the ignorance and profaneness of its inhabitants . . . In this benighted place the Sabbath was openly profaned, and the most holy things contemptuously trampled underfoot." Benjamin Baugh recalled in 1839 that Madeley in 1760 "was

11. L. T. Nyberg, "A Short Sketch of the Awakening in and about Leominster down to May 12 1769." John Rylands University Library. Eng MS 1069 (2).

12. Barrie Trinder, "Schisms and Divisions: The Origins of Dissenting Congregations in Banbury 1772–1860," *Cake & Cockhorse* 8 (1982) 207–21.

13. Barrie Trinder, *The Market Town Lodging House in Victorian England* (Leicester: Friends of the Centre for English Local History, 2001).

overspread with darkness, ignorance and sin." Another Wesleyan wrote in 1858 that in the Coalfield in about 1803 "the tide of impiety reached its highest point."[14] There is a temptation to enjoy the repetition of this kind of rhetoric, which cannot be accepted as a valid description of a complex community, any more than railway navvies can be disparaged as Irishmen who habitually became intoxicated.

"Colliers" and "miners" are words too readily subject to stereotypical interpretation, conjuring images of sweaty, sparsely clad, helmeted men living in isolated villages of terraced housing clustered round pit headstocks with a few pubs or chapels. There were many such villages, but many miners lived in cities, in Newton Heath in Manchester or Hunslet in Leeds. Others occupied scattered open settlements on heaths and commons, such as Kingswood, north of Bristol, whose colliers so influenced the thinking and missioning of John Wesley and George Whitefield. John Fletcher described Ketley (or Coalpit) Bank, one of the archetypal open settlements in the Coalfield, as "this Kingswood of Shropshire."[15] Examination of the buildings in which working men lived in the eighteenth century, and analysis of their probate records has shown that many of them occupied cottages within enclosures of an acre or so that provided an element of self-sufficiency, enabling them to keep a pig and sometimes a cow, to grow small crops of grain, flax, and hemp, and to make butter, brew beer, and spin linen yarn. Wills provide evidence that cottages were extended into short, irregular terraces to accommodate successive generations of families. The availability of accommodation that encouraged early marriage and the growth of population in the eighteenth century owed relatively little to large-scale inward migration. While the livings of most of those who lived on the slopes of the Severn Gorge depended on coal, not all were involved in the extraction of minerals from underground workings. There were boatmen who carried coal and other commodities on the River Severn, burners of lime, potters and makers of bricks and tobacco pipes who burned coal in their kilns, together with those who provided the infrastructure of mining, ropemakers, carpenters who built gins and headstocks, candlemakers, and blacksmiths who forged picks and shovels.

14. Fletcher, *Works*, vol.1, 63; Benjaman Baughen, "Wesleyan Methodism in Coalbrookdale to 1836" (MS, Shropshire Archives, Madeley Vicarage Collection); W. H. Barclay, *The History of Wesleyan Methodism at Lawley Bank* (Lawley Bank, 1858) 3.

15. Forsaith, *Unexampled Labours*, 211.

It is important to understand the miner's working context. Areas of mineral-bearing land were leased from landowners, who profited from royalties, by the ironworking companies, who struck agreements for the working of particular pits with subcontractors called charter masters, or "butties," who managed the extraction of the minerals and employed the miners. By tradition, butties were rich, gluttonous, and illiterate, but there is much evidence that they were leaders of the community outside the working context. Some kept public houses while others were Methodist trustees and class leaders. Fletcher eloquently showed his appreciation of the dangers of work underground:

> To go no further than this populous parish; with what hardships and dangers do our indigent neighbors earn their bread! See those who ransack the bowels of the earth to get the black mineral we burn; how little is their lot preferable to the Spanish felons who work the golden mines? They take their leave of the light of the sun, and, suspended by a rope, are let down many fathoms perpendicularly towards the centre of the globe; they traverse the rocks through which they have dug their horizontal ways. The murderer's cell is a palace in comparison of the black spot to which they repair; the vagrant's posture in the stocks is preferable to that in which they labour. Form, if you can, an idea of the misery of men kneeling, stooping, or lying on one side, to toil all day in a confined place, where a child could hardly stand; whilst a younger company, with their hands and feet on the black dusty ground, and a chain about their body, creep and drag along, like four-footed beasts, heavy loads of the dirty miner, through ways almost impassable to the curious observer. In these low and dreary vaults all the elements seem combined against them. Destructive damps, and clouds of noxious dust, infect the air they breathe. Sometimes water incessantly distils on their naked bodies; or, bursting upon them in streams, drowns them, and deluges their work. At other times, pieces of detached rocks crush them to death; or the earth, breaking in upon them, buries them alive. And frequently sulphureous vapours, kindled in an instant by the light of their candles, form subterraneous thunder and lightning. What a dreadful phenomenon! How impetuous is the blast! How fierce the rolling flames! How intolerable the noisome smell! How dreadful the continued roar! How violent and fatal the explosion![16]

16. Fletcher, *Works*, vol. 8, 261–62.

Mining coal became more dangerous in Shropshire in the late eighteenth century as miners increasingly encountered methane gas, but many of the day-by-day deaths of miners were less dramatic, caused by falls of rock in workings or by breakages of ropes when ascending or descending shafts. The nearness of death in the pits influenced the nature of religion in the coalfields and may explain the brutality of animal cruelty sports. The dangers of working underground, like those of military conflict, could create a strong sense of comradeship, and miners' feelings towards their occupation and their employers could often be ambiguous. They might show pride in being miners, expressed in communal conflicts with bargemen or the tradesmen of the market town of Wellington. They certainly showed communal solidarity when disaster struck, or when they sought to alleviate grievances. They might complain, as they did during the Chartist-inspired strike of 1842, about malpractices by charter-masters, but could nevertheless display solidarity with the groups with whom they worked and with the charter-masters who managed them. They could show hostility towards ironmasters and landlords, as they did at a time of food shortage in 1782 during Fletcher's ministry—and by the nineteenth century that hostility might be expressed in terms of class conflict—yet on other occasions they could display loyalty and even affection towards the wealthy, accepting the bounty provided by families like the Darbys, the Leveson-Gowers, and the Foresters on national occasions or at family weddings or comings-of-age.[17]

In Shropshire as elsewhere the Industrial Revolution changed the lives of women as well as men, and Fletcher and other Evangelicals had opinions about the appropriate employment of women, which tended in the next generation, in the time of Charles and Lucy Cameron, to a view that the most desirable occupation for the daughter of a working man was that of domestic servant in a middle-class household.[18] Fletcher believed that working-class women required supervision. He wrote to Charles Wesley in 1763 that "A pious and zealous wife . . . could be more useful among the women of my parish who seem to have great need of an Inspectoress."[19] In many households women carried out the multitude of tasks which made their families partially self-sufficient: dairy

17. Trinder, *Revolution*, 201–2.
18. Ibid., 194–95, 200, 211.
19. Forsaith, *Unexampled Labours*, 183.

work, brewing, preparing bread, laundry work, and spinning hempen and flaxen yarn. One eighteenth-century Shropshire probate inventory lists "implements of *huswifery* with flax undressed."[20] Such tasks were carried out in the brewhouses or washhouses which formed parts of many houses in the district. They can be identified in the older cottages, and are mentioned in many probate documents. They were also incorporated in housing built by ironmasters. There are ten front doors to the houses in Carpenters' Row, Coalbrookdale, eight of which gave access to dwellings, and two to brewhouses, each of which was shared by four families. Miriam McDonald defined the brewhouse as "a reserved part of the domestic space used by women . . . an easily slopped-out area . . . (with) access to water, a boiler and an area big enough to take the array of wooden tubs and vessels needed."[21] Many women worked outside the home. They did not go underground in coal mines but many were employed on the surface where they were subject to ever-present dangers. Mary Fletcher recorded the death of a pit bank girl in 1805 who supposedly said that she would be keeping her coming wedding night in Hell, but before the marriage took place slipped at the mouth of a pit and was dashed to pieces.[22] In the nineteenth century many women worked at potteries, their most characteristic occupation being the tedious burnishing of the gilt on porcelain, but few were so employed before 1800, and hardly any during Fletcher's ministry.

The most commonplace female occupation was the picking of nodules of iron ore found in clay which was mined by the longwall system and left exposed to the weather on heaps. Women collected the nodules and carried them in baskets on their heads to be loaded on to tramroads that took the ore to the furnaces. A recording of one of the last of the pit bank girls who began work in the 1890s suggests that the women controlled their own working lives, and were not subject to supervision by men, beyond the obvious obligation on the group to deliver certain quantities of ore by particular times. The ability to carry heavy weights on their heads was utilized by many pit girls during annual migrations to the market gardens west of London, where they first helped with the

20. Trinder and Cox, *Miners & Mariners*, 73, 86.

21. Miriam McDonald, "The wash-house: an archaeological and functional evaluation with special reference to the 'brew'us' of the Ironbridge/Coalbrookdale area," MSSc diss., Ironbridge Institute, University of Birmingham, 1989.

22. Henry Moore, *The Life of Mrs. Fletcher* (Birmingham: Peart, 1817) 339.

hay harvest and then carried fruit to markets in the center of the city, remaining until October when they returned for the wakes at Oakengates. They could earn high wages, as much as nine shillings per day, and their consequent independence was the subject of Evangelical criticism and disparagement. Lucy Cameron thought that the girls brought back "many fine clothes, as well as money, which they have gained, some by honest industry alone, but many, it is feared, in a different way."[23]

John and Mary Fletcher were well acquainted with pit girls able to carry heavy loads on their heads who took part in the annual migration to London. On the eve of the haymaking season in May 1765 John Fletcher sent a letter to Charles Wesley observing "The Bearer is a woman of our Society who is going to London to work in the Gardens. She belongs to a parish next to mine—When she comes back I expect a letter by her." "The Gardens" was a phrase commonly used to indicate the market gardens west of London, and it is clear that a woman accustomed to going to work there was a trusted member of Fletcher's congregation. Mary Fletcher wrote the obituary of Mary Barnard, who never learned to read but regularly attended class meetings at Ketley Bank, where she lived, and Sunday services at Madeley. She compared the relief of the burden of sin brought by her acceptance of Christ with the relief that came from leaning on a mile post when carrying a *burn* (i.e., a burden) on her head.[24]

Fletcher's parishioners had identities arising from where they lived and from their occupations, but also from the ways in which they spent their non-working time. Evangelicals tended to see a sharp division between awakened sinners and believers and the unbelieving and impenitent, who indulged in a familiar list of activities, such as tippling at public houses, dancing and attendance at wakes, theatrical performances, bull-baiting and cockfighting. The archetypal autobiography or obituary of a Methodist, in the broad sense of that word, describes a sinful adolescence and early adulthood followed by conversion and the taking up of different secular activities as well as religious observances. Thomas Handley of Coalbrookdale spent his youth "following the multitude to do evil, particularly in revelling and what are called *pastimes*, where he was accustomed to divert himself and his thoughtless companions by playing on the fiddle" but was converted after his mother's

23. Trinder, *Revolution*, 169–70.

24. Forsaith, *Unexampled Labours*, 215; *Methodist Magazine* (1800) 221.

prayers, and always refused to visit "those places of vain amusement which he had previously attended."[25] John Fletcher described dancers as "profusely perspiring and violently fatiguing themselves in skipping up and down a room for a whole night, and ridiculously turning their backs and faces to each other an hundred different ways" and reproved "daughters of Jezebel" by whom he meant mothers who took their daughters dancing.[26] We know little of Fletcher's attitude to religious music, although within a few months of his death, Madeley's churchwardens were given authority to create a singers' pew in front of the west gallery. Many insights into music and broader aspects of popular culture arise from the tune books of a Wellington musician and seedsman, John Moore, which date from about 1840. Moore, like Thomas Handley in his youth, was a fiddler. Gordon Ashman found evidence that he played regularly in church, but he also played a variety of secular music. The tunes include "Come, ye that love the Lord" to the tune "Birmingham," the waltz from Weber's *der Freischütz*, marches, hornpipes, quadrilles, reels, and, as an indication of the deferential aspects of popular culture, a Duchess of Sutherland waltz and a Duke of Wellington march.[27] Music was intricately interwoven with broader patterns of social life. Fletcher's Madeley was regarded as the chief center of Morris dancing in Shropshire. In 1817, during the depths of the economic depression that followed the wars with France, "colliers from Shropshire" drew cartloads of coal to London, Oxford, and Bristol, where they danced the Morris and played tambourines and drums. In the 1830s and 40s, colliers from Broseley annually visited the village of Atcham, home of Fletcher's patrons, the Hills, where they danced the Morris and sought alms. When ice and floods impeded the Severn navigation in January 1861, bargemen paraded through Bridgnorth dancing the Morris and seeking sustenance. Music may be the key to a wider understanding of the social issues of Fletcher's times. Many of his parishioners, and many members of industrial communities throughout Britain, assumed at different times both religious and secular identities. They comprised the "occasional hearers" or "hearers only" listed in church records. Just as John Moore played Charles Wesley's hymns and jigs for convivial

25. *Methodist Magazine* (1805) 505.

26. Fletcher, *Works*, vol. 2, 77.

27. Gordon Ashman, *The Ironbridge Hornpipe: A Shropshire Tune Collection from John Moore's Manuscripts* (Blyth: Dragonfly Music, 1991).

gatherings, so many people listened to Fletcher's sermons, and, without sinking into the depths of depravity imagined by some Evangelicals, participated in wakes, watched theatrical performances, and tippled in public houses. Some fervent men and women devoted their lives entirely to seeking the salvation of others, or to the organization of bull-baitings or cockfights. On the other hand many did neither, and could at different times identify with both parties.[28]

John Fletcher himself showed empathy with the working conditions of his parishioners, while he condemned activities that would now seem harmless if trifling, as well as many that were not. Some of those who subsequently wrote about his ministry labeled his flock in theological terms, suggesting that Madeley was "remarkable for little else than the ignorance and profanes of its inhabitants," or that its inhabitants were a "blasphemous, drunken, immoral brutal crew." Fletcher felt a call to minister at this particular place at a particular time, one of almost incomprehensible economic expansion and of undoubted social stress. It may be legitimate in trying to understand Fletcher's theology to regard his parishioners as "unbelieving and impenitent," but this can obstruct our understanding of the community to which he ministered, on whose members he left profound impressions. It is as easy to ratchet up revulsion against those who lived in Madeley in the late eighteenth century as it is to exercise a vivid imagination concerning the sexual practices of Victorian lodging house inmates or twenty-first-century students, but indignation does not bring historical understanding. John Fletcher ministered to a complex parish, and to understand it requires patient dissection of many unconsidered trifles of evidence, and a shunning of rhetoric. Fletcher was important as a pastor as well as a theologian, and to understand the pastor we must try to understand his flock.

28. Trinder, *Revolution*, 199–208.

3

John Fletcher's Silent Bishop

Lord James Beauclerk of Hereford

William Gibson

From 1746 to 1787, the longest single episcopate of the eighteenth century, Lord James Beauclerk (1709–1787) presided over the diocese of Hereford. It was an episcopacy which did not attract much praise. In 1780 Sir Herbert Croft wrote of Beauclerk that "his promotion was as disproportionate to his mediocrity of his talents as the sentiments he adopted were unworthy of the honours he inherited." He conceded Beauclerk had "brilliancy of conversation" but attacked his "depth of understanding" and claimed his thoughts were "either immature or ill-digested." Croft went on that Beauclerk was ostentatious, pedantic, and "forebearing to blend urbanity with science, passed through life with the reputation either of a scholar or a philanthropist."[1] Beauclerk's recent *Oxford Dictionary of National Biography* entry has begun the process of reexamining his life, rescuing his reputation from that of a lackluster undistinguished bishop. William Marshall argues that his episcopate was distinguished by "outstanding conscientiousness" and a "persistent

---

1. Sir H. Croft, *The Abbey of Kilkhampton: or Monumental Records for the Year 1980* (*sic*) (London: Kearsley, 1780) 13. Although the *Hereford Journal* was more generous, claiming that Beauclerk endeared himself to all classes of society. *Hereford Journal*, October 25, 1787.

determination to raise diocesan standards." This is exemplified in his ordinations, in which he was extremely demanding and rigorous but also
regular and accommodating of his clergy. Ordinations will be a significant issue in the assessment of Beauclerk. Marshall concludes that his
episcopate was one of those which made a "conspicuous impact on diocesan life."[2] This is in sharp contrast to the usual dismissal of Beauclerk's
episcopate as containing "little to record" other than squabbles with the
dean and chapter.[3] It is the intention of this essay to consider Beauclerk's
rehabilitation by considering his dealings with the Cathedral, with dissenters, his churchmanship and a less orthodox aspect of his life.

Despite his family background—he was the seventh son of the Duke
of St. Albans, the natural son of Charles II by Nell Gwynn—Beauclerk
had something of a scholarly turn of mind. At Queen's College, Oxford
he graduated BA, MA, BD, and DD.[4] As a bookish and wealthy youth,
he was one of the most consistent subscribers to books and built up an
impressive library over sixty years of collecting.[5] In the fraught Oxford
election of 1736, Beauclerk voted for Robert Trevor, a Whig member of
his own college, rather than William Bromley, son of the long-standing
Tory MP for the University. It is not clear whether Beauclerk voted from
friendship with Trevor or principle. But it was clear from the beginning
that the Tories were going to win, and they did by the huge margin of 329
to 126 votes.[6] With three brothers at court it was unlikely that patronage would not come his way. In 1744 he was made a canon of Windsor

2. W. Marshall, "Lord James Beauclerk," in *Oxford Dictionary of National Biography*
(Oxford: Oxford University Press, 2004). This is a view Marshall pursues in "The
Diocese of Hereford and Oxford, 1660–1760," in J. Gregory and J. Chamberlain, eds.,
*The National Church in Local Perspective: The Church of England and the Regions 1660–
1760* (Woodbridge: Boydell & Brewer, 2003) 200–209.

3. A. L. Moir, *The Bishops of Hereford* (Hereford: Jakemans, 1964) 58.

4. At the time of his inception as MA, the Sheldonian Theatre was the venue for the
performance of Handel's *Athalia*, which 3,700 people attended. *The bee, or universal
weekly pamphlet*, vol. 2 (London, 1733–35) 883.

5. Beauclerk's name appears in an extraordinary number of subscription lists. For
example, Nathaniel Marshall's *Sermons on several occasions, in three volumes*, vol. 1
(London: Bowyer, 1731) 5. In 1766 Beauclerk bought William Stukeley's valuable library of antiquarian books. *Notes and Queries*, 2nd Series, vol. 10 (October 1860).

6. *An exact account of the poll, as it stood between the Hon Mr Trevor and Wm
Bromley Esq; candidates at the late election of the city and University of Oxford* (London:
Gilliver & Clarke, 1737) 20; W. R. Ward, *Georgian Oxford* (Oxford: Clarendon, 1958)
153–54.

and in 1746, aged just 36, he was consecrated bishop of Hereford. He took up residence in the palace, less than a few hundred yards from the birthplace of his grandmother, Nell Gwynn.[7] As will be seen, Beauclerk's career at Hereford was that of a reformer. But his churchmanship was highly conservative.

In 1752, Beauclerk was invited to preach the annual sermon commemorating the martyrdom of Charles I, before the House of Lords. It was a remarkable sermon for two reasons. Firstly, Beauclerk was preaching about his great-grandfather, something no other such preacher could claim. Secondly, as a note in the British Library's copy of the sermon makes clear, he only preached one public sermon as a bishop because "preaching was not within his compass for in his early days his voice was so feeble that his congregation at Windsor . . . could not hear him." He even refused the usual invitation to preach before the Society for the Propagation of the Gospel "which every bishop in his turn is expected to do."[8] The 1752 sermon took its text from 1 Samuel chapter 25, verse 23: "rebellion is as the sin of witchcraft." It was a highly erudite and learned sermon, comparing the wars of the Old Testament with the English Civil War. He argued that such rebellions were disobedience to God, derived from Adam's fall, and were the cause of human misery. In civil societies, rebellion dissolved society and robbed people of security, property, and "life itself."[9] He spoke of the Civil War as having "blackened the British calendar" and "disgraced the annals of our native country."[10] Thus far, Beauclerk's sermon was a standard 30 January sermon which rehashed the usual view of the Civil War. But Beauclerk went further. In speaking of his great-grandfather, he said: "on this day fell a most excellent prince, not indeed by a foreign enemy in the heat of battle, not in the secret recesses of a dungeon, not by the hidden dagger, or more latent

7. *Notes and Queries*, 6th Series, vol. 12, (August 1885).

8. Both these quotations are from the notes in the British Library copy of Beauclerk's 1752 sermon (shelfmark 694.i.17.6.). On the national stage, besides supporting publishers, Beauclerk's only contribution as a bishop was as a Vice-President of the Guardians of the Asylum for Female Orphans, of which Lord North, the Prime Minister, was President.

9. J. Beauclerk, *A Sermon Preached before the Right Honourable the Lords Spiritual and Temporal in Parliament Assembled, in the Abbey Church, Westminster on Thursday, January 30th, 1752. Being the Anniversary of the Martyrdom of King Charles I* (London: Payne, 1752) 11.

10. Ibid., 15.

poison, but in a manner which no history can parallel, in open day-light amidst thousands of spectators, before his own palace; being arraigned, condemned and executed by his own subjects."[11] Beauclerk argued that the English people "had been industriously taught to speak loudly of grievances" and taxes were represented as "burdensome." [12] The Church was overthrown, the sacraments "neglected or profaned," and clergy "deprived and persecuted."[13] Speaking on behalf of Parliament, he said, "we therefore, the Lords and Commons in Parliament assembled, do hereby renounce, abominate and protest against that impious murder, and most unparalleled treason."[14]

Beauclerk's goal in the sermon was to ensure "men must be strongly induced the like for the future" and "to stand fast in their Christian and constitutional liberty," and he placed an onus especially on the clergy to inculcate "the peaceable doctrines of Christianity; in preaching against faction and rebellion."[15] Echoing the High Church sermons of the Jacobite Bishop Francis Atterbury in 1708–9, he argued that all Christians were subject to civil authority, although he endorsed the "excellency of our government and our constitution in Church and State."[16] Referring to his great-uncle, James II, Beauclerk mentioned that, while in exile, he had adopted "habits and opinions, religious and political, as in succeeding times as well as nigh subverted the religion and liberties of his country." This, argued Beauclerk, was sufficient ground to abandon "the fashion of educating our principal youth abroad . . . and may prove . . . prejudicial to these kingdoms." It risked the estrangement of youth from British laws and religion.[17]

This was an intensely conservative sermon. Despite wrapping itself in the flag of the Glorious Revolution, and repudiating the Catholic principles of his Stuart forebears, Beauclerk was advocating complete

11. Ibid.

12. Ibid., 17.

13. Ibid., 18.

14. Ibid., 20.

15. Ibid., 21.

16. Ibid., 22. For details of Atterbury's sermons on this theme see W. Gibson, *Enlightenment Prelate, Benjamin Hoadly, 1676–1761* (Cambridge: Clarke, 2004).

17. Beauclerk, *A Sermon Preached before the Right Honourable the Lords Spiritual and Temporal*, 23.

subjection of people to the civil power and rejection of the progressive Enlightenment influences of European education.

A year later, Beauclerk asked his friend, William Parker, to preach the annual Three Choirs Festival sermon at Hereford. Parker was rector of Little Ilford, Essex and minister of St Katherine Kree in London, as well as a Fellow of the Royal Society. He was later to be appointed by Beauclerk to the Hereford Cathedral chapter. Parker dedicated his sermon to Bishop Beauclerk and hoped that the Bishop would patronize "that which your encouragement hath introduced into the world." He also thanked the Bishop for his "many civilities and favours." In many ways, Parker's sermon was a relatively customary Pelagian theology of music in the eighteenth century, one which did not see it as an encouragement to sin and regarded pleasure as part of the divine plan for mankind. Parker argued that pleasure came from God, and that music was part of this; God urged man to virtue by way of delight and performance and that the eye and ear were "inlets of pleasure." Hearing, of course, claimed Parker, was also a source of admonition and apprehension of mischief, but the rising and falling of music, the swelling, acuteness, swiftness and slowness of notes "echoes back the several agitations of the soul" and gives mankind satisfaction.

In four respects, however, Parker's sermon was noteworthy. Firstly, perhaps with an eye to the Bishop, Parker claimed that the higher men were placed socially "the warmer the sense of gratitude ought they to cherish . . . towards the God who raised them and fixt their station in this rank of superiority."[18] Secondly, unlike Beauclerk's sermon before the House of Lords, Parker reveled in continental science and learning. Referring to the anatomical dissection and research of Monsieur Ferreir, a member of the French Royal Academy of Science, Parker recounted that his work showed that the vibrating air from the lungs hit the vocal cords, which "serves as a bow, or as quills" and the vibrations caused the cartilages and muscles "to extend or remit these chords."[19] Thus for Parker, science buttressed faith. Thirdly, Parker argued that, however licentious and immoral some represented the country to be, religious

---

18. W. Parker, *The Pleasure of Gratitude and Benevolence improved by Church Musick, A Sermon Preached at the Anniversary Meeting of the Three Choirs of Gloucester, Worcester and Hereford, in the Cathedral Church of Hereford on Wednesday, Sept 12th, 1753* (London: Fletcher, 1753) 7

19. Ibid., 19–20.

music showed that "we have some religious still left in our country."[20] Finally, Parker analogized the musical harmony of the festival with the aspiration for social harmony which he took as the aim of those attending; such social harmony which would protect the interests of the poor and afflicted children. Such aims would, suggested Parker, encourage his congregation to good works.

The centerpiece of Beauclerk's episcopate was his turbulent relationship with the Cathedral. Hereford Cathedral had always enjoyed a wayward independence from its diocesan, claiming from the Middle Ages to be exempt from the bishop's jurisdiction.[21] In 1677 Bishop Herbert Croft held a visitation of the Cathedral but only with the cooperation of his friend the dean, George Benson. This personal arrangement did not concede the Cathedral's right to exemption from episcopal jurisdiction. However, in July 1765, Bishop Beauclerk cited Croft's visitation as grounds to hold his own visitation. Beauclerk planned a thorough visitation of the chapter, the fabric of the Cathedral, the dean and canons, the vicars choral and organists and St. Ethelbert's hospital—a diocesan almshouse. It seems likely that the dean and chapter had sensed that Beauclerk was not a bishop to be resisted, and accepted his authority. Nevertheless they did not at first appreciate the strength of his determination to reform the Cathedral. Canon Humphrey Wishaw, who was the residentiary unlucky enough to respond to the Bishop's seventy-seven visitation queries, casually responded that "it is possible several things may not be in so good a condition as is to be wished." He also mentioned that "the dean is seldom here."[22] In other respects, the chapter seemed to be in good order. The Three Choirs Festival, with the Cathedrals of Gloucester and Worcester, had maintained a strong choir and organist. There was monthly communion, regular preaching, as well as weekly divinity lectures, and the archives, library, school, and financial arrangements of the Cathedral seemed to be well organized. In a separate visitation of the choir school in September 1765, Beauclerk enquired in such detail that he was able to elicit the information that the choir was not furnished with sufficient copies of the *Book of Common Prayer*.[23]

20. Ibid., 23.

21. Attempts had been made by bishops in 1559 and in the seventeenth century to hold episcopal visitations, but to no avail.

22. Hereford Cathedral Archives (hereafter cited as HCA), MS 1543.

23. The most recent history of the Cathedral does not adequately cover the

However well the Cathedral chapter felt it had acquitted itself in the visitation, it did not achieve the high standards demanded by Beauclerk. On November 14, 1765, after taking some time to think about his response, Beauclerk issued orders and injunctions in response to his visitation. Beauclerk began by ratifying and confirming "all and every" injunction issued to the Cathedral by Bishops Croft and Bisse.[24] But he then issued nineteen of his own injunctions and orders. These were astonishingly detailed and thorough. They included that the licenses to preach should be examined for all preachers in the Cathedral; the organist's salary was to be regularized and include payment for the teaching of the choristers; the dean and chapter should exercise proper oversight of the clerk and vergers; books should be bought for the choir; a catalogue should be made of the Cathedral library; deacons should not be permitted to officiate at morning prayer; and the vicars choral should attend morning prayer. A number of injunctions were imposed on the dean and chapter for the parishes over which they exercised peculiar or exempt jurisdiction. These included insistence that the chapter visit the parishes once a year, that they check the maintenance of the chancels in these churches, and that proper arrangements for preaching be made. Beauclerk was also keen to ensure that the financial arrangements of the chapter were managed with probity. He ordered that the lease and tithes of the parish of Yarkhill should only be renewed according to the statutes and that "Henry Poole be called to account and forced to give satisfaction for all trees he has fallen and sold at Kempley."[25]

Not content with issuing such orders, Beauclerk added an extraordinary rider: "For as much as all or the greatest part of the members of the said Cathedral by their answers to the articles exhibited to them in our said visitation seem to be unacquainted with the foregoing orders and injunctions, we do hereby order and injoin that the same be severally registered and recorded in the present act book." Moreover, omissions to the responses made about the fabric of the Cathedral were to be made up with a proper report on the fabric "within and without." Robert Breton, Archdeacon of Hereford and Master of St. Ethelbert's Hospital, had not fully answered ten queries and "totally neglected" to answer eight and

---

visitation of 1765. G. Aylmer and J. Tiller, eds., *Hereford Cathedral, A History* (London: Hambledon, 2000) 132.

24. Phillip Bisse had visited the Cathedral in 1716.

25. HCA, MS 1554.

was ordered to give "full, plain and explicit answers" in writing to the Bishop's commissary by the following January. If the chapter thought that Beauclerk was not serious they were disabused when, in June 1766, he ordered the chapter act book to be checked to ensure that his injunctions and orders had been copied into them as he had ordered.[26]

As late as 1770, however, the chapter was still chafing at the episcopal visitation of 1765 and appealed to the archbishop of Canterbury. Nevertheless, the visitation had galvanized the chapter, and in the years after the visitation, the Cathedral bought books, repaired windows, surveyed and repaired the organ and bells, repaired the fabric, and exercised greater control over the vicars choral.[27] As will be seen, Beauclerk was happy to contribute to these repairs. The visitation of 1765 was not the only business Beauclerk had with the chapter. In 1768, after a long dispute, Beauclerk persuaded the chapter to set aside the Cathedral timber yard and use it as the site for a school for the choir. The Bishop, in an attempt to conciliate the chapter, agreed to give them access through his premises and pay the costs of moving the timber yard.[28] In 1771 there was also a dispute between the dean and chapter and the bishop over the use of canonical houses, the latter standing on the traditional statute use of the houses. An appeal to the archbishop of Canterbury was to no avail.[29]

Beauclerk was the bishop who had to face the greatest crisis in the Cathedral's history, the collapse of the west end in 1786. The most recent history of the Cathedral accuses Beauclerk of being obstreperous and obstructive in his dealing with the chapter following the collapse.[30] In fact, a thorough examination of the papers shows that Beauclerk was simply exercising proper prudence. In January 1787, in response to an appeal from the dean and chapter on the rebuilding, Beauclerk mildly asked for a proper valuation of the chapter's income—since the chapter was claiming it had no money to contribute to the repairs. The chapter sent some information to Beauclerk, but omitted the crucial income it could derive from timber, which the Bishop then asked for. In March 1787 Beauclerk said he would be happy to issue the appropriate faculty for repairs and

26. Ibid., MS 1577.
27. Ibid., Dean and Chapter Act Book 1768–1801.
28. Ibid., MS 5703.
29. Herefordshire Records Office, BN/30/13.
30. Aylmer and Tiller, *Hereford Cathedral*, 140.

for seeking authorization of a church brief from the archbishop, when he had also seen full estimates of the costs of repair. Finally, when the dean and chapter submitted the details of their income and the full costs of repair, Beauclerk agreed that they could raise a voluntary subscription to make up the £5,000 shortfall in the costs.[31] It is quite clear that Beauclerk was not being obstructive; he was simply being businesslike and thorough in ensuring that the chapter contributed to the repair of its own building.

Beauclerk's stern treatment of the Cathedral places him in the reforming tradition of eighteenth-century bishops, who were determined to ensure that the proper duties of the clergy and church officers were effectively discharged.[32] In his oversight of the Cathedral, he also used his powers of patronage to ensure that the most impressive clergy were promoted to the senior dignities. Among those he appointed to the Cathedral chapter were Francis Webber and Nathaniel Wetherell (who had both been heads of Oxford colleges)[33] and William Parker, a noted theologian whom Beauclerk had known at Oxford and whom he invited to preach the Three Choirs Festival sermon in 1753. He also appointed a number of future bishops to the chapter, including John Ewer and Shute Barrington,[34] and a number of scions of noble and gentry families, including John Harley, Henry Egerton, and Peter Rivers Gay.[35]

Beauclerk's reform of Hereford Cathedral is representative of his approach to the discharge of his duties as bishop. He was not particularly interested in attendance on the House of Lords, preferring to pay attention to the detail of diocesan life. His rigor in ordinations was important, insisting on the proper arrangements of ordinands' testimonials, qualifications, and titles. Beauclerk had to be personally convinced of the validity of acting in cases where ordinands were below the canonical age. He carried out visitations in person and even signed schoolmasters'

31. HCA, Dean and Chapter Act Book 1768–1801 (records for 1786–88).

32. See, for example, W. Gibson, "A Hanoverian Reform of the Chapter of St David's," *The National Library of Wales Journal* 25:3 (1988), and Gibson, "An Eighteenth Century Paradox: The Career of the Decypherer-Bishop Edward Willes," *The British Journal for Eighteenth Century Studies* 12:1 (1989).

33. Webber had been rector of Exeter College and Wetherell master of University College, Oxford.

34. Later bishops of Llandaff and Durham.

35. F. T. H. Havergall, *Fasti Herefordienses,* (Edinburgh: Jones, 1869) passim. Sir Peter Rivers added the surname Gay to his own later in the century.

licenses. In June 1757 one curate was called before the Bishop in person, rather than before the judge of his consistory court, to answer charges of neglect of duty. In fact Beauclerk stands out as the bishop of Hereford who most impressed the most recent historian of the diocese.[36]

Beauclerk clearly played a significant role in John Fletcher's life. On March 6, 1757, Beauclerk ordained Fletcher a deacon at the Spring Gardens Chapel, Westminster. He also issued letters dimissory for Fletcher's ordination as priest, which took place a week later by Bishop John Egerton of Bangor.[37] The Methodist historian William Davies made much of the "lax practices" of Georgian ordinations, but omitted the fact that by tradition some clergy were reasonably ordained deacon and priest in less than the canonical two years. In cases where travel to London or to the diocesan cathedral for ordination would cause hardship, letters dimissory were properly used.[38] Also, in such cases as that of Fletcher, where the bishop was assured of the learning and education of the candidate, this was regarded as legitimate. Fletcher's certificate of ordination makes clear that he was "of the University of Geneva," rather than ordained as a nongraduate "literate" clergyman.[39] In short, the circumstances of Fletcher's ordination by one of the most rigorous bishops, as far as ordinations were concerned, does not support Davies' thesis of a lax Georgian episcopacy. But the affair raises the question of whether Beauclerk knew of Fletcher's Methodism.

Certainly, Fletcher himself was anxious that Beauclerk, despite having ordained him, might prevent his admission to the living of Madeley, which the incumbent had agreed to resign (to be appointed to the living of Dunham in Cheshire) to make way for Fletcher. In December 1758, Fletcher wrote to Charles Wesley of his anxiety: "the Bishop to whom I am, or shall be, known for a Methodist may refuse to institute

---

36. W. Marshall, *Church Life in Hereford and Oxford: A Study of Two Sees, 1660–1760* (Lancaster: Carnegie, 2009) 163, 198–99.

37. W. R. Davies, "John Fletcher's Georgian Ordinations and Madeley Curacy," *Proceedings of the Wesley Historical Society* 36 (1967–68) 139. On the same day that he was priested, John Fletcher assisted John Wesley at the Eucharist. R. F. Skinner, *Nonconformity in Shropshire 1662–1816: A Study in the Rise and Progress of Baptist, Congregational, Presbyterian, Quaker and Methodist Societies* (Shrewsbury: Wilding, 1964) 59.

38. See, for example, the case of Jersey ordinands in W. Gibson, *Enlightenment Prelate*, 267–68.

39. Davies, "John Fletcher's Georgian Ordinations," 140.

me after all."[40] Three months later Fletcher wrote to Charles Wesley that the wife of the patron of the living had told him that "the Bishop will never institute me there."[41] And on September 26, 1760, Fletcher wrote to Wesley that his entry to Madeley parish had been beset with problems. The bishop of Lichfield and Coventry, Frederick Cornwallis, had been sluggish in signing the testimonials required for his appointment, though he did so eventually. But more alarmingly, the bishop of Hereford's chaplain had witnessed some of Fletcher's preaching at West Street Chapel in London, where Fletcher had given his Methodism free rein. Consequently, the chaplain seemed likely to object to Fletcher's appointment. Moreover, and this was perhaps a stratagem, questions had been raised about Fletcher's naturalization and therefore whether he could be appointed to a Church living.[42] In the event, Fletcher's admission to Madeley went ahead. Indeed, Beauclerk seemed to want to avoid undue inconvenience to Fletcher; Fletcher wrote to Lady Huntingdon in October 1760 that "the Bishop having unexpectedly sent me word to go to him for institution without delay, if I would not be at the trouble of following him to London, I set out in haste for Hereford, where I arrived the day before his Lordship's departure."[43]

But, according to one account, Fletcher's institution happened more by circumstance than judgment. It was Sir Peter Rivers Gay, a baronet, who was prebendary of Moreton Cum Waddon as well as Beauclerk's chaplain, who played a key role in John Fletcher's appointment to Madeley.[44] According to William Parlby's account, Beauclerk would be likely to refuse to confirm Fletcher's appointment to the living by the patron, Edward Kynaston, if Rivers Gay objected to Fletcher's preaching in London and to his connection with John Wesley. According to

---

40. Peter S. Forsaith, ed., *"Unexampled Labours": Letters of the Revd John Fletcher to leaders in the Evangelical Revival* (Peterborough: Epworth, 2008) 57.

41. Ibid., 61–62.

42. Ibid., 113. In fact, by an Act of 1709, foreign Protestants who conformed to the Church of England were thereby naturalized.

43. Fletcher to the Countess of Huntington, October 28, 1760, Methodist Archives and Research Centre, John Rylands University Library, The University of Manchester: Fl. vol. 2, fols. 57–61.

44. Rivers Gay was something of an eccentric, who by 1773 was depicted turning the garden in front of the Royal Crescent in Bath into a vegetable garden. Bath Central Library, image ref. 13553 and included in Christopher Anstey's *Ode on an Evening View of the Crescent at Bath* (Bath: C. Anstey, 1800).

Parlby, when Fletcher got to Hereford for his meeting with Beauclerk, he arrived some time before Rivers Gay, who was not therefore able to object to Fletcher's appointment. It was a close-run thing, for after the Bishop had confirmed Fletcher's appointment to Madeley, Fletcher "met him [Rivers Gay] at the door of the Bishop's room, and a wig I had on that day prevented his recollecting who I was."[45] It is probable, given Beauclerk's meticulousness and willingness to ordain Fletcher deacon, and issue letters dimissory to Bishop Egerton, that the Bishop knew of Fletcher's Methodism and did not object to his views.

Thereafter, however, Fletcher remained anxious about his relationship with Beauclerk. In July 1762, Fletcher presented a Catholic at the Bishop's visitation, and not without some trepidation. On that occasion he told Charles Wesley that he had the "boldness" to attend the visitation dinner with the Bishop.[46] Presumably he did not expect to be welcomed by Beauclerk. By November 1762, he told John Wesley that his "exhorting in houses," as he called it, although only in his own parish, grew to such a height "that I felt obliged to lay my reasons for it before the Bishop, but his Lordship very prudently sends me no answer. I think he knows not how to disapprove & dares not to approve this Methodist way of proceeding."[47] Skinner took this silence to be Beauclerk's tacit acceptance of Fletcher's activity.[48] Three years later, Fletcher wrote that his field preaching had "raised a storm" and he wrote that "the Bishop has not yet called me to give an account of my conduct."[49] Nevertheless, Fletcher retained a commitment to episcopal authority, and in May 1769, he wrote to the Countess of Huntington that he had written to ask the Bishop's permission to leave his parish for a short time to travel to Switzerland.[50]

---

45. Herefordshire Records Office AW 57/1 MSS titled "The Founders of Methodism: Their Journeys into Herefordshire," by W. Parlby, 76. Skinner repeats this story; Skinner, *Nonconformity in Shropshire*, 60.

46. Forsaith, *Unexampled Labours,* 150.

47. Ibid., 166.

48. Skinner, *Nonconformity in Shropshire,* 71

49. Forsaith, *Unexampled Labours,* 221.

50. Ibid., 247. Two years previously in Sept. 1767 Fletcher had sought to obtain permission from Beauclerk to install a curate to assume the responsibilities of the parish. At that time he said he sought the permission unsuccessfully and when he heard that the bishop was visiting Shropshire for his visitation, he also found that the bishop refused to see him. Lettre De Jean G. De La Flechere A Sa Mere, *Feuille Religieuse du*

Beauclerk's silence toward Fletcher remains an enigma, perhaps because Beauclerk had serious concerns about the behavior of those denominations outside the Church. In 1777 Thomas Warter, rector of Cleobury North, was chosen by Beauclerk to preach the sermon at the bishop's visitation.[51] Warter aimed to "rescue their [the clergy's] profession from obloquy and contempt" and "support the dignity of their employment." Understandably, given that Beauclerk was his diocesan, he praised the "disinterested labours" of those clergy of "independent fortunes," but argued that the general problem for the clergy could not be removed "without the interposition of the legislative powers." [52] Warter argued that St. Paul had been opposed by factions who misrepresented him and similarly parishioners would gain little benefit from clergy who were opposed.[53] He exhorted the clergy to show their faith by "their works and . . . evidence of the purity of their doctrines by the moral goodness of their lives."[54] He was especially concerned with those Calvinist preachers, presumably spilling over from Wales, who "in their systems exclude good works as of little consequence in religion" and urged the clergy to "persevere in exhorting to virtue."[55] He also warned that they should not recommend to their parishioners "reliance on the powers of unassisted nature."[56]

Speaking of the "mysteries of Godliness," he urged the clergy that "the prudent and rational minister will proceed with humility and caution; he will consider himself as a steward and not as a proprietor, as a servant and not as a master."[57] Such irenic behavior did not extend to Dissenters. Of these he said: "Let them reflect on the unreasonableness of their behaviour, when they depreciate the settled worship and orders

Canton de Vaud (Geneva: Vignier, 1830) 25–31. I owe this reference to the Reverend D. R. Wilson.

51. Warter dedicated the sermon to Beauclerk also.

52. T. Warter, St Paul's Vindication of himself: A Pattern for Christian Ministers: A Sermon Preached at a Visitation held by the Lord Bishop of Hereford in the Parish Church of Ludlow, July 9th, 1777 (Ludlow: Turner, 1778) vi, vii.

53. Ibid., 10.

54. Ibid., 12.

55. Skinner, Nonconformity in Shropshire, 83–91, points out that Shropshire possessed a cadre of evangelical clergy in the second half of the eighteenth century, and it may have been this group that Warter was anxious about.

56. Warter, St Paul's Vindication of himself, 16–17.

57. Ibid., 19.

of the Church, when they uncharitably judge and revile her ministers, and would persuade their deluded followers that our office is useless, and our doctrines unedifying."[58] He was realistic to appreciate "that part of our office which relates to the reprehension of sin is generally unwelcome" and that the just rights of the clergy were the subject of prejudice.[59] But more worrying to Warter was the Dissenters' "ministrations of laymen," which he described as "injurious to the cause of virtue and open a wide door to licentiousness and disorder." With an eye to some Dissenters' role in supporting the American revolutionaries, something that Methodists did not entertain, Warter denounced the Dissenters' promotion of "unhappy divisions in the British Empire." Perhaps also with an eye to the Bishop, Warter also reminded the clergy that "there was a time when our Church and Nation and the cause of Religion itself severely felt the bad effects that proceed from enthusiastick babble. How many families have reason to regret the calamities that harassed the nation about the middle of the last century"?[60]

Warter's concerns about Dissent were that it spread "wildest fanaticism" and "the greatest degree of credulity" as well as intoxication with religious fervor and "incoherent effusions" which led people to gather round "every ignorant pretender." He questioned those who were "leading them into separate congregations" whether they were acting in the best interests of the people, God, and the nation.[61] He argued that clergy should not be surprised when they were treated in the same way as Christ and that they had no choice but to emulate him in their lives and doctrines. In doing so, they should oppose the Dissenters. He urged: "Brethren, be it our joint concern by all honest means to countermine them in their designs: let us shew our zeal for the established Church."[62] Referring to Dr. William Dodd, recently executed for forgery, he said that considering the number of clergy, "it cannot be surprising that there should be some blemishes," but the majority should offer "the wholesome influence of a good example."[63] Warter had the opportunity to attack Methodism, but did not. The sermon is explicitly an attack on

58. Ibid., 20.
59. Ibid., 21.
60. Ibid., 22.
61. Ibid., 22–23.
62. Ibid., 26.
63. Ibid., 27.

Dissenters from the Church, and his mention of lay ministrations and of the American Revolution clearly suggests he did not include Methodists with them. Was this because Beauclerk, as he appears to have done, sheltered Fletcher in his diocese? If so, it would not be unique; successive bishops of Bath and Wells permitted the activities of a cadre of evangelical clergy in that diocese.[64]

In Beauclerk, Fletcher may have found himself an ideal diocesan. Unlike Bishops Gibson of London and Lavington of Exeter, who fiercely opposed Methodists, Beauclerk may have had reasons to be silent about Methodism.[65] Like John Wesley and other leading Methodists, Beauclerk was a High Churchman. He was also a reforming bishop who sought to urge cathedral and parish clergy to discharge the highest possible standards of duty. Methodists, like Fletcher, needed no urging to expand the nature of their clerical and parish duty. We can infer from Warter's 1777 visitation sermon that Beauclerk, responsible for a diocese bordering on Wales, saw Protestant Dissent beyond the Church as a much greater threat than Methodism within. Moreover, Beauclerk seems to have been tolerant of the views of others, such as William Parker, whose theological and intellectual preferences he did not share. It is therefore a speculation, but a reasonable one, that Beauclerk's consistent and uncharacteristic silence towards Fletcher was in effect tacit approval and sanction of his Methodism.

64. See W. Gibson, "Somerset Evangelical Clergy," *Somerset Archaeology and Natural History* 130 (1986).

65. For Gibson and Lavington, see A. M. Lyles, *Methodism Mocked* (London: Epworth, 1960).

4

Church and Chapel

Methodism as Church Extension

David R. Wilson

I. INTRODUCTION[1]

JOHN FLETCHER,[2] VICAR OF Madeley, wrote to Charles Wesley in March 1761, "Last Sunday all the aisles of my church were full as were the pews."[3] A month later the church was so full that there were "several

---

1. Note on abbreviations: Many references in this essay are taken from the Fletcher-related collections at the Methodist Archives and Research Centre at the John Rylands University Library of Manchester, hereafter MARC, and the Shropshire Record Office, hereafter SRO. Common names of John and Mary Fletcher correspondence (including their own) have been abbreviated in the references for this essay as follows: JF = John Fletcher; MF = Mary Fletcher (née Bosanquet); CW = Charles Wesley; JW = John Wesley; CofH = Selina Hastings, Countess of Huntingdon. All references to and translations of Fletcher's letters in French to Charles Wesley are from Peter S. Forsaith, ed., "*Unexampled Labours*": *Letters of the Revd John Fletcher to Leaders in the Evangelical Revival* (Peterborough: Epworth, 2008), hereafter cited as Forsaith, *UL*. References to John Wesley's *Journal* are from John Wesley, *The Works of John Wesley*, ed. W. Reginald Ward and Richard P. Heitzenrater, Bicentennial Edition (Nashville: Abingdon, 1988–2003), hereafter cited as Wesley, *Works* (BE).

2. John Fletcher (1729–1785), was born in Nyon, Switzerland. He moved to England *c.* 1750 and took orders as priest and deacon on successive Sundays in March 1757. He was inducted to the church at Madeley in 1760 where he served as vicar until his death in 1785.

3. JF to CW, 10 Mar. 1761, MARC: Fl. Vol. 1:10.

people under the windows in the Churchyard who were not able to get into Church."[4] When John Wesley preached in Fletcher's pulpit in 1764, he recorded, "The church would nothing near contain the congregation. But a window near the pulpit being taken down, those who could not come in stood in the churchyard, and I believe all could hear."[5] Such was the effect of Fletcher's tireless efforts in the parish, that accommodating his congregation became a pressing issue. This essay examines his strategies for achieving the Church of England ideal of pastoral provision for the whole parish and the way in which this ideology of church extension formed a foundation on which his widow, Mary Fletcher (née Bosanquet), and his clerical successors would build with considerable success for thirty years following his death.

This essay is a case study in eighteenth-century Anglican "church extension." It is also an examination of the nature and function of eighteenth-century Methodism. For, however much historians have tended to exaggerate Fletcher's connection to John Wesley as his "designated successor,"[6] the fact remains that he practiced the evangelical[7] irregularities of Methodism, capitalizing upon the associationalism of the age[8] to establish religious societies in his parish, and itinerating, first amongst Madeley villages,[9] and then in the surrounding parishes of the

4. JF to CW, 27 Apr. 1761, MARC: Fl. Vol. 1:13.

5. 21 June 1764, Wesley, *Works* (BE) 21:482.

6. Luke Tyerman, *Wesley's Designated Successor: The Life, Letters and Literary Labours of the Rev. John William Fletcher, Vicar of Madeley, Shropshire* (London: Hodder and Stoughton, 1882). For interpretations challenging the suggestion of Fletcher's "successorship," see Peter S. Forsaith, "Wesley's Designated Successor," *Proceedings of the Wesley Historical Society* 42:3 (1979) 69–74; David R. Wilson, "Church and Chapel: Pastoral Ministry in Madeley, c. 1760–1785, with Special Reference to John Fletcher," PhD thesis, University of Manchester, 2010.

7. On the emphases of early Evangelicalism, see D. W. Bebbington, *Evangelicalism in Modern Britain: A History from the 1730s to the 1980s* (London: Routledge, 1989) 1–19.

8. John Fletcher, *The Nature and Rules of a Religious Society Submitted to the Consideration of the Serious Inhabitants of Madeley*, edited by Melville Horne (Madeley: J. Edmunds, 1788) 9.

9. Throughout this essay, the terms *town* and *village* are used interchangeably with regard to the nucleated communities of Coalport, Coalbrookdale, Madeley Wood (later Ironbridge), and Madeley Town. These areas had grown to be larger than agricultural hamlets by the early 1700s. In the eighteenth century Madeley's villages or towns were part of the Madeley Parish settlement, all sharing the same poor rate and being administrated by the same vestry and overseers of the poor until the mid-nineteenth century.

east Shropshire coalfield. For these activities and his zealous preaching (probably more than for his relationship with Wesley) he was denominated by his parishioners as well as by some of the other clergy, "a Methodist, a downright Methodist!"[10] His "Methodism," however, was firmly rooted in the parish, and though Wesley's preachers eventually made their way to Madeley, Fletcher maintained superintendence of them thereafter. Mary Fletcher (1739–1815), raised in the Church of England, was closely connected with Wesley from 1756, and understood herself to be a faithful Anglican and Methodist. Her ministry endeavors in the parish, which she carried out between her arrival in the parish in 1782 and her death in December 1815, considerably expanded the work of her late husband.

The juxtaposition of these two emphases—church extension and Methodism—may seem paradoxical, for the former is an emphasis on "Established" or "church" religion, while the latter is an emphasis on what has often been construed as an ever-separating movement of "chapel" religion, supposedly in competition rather than cooperation with the Church of England. Alan Gilbert, for example, asserted that there was a "bitter confrontation" based on an inverse relationship between church and chapel characterized by the decreasing relevance of the Establishment and the increasing "capacity of Evangelical Nonconformity

---

The use of *town* or *village* follows Peter Clark and Jean Hosking, *Population Estimates of English Small Towns 1550–1851*, Working Paper No. 5, rev. ed. (Leicester: Centre for Urban History, University of Leicester, 1993) iv: "The town area is . . . smaller than the total of the parish (parish or parishes) within which the town was situated." Perhaps more importantly, the term is consistent with contemporary usage. John Fletcher wrote early in his tenure at Madeley, "I have frequently had a desire to exhort in Madeley-Wood, and Coalbrook-Dale, two villages of my parish," quoted by Joseph Benson, *The Life of the Rev. John W. de la Flechere*, 2nd ed. (New York: Bans & Mason, 1820) 78–79; and Madeley resident George Perry wrote in the late 1750s, "The VILLAGE . . . is called COALBROOK." Quoted in Barrie Trinder, *The Most Extraordinary District in the World: Ironbridge and Coalbrookdale* (Chichester: Phillimore, 2005). The *Victoria County History* volumes on Shropshire use the term *settlements* very loosely in reference to the villages of Madeley parish. While denoting the movement of "settlers" to the area into nucleated towns, reference to these as settlements is uncommon in contemporary eighteenth-century usage related to Madeley, and technically, the parish as a whole was the only settlement until the 1800s.

10. JF to CofH, 6 Jan. 1761, MARC: Fl. Vol. 2:67–71; Fletcher was implicated in the St. Edmund Hall controversy over the expulsion of six students, one of which, a James Matthews, was reputed a Methodist in association with Fletcher. See Richard Hill, *Pietas Oxoniensis: Or, a Full and Impartial Account of the Expulsion of Six Students from St Edmund Hall, Oxford* (London, 1768) 8–9.

to satisfy widespread individual and communal needs."[11] Another way of explaining this relationship has been to contrast Established "church" religion with popular "chapel" religion, which in the conventional view has been categorized as "the non-institutional religious beliefs and practices, including unorthodox conceptions of Christian doctrine and ritual prevalent in the lower ranks of rural society."[12] This construal has tended to reify religion into static categories which resist any fluctuation. Such categorization suggests that Anglican churches not only did not reach the masses, but by definition, they never could, for popularization existed only outside of institution.[13]

However, several studies conducted in the last two decades have revealed that religious participation was in fact much more fluid. As W. M. Jacob has observed, "There is evidence that the relationship was often relaxed and that the boundary between the church and dissent was porous to the extent that many dissenters attended their parish churches from time to time and that some Anglicans attended dissenting meeting houses."[14] Patterns of religious practice in Madeley appear not only to confirm a permeability between church and chapel, but even more, they indicate that the Establishment was in some instances quite capable of assimilating Methodist or "chapel" strategies for developing Anglican piety. During Fletcher's incumbency, his pastoral industriousness manifested itself in the expansion of the regular services of the church, the setting up and management of local religious societies, and itinerating within his parish, all aimed at bringing the church to the people in their respective villages, workplaces, and families—that is, he sought to establish the church as "popular religion." Following his death, far from a dissension from his practice, his widow, together with the curates of

---

11. A. D. Gilbert, *Religion and Society in Industrial England: Church, Chapel, and Social Change 1740–1914* (London: Longman, 1976) 8, 69.

12. Jim Obelkevich, *Religion and Rural Society: South Lindsey 1825–1875* (Oxford: Clarendon, 1976) 305–6.

13. Ibid. A critique of Obelkevich's categories as oversimplified is made briefly in Hugh McLeod, "Recent Studies in Victorian Religious History," *Victorian Studies* 21:2 (1978) 249–50.

14. W. M. Jacob, *Lay People and Religion in the Early Eighteenth Century* (Cambridge: Cambridge University Press, 1996) 6; Gail Malmgreen, *Silk Town: Industry and Culture in Macclesfield 1750–1835* (Hull: Hull University Press, 1985) 158–59; Jeremy Gregory, *Restoration, Reformation and Reform, 1660–1828* (Oxford: Oxford University Press, 2000) 273.

Madeley and the visiting Wesleyan preachers, carried this aim even further. In the eighteenth-century industrializing parish of Madeley, any clear distinction between Established religion and popular religion—church and chapel—is elusive at best. Indeed, it is the thesis of this essay, that chapel religion in Madeley is best represented by John and Mary Fletcher's own variation of localized Methodism which operated largely as an auxiliary to the church, and in that as a form of "unofficial" Anglican church extension.

Madeley, a parish of roughly twenty-eight hundred acres, consisted of three relatively nucleated villages: Madeley (Town), where the church, St. Michael's, was (and is still) located; Madeley Wood, about two miles to the southwest near the River Severn; and Coalbrookdale in the western part of the parish, approximately three miles from the church. The latter two villages had risen up around mining industries, iron founding, and river trade, while the old town of Madeley was largely surrounded by agricultural land. The majority of the two thousand inhabitants upon Fletcher's arrival in 1760 lived in Madeley Wood and Coalbrookdale. There were no official parochial chapels or chapels of ease[15] in the parish, and thus the old church, a Norman building which seated six hundred, could accommodate just over half of the parish in two services. In the following fifty-five years the population rose to over five thousand, presenting the church with a considerable challenge of providing for the spiritual needs of the whole parish.

Church Services

It would be somewhat pointless to talk of church extension if basic pastoral duty was not already being performed in the parish, for otherwise, the former is merely an exchange for the latter, and no real extension would have taken place. It is worth noting briefly, therefore, Fletcher's and his successors' regular pastoral duty. The Establishment pastoral ideal, as Henry Rack has summarized, was a parish in which the "parson . . . held two services on Sunday, preaching two sermons; and theoretically read morning and evening prayer daily or at least on Wednesdays,

---

15. Parochial chapels were unbeneficed places of Anglican worship which also had the rights of baptizing and burying, whereas chapels "merely of ease" did not have rights of baptism or burial, nor was it beneficed. Both were intended to make attendance at worship in the church more convenient for those who lived remote from the parish church. Richard Burn, *Ecclesiastical Law* (London, 1763) 1:275–77.

Fridays and Feast days . . . Communion would be administered at least three times a year."[16] How well was this ideal achieved at Madeley?

Fletcher preached his first sermon in Madeley on 26 October 1760.[17] Attendance was sparse; only about 160 people attended. Half as many attended his second sermon.[18] Yet, only a month later he wrote, "I have had four opportunities to proclaim [the gospel] . . . since I was inducted . . . The weather and the roads are all so bad, that the way to the church is almost impracticable. Nevertheless, all the seats were full last Sunday."[19] Attendance remained high, prompting him to begin regularly preaching a sermon at Sunday evening prayer from April of the following year; the second service had been without a sermon until this point. After the service he catechized the children and any others who wished to attend, and the afternoon service followed.[20] He instituted Friday evening lectures, which drew many more parishioners than he had anticipated: "The number of hearers at that time," he wrote, "is generally larger than that which my predecessor had on a Sunday."[21] In addition to daily prayers, Wednesdays[22] (and possibly Fridays) were kept as fast

16. Henry D. Rack, *Reasonable Enthusiast: John Wesley and the Rise of Methodism* (London: Epworth, 1989) 16; for eighteenth-century expressions of these ideals, see Archbishop Thomas Secker's *Eight Charges Delivered to the Clergy of the Dioceses of Oxford and Canterbury* (London, 1769). Related canons of the Church of England are to be found in Gerald Bray, ed., *The Anglican Canons 1529–1947* (Woodbridge: Boydell, 1998) see esp. can. 1603/14–16, 21, 45.

17. See JF to CW, 7 Nov. 1760, MARC: Fl. Vol. 1:12; JF to CofH, 19 Nov. 1760, MARC: Fl. Vol. 2:63–65.

18. JF to CofH, 19 Nov. 1760, MARC: Fl. Vol. 2:63–65.

19. Ibid.; *Victoria County History*, Shropshire, 11:240, 319 (hereafter *VCH*); William Marshall, "The Dioceses of Hereford and Oxford," in *The National Church in Local Perspective*, ed. Jeremy Gregory and Jeffrey S. Chamberlain (Woodbridge: Boydell, 2003) 197–222.

20. 22 Jul. 1764, Wesley, *Journal*, 5:87; JF to CofH, 6 Jan. 1761, MARC: Fl. Vol. 2:72. Fletcher continued this practice to the end of his life. See MARC: MAM Fl. 19/5/2.

21. Ibid.

22. See JF to CW, 5 Jan. 1763, MARC: Fl. Vol. 1:15, in *UL*. See Forsaith's note, p. 173, n.147. Fletcher, even prior to his "conversion," kept weekly fast days. Mary Fletcher, *A Letter to Mons. H. L. de la Fléchère* (London: R. Hindmarsh, 1786) 9.

days.[23] Monthly communion (celebrated the first Sunday of the month)[24] in Madeley was the rule, in addition to three feast days, surpassing the canonical minimum.[25] These patterns appear to have been maintained throughout Fletcher's incumbency, even by his curate during the three-and-a-half years Fletcher was away from his parish convalescing from a consumptive disorder.[26] Fletcher married Mary Bosanquet in November 1781, and returned with her to Madeley in 1782 for three short years of ministry together. Mary Fletcher recorded his pastoral devotion to the last in a biography she was writing (but never completed) of her late husband: "that Last Sabath morning yt ever he was at church . . . when seeing his great weakness & dying looks I begd him to refrain this one day—he answerd . . . 'my dear these 25 years however ill I have never once omited my duty in the church if at home & shall I miss them this day? then w[it]h a smile he added no no not this day fear no the Lord will bring me thro.'"[27]

Fletcher performed his full duty that Sacrament Sunday after which his health declined; he died of a fever the following Sunday, 14 August 1785. In June 1786 the new vicar, Henry Burton,[28] a nonresident

23. Just to the northwest of Madeley in the neighbouring, larger parish of Wellington, a similar pattern of worship services was common: two Sunday services, each with a sermon, were provided during the summer, while in the winter only the morning service had a sermon, and Wednesday and Friday Prayer was provided throughout the year. See *VCH*, Shropshire, 11:240. On fasts and feast days, see W. M. Jacob, *The Clerical Profession in the Long Eighteenth Century, 1680–1840* (Oxford: Oxford University Press, 2007) 181–92; F. C. Mather, "Georgian Churchmanship Reconsidered: Some Variations in Anglican Public Worship, 1714–1830," *Journal of Ecclesiastical History* 36:2 (1985) 276. These regular days of fasting were kept by Fletcher in addition to special fasts decreed by the Crown, which Fletcher promoted both locally in his parish as well as nationally. John Fletcher, *The Bible and the Sword* (London: Hawes, 1776). For a fuller study of communion practice in Madeley, see Wilson, "Church and Chapel," 91–94.

24. This is inferred from those of Fletcher's letters which mention Sacrament Sundays, as well as from records in Madeley which clearly indicate that first Sundays were Sacrament Days beyond the end of the century. See JF to CW, 4 Dec. 1775; JF to Mrs. Thornton, 3 Mar. 1783; Pocketbooks of Mary Tooth, MARC: MAM Fl. 25.

25. For a comparison of parishes, see Lichfield Joint Record Office: Parish Returns 1772; Mather, "Georgian Churchmanship," 273–74; *VCH*, Shropshire, vols. 10 and 11.

26. JF to Bishop Beauclerk, 22 Mar. 1777, MARC: MAM Fl. 36/2/6.

27. MARC: MAM Fl. 19/5/2.

28. Henry Burton (c. 1757–1831) was vicar of Madeley 1786–1831. He was also Rector of Sutton near Shrewsbury. J. Venn and J. A. Venn, *Alumni Cantabrigienses. A Biographical List of All Known Students, Graduates and Holders of the University of Cambridge, from the Earliest Times to 1900, Part II*, 6 Volumes. (Cambridge: Cambridge

pluralist, employed a curate for Madeley. Mrs. Fletcher was graciously allowed by Burton to remain in the Vicarage at Madeley, and more remarkably he offered her the opportunity to appoint the curates. John Fletcher had expressed to Mary that he desired their friend and his erstwhile curate Melvill Horne[29] succeed him, and on 21 June 1786, at Mrs. Fletcher's recommendation, he was so appointed. Horne's ministry worked in tandem with Mrs. Fletcher's, and when in 1792 he was called away to be a missionary in Sierra Leone, she and the parishioners were very disappointed. Again allowed to recommend a curate,[30] and after no small pains were taken to find the best person, Fletcher chose Samuel Walter, whom Burton duly appointed. Walter served as curate until the final year of Mary Fletcher's life. In terms of regular (i.e., canonical) performance of services, both Horne and Walter were assiduous, keeping Fletcher's pattern, including full duty on Sundays and monthly communion.[31] Any form of extension of the church, then, was not in exchange for regular canonical duty, but an expansion of it.

Church Extension: Defining the Problem

In addition to an Establishment *clerical* ideal there was a *parochial* ideal rooted in the medieval system of parishes as units "of ecclesiastical administration and pastoral care," individual bounded areas "large enough in population and resources to support a church and its priest, and yet small enough for its parishioners to gather at its focal church."[32] This ideal has informed studies of church extension which have typically focused primarily upon church-building activity by the Establishment. The term "church extension" seems to have originated in the last decade

---

University Press, 1922–27) 1:468. Fletcher was actually succeeded immediately by Edward Kynnaston, a relative of the patron of the benefice, but Kynnaston served only temporarily until a long-term replacement could be found.

29. Horne was the nephew of Nathaniel Gilbert (1721–74), the first Methodist missionary to Antigua. Gilbert's son, and Horne's cousin, Nathaniel Gilbert Jr. (1761–1807) was ordained in the Church of England and served as curate to Fletcher in Madeley for a short time.

30. Draft letter of MF to "Rev'd Sir," 26 March 1792. MAM Fl. 38/1/23.

31. For communion patterns during Walter's curacy, see Mary Tooth's Pocket Books, at MARC: MAM Fl. 25/1–31.

32. N. J. G. Pounds, *A History of the English Parish* (Cambridge: Cambridge University Press, 2000) 3.

of the eighteenth century.[33] Thomas Chalmers, known for his work on church extension in Scotland, reflected in 1821, that in order to bring the number of non-churchgoing population back into attendance upon the services of the church, "what a rapid process of church-building this would imply. More would need to be done in this way . . . than there has been done altogether since the first erection of them."[34]

Taking up this criticism of the damage resulting from the lethargy of the eighteenth-century church, Virgin has asserted that it was "just as well" that the masses did not "show any great enthusiasm for the services of the Church of England," for, "had they all decided to attend, there would have been nowhere to put them."[35] The problem of not only a lack of accommodation, but of unwieldy and extensive parishes in need of reform, was a real one. Madeley, for example, was often described as large and populous,[36] and industrialization compounded needs for pastoral care. It has been fashionable for historians to interpret this problem through the lens of the building initiatives and subdivisions taken up by nineteenth-century reformers. Geoffrey Best asserted that such was the essential and necessary response to the dilapidated parochial machinery.[37] Virgin refers to this as one of the "central problems" left "largely untouched" until such reforms as the Church Building Act of 1818,[38] and Gilbert's conclusions that the Established Church lost ground, largely to

33. Here, the obvious association of the term might be with Thomas Chalmers, clergyman of the Scottish Kirk, who chaired the Committee for Church Extension, and published numerous treatises on the subject, epitomizing the nineteenth-century critique of the Hanoverian Church to reform itself according to the expanding population and changing demographic needs of industrial society. On the history of church-building and developments concerning "church extension," see Robert Phillimore, *The Ecclesiastical Law of the Church of England* (London, 1895) 1638–1748.

34. Thomas Chalmers, *The Christian and Civic Economy of Large Towns* (Glasgow: Stark, 1821) 129; D. King, ed., *Two Lectures, in Reply to the Speeches of Dr. Chalmers on Church Extension* (Glasgow: David Robertson, 1839).

35. Peter Virgin, *The Church in an Age of Negligence: Ecclesiastical Structure and Problems of Church Reform 1700–1840* (Cambridge: Clark, 1989) 5.

36. On parish size and population, see D. M. Palliser, "Introduction," in *Parish, Church and People: Local Studies in Lay Religion 1350–1750*, ed. S. J. Wright (London: Hutchinson, 1988) 19. On Madeley specifically, see comments by Benson, *The Life of the Rev. John W. de la Flechere*, 101.

37. G. F. A. Best, *Temporal Pillars: Queen Anne's Bounty, the Ecclesiastical Commissioners, and the Church of England* (Cambridge: Cambridge University Press, 1964) 193–96.

38. Virgin, *Church in an Age of Negligence*, 3, 143.

the chapel religion of New Dissent and Methodism, rely partially on a critique of the church's "failure" to provide adequate accommodation: "This was the crux of the Anglican failure . . . Little was done between the reign of Queen Anne and the second quarter of the nineteenth century to enlarge the Church of England as a religious service organization . . . The facilities at its disposal, measured in terms of personnel or in terms of accommodation for religious worship, increased only marginally, if at all."[39]

However, as Arthur Burns has illustrated in his analysis of Diocesan reform in the nineteenth century, critiques by historians on the lack of systematic reform before the Tractarians, have eschewed the fact that throughout the eighteenth century, reform was taking place at various levels from the diocese down to the parish itself.[40] One example is to be found in Mark Smith's examination of Anglican chapel-building and pastoral activity in Oldham and Saddleworth, in which he concluded that the "Unreformed" Establishment's "failure to subdivide . . . may have helped to create a culture of church extension" as a foundation on which the nineteenth-century "Reformed Establishment" could build.[41] His conclusions are much more optimistic than the conventional view regarding the ability of the church to rise "to the challenge of its new circumstances with surprising vigor and imagination."[42]

It is a similar vigor and imagination which energized the Fletchers' efforts at extending the reach of the church. In Madeley, however, church extension is elusive if we look only to material success, that is, to the official forms of it to be found in the building of new churches, new chapels, or the redrawing of the parochial map.[43] There were ways of extending

39. Gilbert, *Religion and Society*, 27–28; Henry O. Wakeman, *An Introduction to the History of the Church of England* (London: Rivingtons, 1908) 432.

40. Arthur Burns, *The Diocesan Revival in the Church of England, c. 1800–1870* (Oxford: Clarendon, 1999) 16–17, 41–43, 76–78.

41. Mark Smith, *Religion in Industrial Society: Oldham and Saddleworth, 1740–1865* (Oxford: Oxford University Press, 1994) 41–42.

42. Smith, *Religion in Industrial Society*, 34.

43. On the issue of "success" and "failure" regarding reform movements in the early modern period and the need to examine the local (e.g., local setting, space, culture, discourse between local realities and institutional ideals) not just the universal (e.g., institutional ideals and propagation of those ideals), see Edmund Kern, "The 'Universal' and the 'Local' in Episcopal Visitations," in *Infinite Boundaries*, ed. Max Reinhart, vol. 40 (Kirksville, MO: Thomas Jefferson University Press, 1998) 35–54.

the reach of the church that took place outside of conventional official means, primarily represented by ideals and practice of pastoral care. Thus, even though with regard to east Shropshire specifically, as Barrie Trinder has noted, only one church was rebuilt, two were replaced by new construction, and one chapel of ease was built, in the second half of the century,[44] this was not necessarily indicative of the church losing ground. Certainly in Madeley, the fact that a new church was not built until the last decade of the century hardly indicated that the Church was in decline or neglected. Conversely, the situation prompted and was met by considerable pastoral energy and imagination which went a good way towards augmenting both the range and effectiveness of the Church in this period. This dimension of church extension is to be seen in the extent to which Fletcher and his successors understood themselves as competing with not only nonconformity, but with irreligion, and the means by which they sought to evangelize a yet un-Christianized Britain.[45] Indeed, to look only to the numbers of church buildings erected by the Establishment in the eighteenth century for an estimation of its effective outreach, is to underestimate the creative ways in which some of the local clergy worked to meet the need to bring the full ministry of the Church to their flocks, in spite of a lack of official accommodation.[46]

II. CHURCH EXTENSION 1760–1785

Expanded Church Services

Church extension in Madeley was accretive, building upon the canonically prescribed duties as opportunity presented or demanded—or, as Fletcher saw it, as providence opened the door.[47] According to Overton

44. Barrie Trinder, *The Industrial Revolution in Shropshire* (London: Phillimore, 1973) 297 (hereafter *Indus. Rev. Salop.*) On the chapel of ease at Jackfield, see Joseph Plymley, "Archdeaconry of Salop," British Library: Add. MS 21018.

45. Cf. JF Sermon, Acts 5:42, MARC: MAM Fl. 20/14; Gregory, *Restoration, Reformation, and Reform*, 234.

46. Robin Gill has submitted, that *over*-accommodation actually deters growth in church attendance—a significant challenge to the conclusions drawn by Currie, Gilbert, and Horsley's *Churches and Churchgoers: The "Empty" Church Revisited* (Aldershot: Ashgate, 2003) esp. 7–10; R. Currie, A. Gilbert, and L. Horsley, *Churches and Churchgoers* (Oxford: Oxford University Press, 1977).

47. Cf. JF to CofH, 27 Apr. 1761, MARC: Fl. Vol. 2:6; JF to CW, 27 Apr. 1761, MARC: Fl. Vol. 1:13.

and Relton, "The numerous week-day services [in the eighteenth century] . . . soon became a vanishing quantity."[48] Yet in striking contrast to this and other claims that the bare minimum of perfunctory duties became the standard practice of the clergy,[49] and that the later eighteenth century evidenced a steady decline in church services,[50] Fletcher moved well beyond the minimum, gradually expanding his ministry year by year. His weekday preaching increased early on and remained steady thereafter. As Joshua Gilpin[51] testified: "Not content with discharging the stated duties of the sabbath, he counted that day as lost, in which he was not actually employed in the service of the church[.] As often as a small congregation could be collected, which was usually every evening, he joyfully proclaimed to them the acceptable year of the Lord."[52] This was no hyperbole, and the early vigor with which Fletcher embarked upon performing his duty was indicative of his concern to provide the opportunity for all of his parishioners to attend divine worship. Fletcher admonished ministers who made excuses "that they neglect to proclaim that Gospel during six days in the week, lest they should be unprepared . . . upon the seventh."[53] He described his own routine thus: "I am insensibly led into exhorting sometimes, in my house and else where. I preach [S]unday mornings and Friday evenings; and Sunday evening, after catechizing or preaching to the children, I read one of the Homilies, or a sermon."[54] Even though neither Wesley nor his preachers had spent any time in Madeley up to this time, it did not take long for his parishioners to associate his zeal and evangelical doctrines with Methodism.[55] Already in November 1760 he wrote that the parishioners had begun

---

48. J. H. Overton and F. Relton, *The English Church* (London: Macmillan, 1906) 63.

49. Anthony Russell, *The Clerical Profession* (London: SPCK, 1980) 64–65.

50. Ibid., 54.

51. Joshua Gilpin (*c.* 1755–1828) was one of Fletcher's curates and later became vicar of the Shropshire parish of Wrockwardine. He authored a biography of Fletcher which was appended to Fletcher's *Portrait of St. Paul*, which Gilpin translated and edited for publication. 2 vols. (Shrewsbury: Eddowes, 1790).

52. Gilpin, *An Account of the Rev. John Fletcher*, 185–86.

53. Fletcher, *Portrait*, 1:361; JF to CW, 14 Sep. 1759, MARC: Fl. Vol. 1:4, copy at MAM Fl. 36/5.

54. JF to CofH, 27 Apr. 1761, MARC: Fl. Vol. 2:74. Cf. William Grimshaw to JW, 20 Aug. 1747 in J. W. Laycock, ed., *Methodist Heroes in the Great Haworth Round* (Keighley: Wadsworth, 1909) 55–56.

55. JF to CW, 12 Oct. 1761, MARC: Fl. Vol. 1:84.

to call his "meeting"—that is the Sunday church service—a "Methodist one, I mean the Church."[56]

Fletcher believed that "all pastors, should give evening instructions to those who have been engaged, through the course of the day, in their different callings."[57] Weeknights, he conceived, lent themselves particularly well to spiritual reflection, and services offered during the week competed with the communal solidarity offered by the alehouse.[58] He hoped that these services might well "prevent many young persons from mixing with that kind of company, and frequenting those places, which would tend to alienate their minds from religion and virtue."[59] Extension of the ministry of the church via competition was part of his parochial paradigm. For example, by 1764, Madeley's church schedule also included Monday night services.[60] Fletcher's choice of Mondays was actually quite strategic in attempting to offer a religious alternative to the alehouse. The colliers and iron workers who were paid fortnightly often recreated on what were known as "Reckoning Mondays," usually by gathering for drinking fests.[61] Scheduling weeknight preaching on these days would have coincided better with industrial workers' schedules than other nights.[62] By taking advantage of the Monday-night availability of the colliers and miners, Fletcher seems to have overcome obstacles presented by industrialization which, as Mather has shown, could in some areas only be "solved by substituting informal evening gatherings—cottage lectures, schoolroom services and class meetings—for the regular worship of the parish church."[63] And when still some did not come, Fletcher went to them: "I preach every morning," he explained, "to the colliers of Madeley Wood, a place that can vie with Kingswood for wildness."[64] The idea of expanding services was not mere pastoral

56. JF to CofH, 19 Nov. 1760, MARC: Fl. Vol. 2:4.

57. Fletcher, *Portrait*, 1:369.

58. JF to CofH, 10 Sep. 1763, MARC: FL. Vol. 2:9.

59. Ibid.

60. 23 Jul. 1764, Wesley, *Works* (BE) 21:481.

61. *Indus. Rev. Salop.*, 346. E. P. Thompson expounds on laborers' "Saint Monday" on which they drank "their earnings from the previous week." "Time, Work-Discipline, and Industrial Capitalism," *Past and Present* 38 (1967) 72–75.

62. One-quarter of the marriages in Madeley during Fletcher's incumbency took place on Mondays. Madeley Marriage Registers, SRO: P-180/A/3/2.

63. Mather, "Georgian Churchmanship," 278–79.

64. JF to CofH, 10 Sep. 1763, MARC: FL. Vol. 2:9.

speculation, for he knew his parishioners could confirm it in his practice, and he called upon their testimony of his labors when he wrote in 1774: "Now I appeal to every impartial hearer . . . whether I ever so much as hinted that we ought not to endeavour so to despatch our worldly business, as to hear [if possible][65] the word preached or expounded both on Sundays and working days: whether I have intimated that we can live in the neglect of God's ordinances, and break his Sabbaths, without bringing upon ourselves swift destruction."[66]

Thus the first phase of church extension was his reputedly "Methodist" zeal for declaring the gospel at every opportunity and in every place,[67] that all would come to saving faith and worship God in "spirit and in truth." This, however, raises the question, If every person was to attend divine worship, but the church would only contain half the parish in two services, how was this to be accomplished? The next phase of church extension then required some innovation, though concordant with a long English tradition of gathering believers together into religious societies.[68]

Madeley Religious Societies and the "Chapels"

Lack of new venues for preaching and fellowship in the absence of chapels was an obvious obstacle to Fletcher, who wanted to reach out to the villages of his parish from the beginning. His answer to the need for accommodation was to look for the opportunity to take the church to the people rather than trying just to get people to the church. The first such opportunity came in 1761. "I have often had a desire," he wrote, "to exhort at Madeley Wood & the Dale . . . but I did not dare to run before I saw the door open: it is now opening, a little society of about 20 or 30 people has come together . . . in the 1st of those places, and another of some 20 in the second."[69] He frequently urged upon his parishioners

65. Brackets in the original.

66. John Fletcher, *First Part of an Equal Check to Pharisaism and Antinomianism* (Shrewsbury: Eddowes, 1774) 68–69.

67. Fletcher, Manuscript Sermon, Acts 5:42, MARC: MAM Fl. 20/14/2.

68. Fletcher, *Nature and Rules*, 7–10; cf. John Spurr, "The Church, the Societies, and the Moral Revolution of 1688," in *The Church of England c. 1689–c. 1833*, ed. John Walsh, Colin Haydon, and Stephen Taylor (Cambridge: Cambridge University Press, 1993) 127–42.

69. JF to CW, 27 Apr. 1761, MARC: Fl. Vol. 1:13.

the command of Hebrews 10:25, not to forsake assembling together, and it is clear that what was often referred to by churchmen as "social worship" was part of Fletcher's evangelical ethos.[70] The importance of religious societies in Fletcher's life actually predated his contact with the Methodists: "When I was sixteen," he explained to Charles Wesley, "I began . . . to strive in earnest to grow in holiness . . . I was also convinc'd of the necessity of having a Christian friend . . . I at last . . . met with 3 Students who formd with me a religious society: we met as often as we could to confess one an other our sins to exhort read & pray, and we would . . . perhaps have been what the Methodists were at Oxford."[71]

The societies in Madeley in some ways reflected Wesley's Methodism, but there was an explicit clerical and Anglican emphasis in Fletcher's societies more reminiscent of the early Anglican religious societies of Horneck and Woodward.[72] Fletcher drew up rules for them, which, like Wesley's, specified the resquirement for membership as a "sincere desire to flee from the Wrath to come."[73] However, Fletcher qualified this statement with the condition, "and to seek Salvation from the Servitude of Sin, according to the Gospel and the Thirty-nine Articles of the Church of England; especially the Ninth, Tenth, Eleventh, Twelfth and Thirteenth;[74] which are earnestly recommended to the Perusal of every person who would be a member." Fletcher's societies, also like Wesley's, were to be spiritual associations and thus non-stratified, whose members were admitted upon their confession of their desire for salvation, "according to the Articles of the Church of England . . . be they high or low, old or young, learned or unlearned."[75] Fletcher summarized what constituted a religious society according to the means which the "Church recommends, in the first Exhortation of the Communion Service . . . Such a Society then, is only a Company of People who . . . require, as says our Church, farther Counsel and Comfort for the quieting

---

70. JF to Thomas York and Daniel Edmunds, Nov. 1777, in John Fletcher, *Posthumous Pieces of the Late Rev. John William de la Flechere*, edited by Melvill Horne (Madeley: Edmunds, 1791) 31–33 (hereafter *FL*).

71. JF to CW, 10 May 1757, MARC: Fl. Vol. 1:65.

72. Cf. JF to [Lord Gower], n.d., MARC: MAM Fl. 36/4/6.

73. Cf. Wesley, *Works* (BE) 9:69–75.

74. "Of Works Before Justification," *Book of Common Prayer*.

75. Fletcher, *Nature and Rules*, 15.

of their awakened Consciences, and meet to consult, read and pray with their Ministers."[76]

Overton and Relton lamented that "the religious societies, which were to a large extent responsible" for the extension of church services into parish communities in the seventeenth century, had by the middle of the next, "ceased to thrive."[77] Such "chapel" meetings, Gilbert claimed, were now the stronghold of dissenting congregations, or Methodism, which he characterized as "Extra-Establishment" religion, part of a "new, expansionist, chapel-based movement" known as "Evangelical Nonconformity."[78] The Establishment, on the other hand, was allegedly, due to the constraints of an outmoded parochial system and clerical lethargy, incapable of assimilating the currents of Evangelicalism and thus unable to compete in the market-situation presented by "chapel religion." In Madeley, however, the growth of evangelical chapel communities was rather indistinct from the growth of church communities in the parish, for it was the parish incumbent who established and managed both. Indeed, the growth of "extra-establishment" communities may be seen as the fruits of Fletcher's conscientious attempt to fulfill the church's ideal of pastoral care through a ministry of church extension by which he became familiarized with his parishioners, fostered their spiritual growth in their local village communities, and built an informal parish infrastructure to support this expansion. In this context, then, "extra-Establishment" might be better described as *extra* Establishment, where the ministry of the church took on forms subsidiary to its liturgical services and gradually extended from its center in Madeley (Town) to the outlying villages where the largest part of the population lived and continued to increase throughout the century.

Another indication of the strong Anglican character which instructed his management of societies from inception to expansion to multiplication—a key to interpreting his meetings as an extension of the church rather than as extra-parochial social gatherings—is to be found in the conflicts Fletcher was brought into by such "Methodistic" ministry. The first society at Madeley Wood eventually met in "a tall cottage on the edge of the Severn Gorge,"[79] owned by one of his earliest converts,

76. Ibid., 10.

77. Overton and Relton, *English Church*, 63.

78. Gilbert, *Religion and Society*, 51.

79. *Indus. Rev. Salop.*, 269.

Mary Matthews.[80] It soon had acquired the epithet "the Rock Church." This first of his religious meetings proved a testing ground for Fletcher's model of church extension. Two incidents here are noteworthy.

The first offers insight into the format and content of the meetings. About a year after the society had first come together, Thomas Slaughter Jr., a Catholic parishioner, interrupted Fletcher's meeting with a mob. However, Slaughter's behavior in barging in on the Rock Church was judged to be so indecorous, that he was left standing alone, and Fletcher took it upon himself to present him at the Church Court. The incident is significant in its own right, but as regards the Anglican nature of Fletcher's meetings, it is particularly enlightening. In his charge against Slaughter, Fletcher enumerated the offenses he had committed, amongst which two are noteworthy: Fletcher charged him "With prophane behaviour, and open contempt of the Lord's prayer & the Liturgy of our Church"; and with "remarkably interrupting the Vicar while he was praying for the Royal Family, in so much that he found himself obliged to get up from his knees, and make the said Mr. Slaughter walk out of the room, before he could quietly conclude the Collect for the Queen."[81] The implications are clear that at least part of the content of the meetings was the Anglican liturgy. Furthermore, Fletcher was apparently aware of fears that such house meetings might be incubators of Jacobitism, and thus his charge defended the meeting against any such accusation, while simultaneously indicating fear that Catholics such as Slaughter might themselves be Jacobites.

The second incident occurred at around the same time, when the Rock Church meeting was accused of being a conventicle, and Mary Matthews, along with those who met at her house, were presented to the magistrate on that account, for which she was fined £20 by some of the parish "gentlemen," so called. Threats were shortly after made against Fletcher, and some of the accusers actually sent a presentment to the bishop. Fletcher attempted to preempt any judgment by sending a letter to the bishop. He described his defense in a letter to David Simpson, the evangelical incumbent of Christ Church, Macclesfield, who had asked Fletcher about the irregularity and legitimacy of such house meetings:

80. Mary Fletcher, "Account of Mary Matthews," *Wesleyan Methodist Magazine* (1800) 219–22.

81. Slaughter Charge, 11 May 1762, MARC: MAM Fl. 17/19/2.

If the Bishop were to take me to task about this piece of irregularity, I would observe,—

> 1. That the canons of men cannot overthrow the canons of God. 'Preach the word. Be instant in season and out of season.' . . .

> 2. Before the Bishop shackled me with canons, he charged me to 'look for Christ's lost sheep that are dispersed abroad, and for his children who are in the midst of this wicked world;' and these sheep, &c., I will try to gather whenever I meet them . . .

> Some of my parishioners went and complained to the bishop about my conventicles. I wrote to the registrar that I hoped his lordship, who had given me the above-mentioned charge at my ordination, would not be against my following it . . . As I was speaking on the head of preaching in licensed places, or dissenting meeting-houses, with the late Mr. Whitefield, he told me, that when a minister of the church of England did read the common-prayer, there was no law against him[.][82]

Again, it is apparent that Fletcher perceived his religious meetings to be fully within the scope of his calling as a priest in the Church of England, and that the content and form of the meetings only served to build upon and encourage piety and churchmanship. The purpose of the meetings was an integral part of his strategy to extend the reach of the church. Fletcher was never called to account by the bishop, which Fletcher attributed to the strength of his case: "his Lordship very prudently sends me no answer," he wrote to Charles Wesley. "I think he knowns [sic] not how to disapprove; & . . . dares not to approve this Methodist way of proceeding."[83] The societies then, despite a lack of accommodation in the parish church for every inhabitant, helped to provide worship in the local communities. In addition to Mrs. Matthews's house, Fletcher leased a building which he referred to as his "Tabernacle at Madeley Wood"[84] at his own expense of five guineas a year. Then, in 1777, when the opportunity to buy land presented itself, Fletcher used his own resources to buy it and, "to build a house in Madeley-Wood,

---

82. JF to David Simpson, 4 Aug. 1770, in Fletcher, *Works of the Rev. John Fletcher* (London, 1859–60) 9:256–57.

83. JF to CW, 22 Nov. 1762, MARC: Fl. 1:19.

84. This may have been where he preached daily to the colliers of Madeley Wood.

about the centre of the parish, where I should be glad the children might be taught to read and write in the day, and the grown up people might hear the word of God in the evening . . . and where the serious people might assemble for social worship."[85] The society in Coalbrookdale also met in the house of a parishioner, George Crannage. The "Dale," as it was called, was the center of Quaker activity in the parish, and confrontations with one of their ministers, Abiah Darby, who was the widow of the industrialist Abraham Darby II, reveal that the meetings at the Crannages' was similarly built upon the ministry of the church, and the content of the meetings was, along with personal times of sharing spiritual experiences, structured around the liturgy of the Church of England.[86] In 1784 the Fletchers began the construction of a chapel in Coalbrookdale to host their meetings there. Thus, between 1760 and 1785, Fletcher's ever expanding ministry came to encompass all three parts of the parish in which he itinerated, giving clerical leadership and support. Thus Fletcher's "Methodism" was one of pastoral zeal, creatively utilizing his own resources and those of the parish to carry out the parochial ideals of the church.

From the mid-1760s, a Madeley parishioner would have found it difficult to find a day of the week on which the church did not provide some kind of worship service. Anthony Russell concluded that generally, "the policy of multiplying services" in the early nineteenth century was the reestablishment of an "almost totally neglected element" of pastoral duty by eighteenth-century clergy.[87] If this was the case elsewhere, it was not representative of Madeley, for Fletcher's work—sometimes in continuity with the common practices of the coalfield clergy, and sometimes innovative—set the standard for the decades following his death. In 1793, Joseph Plymley, archdeacon of Salop (Hereford Diocese), visited Madeley as part of an assessment of the fabric of churches in his charge. Although the Church was much in need of repair, what impressed Plymley was the pattern of worship which included two services on Sundays, prayers on Saint's Days, and sermons "twice every week on the evenings of working days in rooms appropriated for that purpose." He did not scruple

85. JF to Thomas York and Daniel Edmunds, Nov. 1777, in *FL*.

86. Cf. Abiah Darby's manuscript journal at the Library of the Religious Society of Friends in Britain: MS Vol. 310; see also Fletcher's correspondence with her and various tracts at MARC: MAM Fl. 20/4; copy at MAM Fl. 20/5.

87. Russell, *Clerical Profession*, 66, 75–76.

with the preaching which took place at times in unconsecrated rooms, but acknowledged that it was in "the most populous part of the parish and at a considerable distance from the Church."[88] He was aware of how the pattern in the parish was established, and noted the advantages of such diligence: "This custom originated in the time of Mr. De la Flechere whose zeal for the propagation of Christianity was much adorned by his charity and benevolence. He was a friend of the late Mr. Wesley's. The people are much attached to their evening preachings, and the Quakers . . . encourage it very much, perceiving the good effects it has upon the Workmen, the persons who attend these meetings frequent the Church on Sundays."[89]

III. IMPLICATIONS OF FLETCHER'S MINISTRY FOR CHURCH EXTENSION 1785–1815

Church extension was by no means diminished after John Fletcher's death. Indeed, as Barrie Trinder has observed, a "threefold ministry operated from the vicarage, comprising . . . [the] curate of the parish church, the visiting preachers of the Wesleyan Shrewsbury circuit, and Mary Fletcher . . . Sally Lawrence, and Mary Tooth."[90] There is only space here for a brief overview of the way in which John Fletcher's incumbency helped to create a foundation for church extension. There was considerable intentionality and a sense of divine calling which guided Mrs. Fletcher's next thirty years of ministry in the parish, despite initial uncertainty after her husband's untimely death. She was forty-six years old, and being left to decide whether to remain in the parish, she began to search out a new place to live to make room for the new vicar in the parsonage. She recorded the event in her journal, "3 October 1785 . . . when I had some reason to think this house would be wanted and that I must quit it I begun to consider where I had best to remove too." However, John Fletcher had pleaded with her to stay in the parish if he were to die before her. After submitting herself to God in prayer, she received a notice that "I should never be turned out of this House but might rent it which I received as an answer from the Lord directing my

88. Joseph Plymley, "Archdeaconry of Salop," British Library: Add. MS 21018.
89. Ibid.
90. *Indus. Rev. Salop.*, 271.

way." Permission to remain in Madeley vicarage was to her a providential sign of her call to continue and expand the work of religion in the parish, which she described in her journal: "I never was in any situation in which I had so much opportunity of doing good according to my small abilities as here and that in various ways public and private . . . here I have a great many sweet lively souls to converse with, my meetings are more satisfactory to my self then any place I ever yet settled in . . . I have been more and more convinced my inheritance is appointed of the Lord & that here is the spot I am to fix in."[91]

Ironically, John Wesley attempted on several occasions to coax Mary Fletcher out of Madeley, to live and minister nearer to himself in London, but she was as resilient to his persuasions as her husband had been.[92] So, in Madeley she stayed, and the Fletcher legacy of church extension became hers as much as it was her late husband's. The societies increased from three, one in each part of the parish, to a new minimum of four, and extending to as many as seven meetings a week during some seasons, amongst which she preached and superintended.[93] In 1785 and 1789, she was instrumental in enlarging the Coalbrookdale chapel. In 1788, she had the tithe barn refitted as a preaching house which came to be known by laity and clergy all around as "Mrs Fletcher's Room."[94] When between 1788 and 1797 discussions regarding the poor state of the church fabric led to the demolition of the old and the erection of a new and more commodious church, she not only subscribed, but opened her preaching rooms as de facto chapels of ease. In her selection of curates, she insisted[95] on a willingness to engage in a parish built upon Church Methodism.[96] This included a willingness to not only perform

91. Manuscript Autobiography of Mary Fletcher, MARC: MAM Fl. 23/1.

92. Peter S. Forsaith, "Wesley's Designated Successor"; "'The Devil's Snare': Issues of Ministry and Mobility in a Wesleyan Setting," unpublished paper presented at Point Loma Nazarene University, Faith, Hope and Work Conference (Feb. 2006).

93. See for example MAM Fl. 13/1/106–7.

94. See Mary Tooth to M. Davies, MARC: MAM Fl. 2/9/1.

95. MF to S. Walter, 26 Mar. 1792 extracted in H. Moore, *Life of Mrs. Fletcher*, 2 vols. (Birmingham: J. Peart and Son, 1817) 2:273–74; MF to S. Walter, [c. Jun. 1792] MARC: MAM Fl. 13/1/73.

96. "Church Methodism" was an "aggressively pro-Anglican" manifestation of Methodism represented not least by Charles Wesley. According to Gareth Lloyd, "Church Methodism" may in fact have provided a strong foundation for the success of Methodism after separation, if only by postponing schism until the movement was strong enough to succeed as a denomination, independent of a mother church.

full duty in the church, but to continue Fletcher's legacy by working the whole parish. Both Horne and Walter agreed to this. Two brief quotations summarize well the degree to which Madeley, despite a lack of official church-building activity, became a model of church extension in the second half of the eighteenth century.

When Melvill Horne was departing for Sierra Leone, he attempted to help Mrs. Fletcher secure a faithful successor. He described the situation to a prospective candidate, Joseph Benson:

> The constant inspection of 4000 people if you do it, as I am confident you would do it, will find you constant employment . . . Besides preaching 3 times on Sunday, & 2 every week, saints days &c. an extensive & populous country lies round me . . . My Morning congregation on a fine day is between 3 & 600 wch is as many as the Church can conveniently hold, & in the Evening not more than 200. At Colebrooke Dale at 7 o'Clock I frequently preach to between 2 & 300 & sometimes I have known as many as 400. On the week days however, I am seldom attended by more then 100 either at the Dale, Madeley Wood or Madeley. Near 200 people may be in Society . . . Upon the whole I have been so happy here, & thought myself so honoured in being Minister of Madeley[.][97]

Mary Tooth, who in 1795 came to live with Mary Fletcher in the vicarage,[98] first as a servant, but thereafter becoming the protégé of Mrs. Fletcher, and her eventual successor as leader of Madeley's societies, described the situation in the interim between the destruction of the old church and the completion of the new one:

> Decr 1796 I have now been just one year in Madeley & have found here a people with whom I wish to live & die . . . the church service is only once in three weeks & then held in Mrs. Fletchers Room, the other two Lord's days Mr. Walter is at either Coalbrookdale or Madley-wood. While he is at those places Mrs.

See Gareth Lloyd, "'Croakers and Busybodies': The Extent and Influence of Church Methodism in the Late 18th and Early 19th Centuries," *Methodist History* 42 (2003) 20–32; and more recently, Lloyd, *Charles Wesley and the Struggle for Methodist Identity* (Oxford: Oxford University Press, 2007).

97. Melvill Horne to Joseph Benson, 11 Nov. 1791, MARC: PLP 56/9/2.

98. Mary Tooth came from Birmingham, first for employment in the 1790s, but after finding a spiritual connection with the Madeley societies, removed to live in the parish where she served until her death in 1843. She was an executrix of Mary Fletcher's estate. See Mary Tooth's partial manuscript autobiography at MARC: MAM Fl. 14/1.

Fletcher speaks to the people in her own Room . . . & the people are so well pleased with the arrangement that they are wishing the building of the Church did not go on so fast they do so well without it.[99]

It is clear, especially in light of these accounts, that church extension should be considered as much at the ideological as at the material level. The parish church was rebuilt and opened in 1797, increasing the seating capacity from six hundred in the old church to 1,800 in the new one. In addition, the chapels, though technically unconsecrated, were considered by both the archdeacon and the bishop as de facto Anglican chapels. Thus, in 1818, in an *Account of Benefices and Population*, the population of Madeley was stated as 5,070, an increase of 253 percent since 1760. The *Account* noted an increase in the accommodation of the parish in one church and three chapels—that is, the parish church and the unconsecrated meeting houses in Coalport, Madeley Wood, and Coalbrookdale.[100]

CONCLUSION

Pastoral care in Madeley from 1760 to 1815 was characterized by a gradually extending ministry of church *and* chapel. Chapels, however, rather than being indicative of an ever-separating group of sectaries, operated as a means of Anglican Church extension, making lines between "Establishment" and "Extra-Establishment," difficult to delineate. For John Fletcher, the ministries of church and chapel were not always coextensive. For while he founded societies, preached and prayed extempore, and developed a local ad hoc preaching rota in his own parish which eventually expanded to include stops in neighboring parishes, there were limitations to Fletcher's "Methodism." These limitations, however, were rooted in the same foundations which he believed gave him liberty to practice some pastoral irregularities in the first place—the Canons, Articles, Homilies, and liturgy of the Church.[101] Thus, although he be-

99. Mary Tooth's Journal, December 1796. MAM Fl. 14/1, p. 95.

100. T. B. Clarke, *Account of Benefices and Population; Churches, Chapels, and Their Capacity* ([London], 1818) 95.

101. Cf. for example, Fletcher's defense of his preaching in JF to [Rev. Prothero], 25 Jul. 1761, listed as "John Fletcher's Mini-Manuscript" is at the General Commission on Archives and History of the United Methodist Church, Drew University: 1306–5–3:3.

lieved the canons allowed preaching as he practiced it in house meetings by right of necessity, sacraments were offered only in the actual church.

It was Wesley's claim that Methodism was to be spiritual leaven in the Church of England,[102] but it has often been asserted that the Establishment was too lethargic to either "initiate pastoral developments"[103] or to integrate the strengths of chapel religion, and the parochial infrastructure undermined its ability to extend its reach in even the most basic sense by providing increased accommodation, rendering it a Church of diminishing success when faced with rising population and the sociocultural challenges presented by industrialization. Church-building, however, was not the only (nor ostensibly the best) means of church extension. Fletcher's ministry at Madeley is a demonstration both of the possibility that existed in the parishes under the care of a diligent incumbent to extend the reach of the Church, and of the creative ways in which such potential was exploited. His gradual expansion of pastoral care from the regular services of the church, to weekday services, religious society meetings, and a local Anglican itinerancy in cooperation with Wesleyan preachers, helped lay the foundation for future church extension in Madeley. Mary Fletcher's ministry and that of the curates she appointed only developed these strategies further, and the industrializing parish of Madeley became an example of some of the best parochial work of Anglicanism in the later eighteenth century.

It was first published as *A Letter from the Rev. Mr. Fletcher, to the Rev. Mr. Prothero, in Defence of Experimental Religion*, in *Wesleyan Methodist Magazine* (1821) 17–28, 95–105, and added to the second edition of his collected works in 1825.

102. JW to Mary Bishop, 18 Oct. 1778, John Wesley, *The Letters of John Wesley*, 8 vols. Ed. John Telford (London: Epworth, 1931) 7:326–27; John Wesley, *Minutes of Several Conversations, Between the Reverend Mr. John and Charles Wesley and Others* (London, 1744) 1:14.

103. Jeremy Gregory, "The Eighteenth Century Reformation: The Pastoral Task of Anglican Clergy After 1689," in Walsh, Haydon, and Taylor, *Church of England*, 67–85, at 79.

5

John Fletcher's Links with Mystical Methodists and Swedenborgians

Peter James Lineham

WHEN AND HOW FLETCHER READ SWEDENBORG

THERE IS VERY STRONG evidence that John Fletcher later in his life was fascinated by the ideas of Emanuel Swedenborg. This is a surprising addition to the familiar portrait of this "typical Methodist saint,"[1] characterized by heroic virtue, and it warrants careful assessment.

Emanuel Swedenborg (1688–1772) was a participant in the little known spiritual and mystical Protestant tradition of the seventeenth and eighteenth centuries traced so carefully by W. R. Ward.[2] Modern scholars have interpreted Swedenborg's many Latin volumes with their accounts of visions of angels and the heavens as a search for a new theosophy in the face of the growth of rationalism. A son of a Lutheran bishop in Sweden, he was a recluse who lived his last years in London before his death in 1772. Most readers have reacted as John Wesley did when he first read the seer:

1. T. Alexander Seed, *John and Mary Fletcher: Typical Methodist Saints* (London: Kelly, 1906) 11.

2. See in particular W. R. Ward, *Early Evangelicalism: A Global Intellectual History, 1670–1789* (Cambridge: Cambridge University Press, 2006) esp. 163–69.

> I sat down to seriously consider some of the writings of Baron
> Swedenborg. I began with a huge prejudice in his favor knowing
> him to be a pious man, one of a strong understanding, of much
> learning, and one who thoroughly believed himself. But I could
> not hold out long. Any one of his visions puts his real character
> out of doubt. He is one of the most ingenious, lively, entertaining
> madmen that ever put pen to paper. But his waking dreams are
> so wild, so far remote from scripture and common sense, that
> one might as easily swallow the stories of 'Tom Thumb' or 'Jack
> the Giant-killer.'[3]

Wesley read more of Swedenborg in December 1771 and in April 1779,
and although he was intrigued by the ideas he found, he published
scathing comments on the subject in the *Arminian Magazine* in 1781,
and his evaluation tended to harden against these writings.[4] Whether
or not Charles Wesley read Swedenborg or what he thought of him, remains unknown. Yet Fletcher took a stance which moved in the opposite
direction. The reasons deserve investigation.

Fletcher evidently first read the writings of Swedenborg shortly
after *Heaven and its Wonders and Hell* appeared in an English translation in 1778 (the publication of which spurred Wesley's second round
of comments). This along with *The True Christian Religion*, issued in
English translation in 1781, is the simplest and most accessible of all of
Swedenborg's many writings. Those responsible for the translation were
the Quaker, William Cookworthy, and Rev. Thomas Hartley of Winwick,
who wrote a lengthy preface to the work defending Swedenborg's rationality and theology.[5] In the early 1780s, as a result of reading *The True
Christian Religion*, a new advocate of the seer emerged in the person of
the Anglican minister of St. John's in Manchester, the Reverend John
Clowes (1743–1831), and perhaps his interest was known to Fletcher,

---

3. Nehemiah Curnock, ed., *The Journal of the Rev. John Wesley*, 8 vols. (London:
Epworth, 1938) 5:354–55 [February 23, 1770]. W. R. Ward and R. P. Heizenrater, eds.
Works of John Wesley, 22: *Journals and Diaries V (1765–1775)* (Nashville: Abingdon,
1993) 216–17 [28 February 1770].

4. W. R. Ward and R. P. Heizentrater, eds., *Works of John Wesley*, 22:301 [8 December
1771], *Works of John Wesley* 22: *Journals and Diaries VI (1776–1786)* (Nashville:
Abingdon, 1995) 126–27 [22 April 1779]. "Account of Baron Swedenborg," *Arminian
Magazine* 4 (1781) 46–49.

5. Emanuel Swedenborg, *A Treatise concerning Heaven and Hell* (London: Phillips,
1778) i–liii.

although Clowes disdained the spirit of Fletcher as too "self-active" and his writings as "so much harshness and violence."[6]

Fletcher's interest in Swedenborg was raised controversially by Swedenborgian advocates as early as 1790[7] and aroused debate from that point, especially from Mary Fletcher, who did much to guard her husband's reputation. Still the evidence is strong, for not only did the Swedenborgians who reported his views have links with Fletcher, but their views were borne out by others with quite a different outlook. There is room for divergence of opinion about the attitude Fletcher took to what he read. Yet even according to Mrs. Fletcher, "The first book which he saw contained but little amiss," and she misquoted Wesley's opinion in 1778 that Swedenborg's writings would do neither good nor harm.[8] We know that Fletcher told several friends to take a look at Swedenborg for themselves.[9] A key example of this is his letter to Rev. Bouverot of Geneva in 1783:

> A Swedish gentleman called Baron Swedenborg, published many pieces in England, and declared that he had conversed with angels and spirits for more than forty years, and that with as much familiarity as with men. Some of his works have been translated into English. There is one, of which I have the original Latin by me, entitled "Mirabilis Coeli et Inferni," and which I mean to send you as soon as I shall find a convenient opportunity. It is certain, if believers were more detached from earthly things, and more concentred [*sic*] in Christ by faith, they would converse with angels and with the spirits of the departed saints, as the Patriarchs and first Christians were accustomed to do. There would, indeed, in this, be some danger of following after piety, with a view to such advantage, through a species of curiosity, which, if it ought not to be called the *back door*, yet would not deserve to be entitled the *front*, which consists in a humble faith disengaged from sense and from all self-seeking.[10]

6. Theodore Compton, *Life and Correspondence of John Clowes* (London: Longmans, 1874) 112.

7. See J. W. Salmon's comments in *Magazine of Knowledge of Heaven and Hell* 1 (1790) 238–39.

8. Henry Moore, *The Life of Mrs Mary Fletcher*, 6th ed. (London: Kershaw, 1824) 351–52, citing her journal of 5 March [1807].

9. See P. J. Lineham, "The English Swedenborgians 1770–1840," PhD thesis, University of Sussex, 1978, 52.

10. Luke Tyerman, *Wesley's Designated Successor: The Life, Letters, and Literary*

While Tyerman chooses to pass over this letter "in silence," we must not do so. However, the validity of the evidence cited needs careful assessment. The problem is that all reporters were affected by the later excoriation of Swedenborg and were thus bound on the one side to exaggerate Fletcher's interest or on the other side to minimize it.

WHY DID FLETCHER READ SWEDENBORG?

The idea that Fletcher was open to a heretical and sectarian visionary philosopher is clearly distressing to those who hold Fletcher in high esteem as a model of spirituality. When Robert Fraser in his doctoral thesis argued that Fletcher had developed Swedenborgian sympathies, although he noted that this occurred after Fletcher's key publications had been completed, thus preserving his much-reprinted defense of Arminianism from taint, this scholarship was dismissed out of hand by Laurence Wood.[11] Since recent scholarship on Fletcher has been dominated by those searching for precursors to the Holiness and Pentecostal movements, historians and theologians may find themselves caught up in a battle for current orthodoxy. It is much harder to place Fletcher's views in their original setting.

Fletcher's zeal for spirituality meant that he was constantly exploring various spiritual traditions, and he was not to know that they would subsequently be seen as somewhat unorthodox or inconsistent with Methodist discipline.[12] John Wesley shared an interest in spiritual experimentation, but anxiety for his movement typically led him to tighten discipline to exclude any spiritualities which could become diversions.

Labours of the Rev. John William Fletcher, Vicar of Madeley, Shropshire, (London: Hodder & Stoughton, 1882) 531. This letter is listed with manuscript copy in Patrick Streiff, *Reluctant Saint: A Theological Biography of Fletcher of Madeley* (Peterborough: Epworth, 2001) Appendix: Sources [not paginated] with the reference Methodist Archives and Research Centre: Ce2: Fl Box 36.5. I have not seen this copy.

11. Laurence Wood, "Historiographical Criticisms of Randy Maddox's Response," *Wesleyan Theological Journal* 34:2 (1999) 129. See M. Robert Fraser, "Strains in the Understandings of Christian Perfection in Early British Methodism," PhD diss., Vanderbilt University, 1988, 393. I am grateful to Dr. Fraser for providing me with details from his thesis.

12. See P. P. Streiff, *Jean Guillaume de la Fléchère John William Fletcher 1729–1785: Ein Beitrag zur Geschichte des Methodismus* (Frankfurt am Main: Lang, 1984), which has extensive details of his early contacts on pps. 65–70.

Consequently, Wesley was privately concerned about Fletcher's overemphasis on mysticism because he felt it led Fletcher into an undue passivity in his spirit.[13] Wesley stated his opinion in a letter to his niece three years after Fletcher's death: "The reading of those poisonous writers the Mystics confounded the intelligence of both my brother and Mr. Fletcher and made them afraid of (what ought to have been their glory) the letting their light shine before men."[14]

FLETCHER AS THE MYSTICAL METHODIST

Fletcher's interest in Swedenborg seems to me to be not a late aberration in his thought but an adjunct—although never more than an adjunct—to his broader interest in mystical theology. His references to Swedenborg are sufficiently guarded to show that he was uneasy about the complex philosophical system of Swedenborg's theosophy. He did not like the kind of exclusive allegiance to Swedenborg which became a growing pattern among the Swedenborgians from the 1780s. Mary Fletcher is not an objective source, but something rings true in her report that he had remarked, "Polly, I believe Mr. ____ will be a Swedenborger, and I am very sorry for it."[15] The reason Fletcher cited was not the exotic ideas of heaven which Mary ridiculed or the visionary aspect which Wesley disliked but the Swedenborgian view of the atonement which viewed it as Jesus putting off the imperfections of his body. It is this theology which emerged in Swedenborg's *True Christian Religion* as a clear divergence between him and the Evangelicals, both Arminian and Calvinist.[16] Yet theologies of the atonement were an ongoing debate in the tradition of mystical religion, of which Fletcher was so intense a reader.

Fletcher had a deep knowledge of the mystical traditions. His name occurs on a curious list of mystical readers circulated in 1779, which consisted of a listing of groups of devotees throughout England, including John Clowes in Manchester and various other readers of

13. John Wesley, *A Sermon preached on Occasion of the Death of the Rev Mr John Fletcher* (London: Paramore, 1786) 18 (his wife's comment with footnote by Wesley).

14. Wesley to Sarah Wesley, 26 September 1788, in John Telford, ed., *The Letters of the Rev. John Wesley, A.M.* (London: Epworth, 1931) 8:93.

15. Samuel Noble, *An Appeal in Behalf of an Eternal World*, 6th ed. (London: New Church Missionary & Tract Society, 1867) 251.

16. Ibid.

Jakob Boehme and William Law.[17] There is other evidence of such circles which complemented and contrasted with Methodist links. These circles were closer to the Moravians than the Methodists and included Francis Okely, who was offered the position of master of Trefeca College and was also later fascinated by Swedenborg's writings.[18] John and Mary Fletcher were well aware of these circles of mystics and quietists. The Calvinists circulated accusations that Fletcher was imbued with mystical ideas,[19] as Tyerman reluctantly conceded long ago.[20] But Fletcher was not ashamed of his interest, and vehemently commented in his *Second Check*: "if you think Mysticism is intrinsically bad, you are under a mistake."[21] In his *Fourth Check* he recommended Thomas Hartley's *Short Defence of the Mystics*, perhaps realizing that Hartley was within the Countess of Huntingdon's circle.[22]

Fletcher's enthusiasm for the mystical writers is a key factor in leading to his interest in Swedenborg. There has been sharp debate about how far Fletcher was "tainted with quietistic mysticism" and veered

17. Ralph Mather's "Account of Spiritual Persons to Henry Brooke," in *Correspondence of Henry Brooke*, Walton Collection, Dr Williams Library, reprinted in Christopher Walton, *Notes and Materials for an Adequate Biography of William Law* (London: Printed for private circulation, 1854) 595–96. It is discussed in J. F. C. Harrison, *The Second Coming: Popular Millenarianism, 1780–1850* (London: Routledge & Kegan Paul, 1979) 20–22 and 233, note 32.

18. M. H. Jones, "John William Fletcher (1729–1785) Bi-centenary of his Birth," *Cylchgrawn Cymdeithas hanes*, 14:34 (1929) 75–79. For the Trefeca link see E. Welch, *Spiritual Pilgrim: A Reassessment of the Life of the Countess of Huntingdon* (Cardiff: University of Wales Press, 1995) 113. Note the references to Okely in Fletcher's letters to Charles Wesley in Peter S. Forsaith, ed., *"Unexampled Labours": Letters of the Revd John Fletcher to Leaders in the Evangelical Revival* (Peterborough: Epworth, 2008) 295, 331. For Okely see John Walsh, "The Cambridge Methodists," in *Christian Spirituality: Essays in Honour of Gordon Rupp*, ed. Peter Brooks (London: SCM, 1975) 251–83.

19. Cheshunt College Archives F1/1576: W. Shirley to Countess of Huntingdon, 9 January 1772.

20. L. Tyerman, *Wesley's Designated Successor*, 531–33.

21. Fletcher, *A Second Check to Antinomianism occasioned by a Late Narrative, in Three Letters to the Hon and Rev Author*, Letter 2, in *The Works of the Rev. John Fletcher, Late Vicar of Madeley*, 8th ed. (London: Kershaw, 1826) 1:349.

22. Fletcher, *Logica Genevensis or a Fourth Check to Antinomianism*, Letter 5, in *Works*, 2:16–17. Hartley was by the 1770s also an advocate of the writings of Swedenborg. See Boyd Stanley Schlenther, *Queen of the Methodists: The Countess of Huntingdon and the Eighteenth-Century Crisis of Faith and Society* (Bishop Auckland: Durham Academic Press, 1997) 44, 86.

towards passivity.[23] Arguably, he moved increasingly towards inward religion in the 1770s and 1780s because he observed the politicization of Wesleyanism and the critical tone of its evangelistic activism. He may also have disliked any hint of exclusivism, for he seemed to welcome a diverse range of people with ideas of spiritual religion.[24] It may also have been linked to his "highly principled" approach to life.[25] He wrote to Charles Wesley in 1776: "I had this week a letter from one of the lay preachers, who finds great fault with me for having published in my book on perfection your hymn called the last wish. He calls it dangerous mysticism. My private thoughts are that the truth lies between driving methodism and still mysticism. What think you?"[26]

In effect, he was arguing for an evangelical mystical tradition as an alternative to antinomianism.[27] The species of mysticism which Fletcher favored can be identified from his writings, and from the comments of others. It was a compound of Jakob Boehme, whose writings were reprinted by William Law in later life, and a series of other mystical and "spiritual" writers, including Thomas à Kempis, Johannes Tauler, Miguel de Molinos, and probably other modern writers. These writers were in one sense a pathway to evangelicalism, and in other respects the path away from it. He was well aware that such writers needed to be distinguished from other "false mysticisms":

> I allow there is an extravagant mysticism, by which violence is done to sound criticism, in quitting, without reason, the literal sense of the Scriptures, and running into ridiculous and forced allegories. The authors who incline to this error, for which Origen was reproached, are blameable. But let us distinguish between frivolous mysticism and that which cautiously penetrates the bark or veil of religion to sound its depths, and discover in the sacred oracles a spiritual and heavenly sense, though veiled with

23. Wood, "Historiographical Criticisms," 129.

24. Note also Fletcher's dispute with Mrs. Darby recounted in P. Streiff, *Reluctant Saint*, 12–23. For Swedenborgians, see Lineham, "English Swedenborgians," 131–32.

25. See David Lyle Jeffrey, ed. *A Burning and a Shining Light: English Spirituality in the Age of Wesley*, (Grand Rapids: Eerdmans, 1987) 347.

26. Fletcher to Charles Wesley, 10 October 1775, in Forsaith, *Unexampled Labours*, 332. Also in Melville Horne, ed., *Posthumous Pieces of the Late Rev. John William de la Flechere* (Madeley: Edmunds, 1791) 230, where it is part of a letter dated 11 May 1776.

27. Robert G. Tuttle, *Mysticism in the Wesleyan Tradition* (Grand Rapids: Zondervan, 1989) 138–39. See also Streiff, *Reluctant Saint*, 305–6.

> figures which, in their general acceptance, signify nothing more than common things.[28]

What was the character of the mystical tradition he preferred? When E. P. Thompson claimed that there was an erotic flavor to Methodism, the charge fits more naturally with Moravianism and the mystical writers. They were constantly using the language of emotion as the vehicle of spiritual life. A recent work by Brian Gibbons has argued that the gendered dimension is fundamental to mysticism.[29] Now as many historians have noted, Thompson's analysis of revivalistic religion is a severe distortion. Phyllis Mack has shown that "images of pain and self-abasement" were much more characteristic of Methodist devotion than erotic imagery.[30] Strength in weakness is an important image in the mystics too. Yet the imagery of sweetness is perhaps a distinctive mark of the spiritual tradition linked with *The Imitation of Christ* which Fletcher constantly recommended.

In addition, mystical writers generally advocated a theosophy which viewed personal spiritual struggles as part of a cosmic struggle across time and space. The human as flesh and spirit was a replica of the universe. Fletcher seems to have interpreted the story of Adam as a parable of the universe, and there are many other indications in his writings of the influence of Jakob Boehme and William Law.[31]

Mystical theology, according to Fletcher, offered a way of reading the scriptures to illuminate the meaning of the Scriptures.

> It would be impossible, without this wise mysticism, to understand the Scriptures, which, in many places, offer nothing but a coarse meaning, equally unworthy of the Holy Ghost, and of common sense. For instance, what literal meaning is there in these words of Moses? 'Circumcise the foreskin of your hearts,

28. Fletcher, "On Evangelical Mysticism," in *Works* in 4 vols. (Salem, OH: Schmul, 1974) 1.

29. Brian J. Gibbons, *Gender in Mystical and Occult Thought: Behmenism and its Development in England* (Cambridge: Cambridge University Press, 1996). This fine work takes the story of the followers of Böhme as far as Swedenborg, but neglects its sympathizers among the Methodists.

30. E. P. Thompson, *Making of the English Working Class*, rev. ed. (Harmondsworth: Penguin, 1968) 385 ff. Phyllis Mack, "Religious Dissenters in Enlightenment England," *History Workshop Journal* 49 (2000) 2.

31. Nicholas Manners, *A Full Confutation of the Rev John Fletcher's Appeal: Remarks on the Writings of the Rev John Wesley.* (Hull: Briggs, 1789) lv.

and harden not your necks. The Lord will circumcise your hearts that ye may love him with all your soul.' And what literal sense can we fix to the words of David, when he says, 'The Lord is my rock and my fortress, my buckler, and the horn of my salvation?' All the sacred writers may be cited to prove the necessity of admitting mysticism in the manner it is done in the following work.[32]

It is these themes which may have drawn him to the Swedenborgian doctrine of correspondences, which constructed comprehensive analogies between the natural, the spiritual, and the heavenly realms, for supposedly he was thinking of writing a book on the idea of "correspondences" himself—a way of reading the bible "spiritually."[33]

FLETCHER'S MILLENNIALISM AND DOCTRINE OF PERFECT LOVE

Fletcher's Arminianism was at the heart of his theological values, but his reputation as Wesleyan flag bearer was earned primarily by John Wesley's search for a successor and by his increasingly vehement defense of Wesley in his series of *Checks to Antinomianism*. Actually, Fletcher's relationships with the Wesleyan connexion were ambiguous, and this was partly because of his sponsorship of other spiritual themes and people with outlooks which differed from those of Wesley. This was to some extent evident in his ministry at Madeley. John Wesley might have been surprised at some of what Fletcher dispensed to his parishioners.

Fletcher defended the 1763 millenarians (Bell and Maxfield) in a letter to Wesley.[34] Fletcher had early contact with Maxfield in 1758 and after the split sought to persuade Wesley to renew links with him.[35] He invited Maxfield to preach for him after he had been expelled from the London Society.[36] Fletcher's links with Henry Brooke are particularly

32. John Fletcher, *A Poem entitled Grace and Nature . . . translated by Miles Martindale* (Leeds: Printed for the translator, 1810) xxiv. In some editions of Fletcher's *Works* as "On Evangelical Mysticism." Originally in French as "Discourse Préliminaire," in J. G. De la Fléchére, *La Grace et la Nature, Poëme*, 2nd ed. (London: Hindmarsh, 1785) xxiii–xxiv. Many thanks to Peter Forsaith for tracking down this elusive source.

33. Noble, *Appeal*, 254.

34. W. Stephen Gunter, *The Limits of Love Divine* (Nashville: Kingswood, 1989) 216. See Streiff, *Reluctant Saint*, 135–39.

35. Tyerman, *Wesley's Designated Successor*, 33.

36. Peter S. Forsaith, *John Fletcher* (Peterborough: Foundery, 1994) 17.

interesting for they reflected their shared millenarian interests.[37] Brooke's sympathy with Law's ideas seems to have interested Fletcher.[38]

Fletcher's eagerness for the fullness of the Holy Spirit both for himself and for others has some relevance to the issue.[39] He was profoundly focused on the doctrine of perfect love.[40] Fletcher placed this in the context of the church emerging into a new Pentecostal age, and of an age of special grace awaiting those whose spiritual lives were renewed. This attitude moved beyond anything that Wesley would have approved, seeming to embrace "enthusiasm," although it was tempered by an emphasis on practical holiness.[41] Wesley told Fletcher: "It seems our views of Christian perfection are a little different, though not opposite."[42] Writing to Mary Bosanquet some years before their marriage, Fletcher defined the distinction: "I would distinguish more exactly between the believers baptized with the Pentecostal power of the Holy Ghost, and the believer who, . . . is not yet filled with that power."[43] Thus his doctrine of the dispensations gave him a distinctive interpretation of salvation history.[44] Henry Brooke said that "Mr. Fletcher seemed to think that all professing Christians lived *now* in and under an Ante-Pentecostal dispensation . . . that the church is *now* in the wilderness although just on the *eve* of coming forth again in much more abundant power and glory."[45]

37. Tyerman, *Wesley's Designated Successor*, 552.

38. I. D'Olier, *Memoirs of the Life of the Late Excellent and Pious Mr. Henry Brooke* (Dublin: Napper, 1816) 40, 159, 194.

39. [A. C. H. Seymour], *The Life and Times of Selina Countess of Huntingdon*, 2 vols. (London: Painter, 1844) 2:102–5, based partly on James Macdonald, *Memoirs of the Rev. Joseph Benson* (London: Blanshard, 1822) 16–17.

40. Gunter, *Limits of Love Divine*, 214.

41. See Donald Dayton, "John Fletcher as John Wesley's Vindicator and Designated Successor? A Response to Laurence W. Wood," *Pneuma* 26 (2004) 356. See also Isabel Rivers, *Reason, Grace and Sentiment: a Study of the Language of Religion and Ethics in England, 1660–1780*, vol. 1 *Whichcote to Wesley* (Cambridge: Cambridge University Press, 1991) 234–47.

42. Wesley to Fletcher, 22 March 1775, Telford, *Letters of John Wesley*, 6:146.

43. Fletcher to Mary Bosanquet, 7 March 1778, cited in Tyerman, *Wesley's Designated Successor*, 411.

44. See Randy Maddox, "Wesley's Understanding of Christian Perfection," *Wesleyan Theological Journal* 34 (1999) 92–95. But see in response Wood, "Historiographical Criticisms," ibid.

45. I. D'Olier, *Henry Brooke*, 125.

The implication of this is seen in his expectation in a new experience of connections and effluxions from heaven to earth. It was this that made him look with interest at all claimants to heavenly inspiration.

THE SEARCH FOR THEOSOPHY

Joshua Gilpin's translation of Fletcher's *Portrait of St. Paul* was seen by Mrs. Fletcher in her old age as suggesting that her husband was sympathetic to Swedenborg.[46] Very probably she was upset by comments in the life of Fletcher, which was appended as notes to the early editions.[47] There is also a logic in the latter part of this posthumous publication that true Christian believers needed to find a way between the enthusiasm of the Convulsionaries and the rationalism of the Enlightenment. Fletcher seems to have expected that there will be an age of the Spirit, when a true Christian philosophy will illuminate faith. Such interests would have led him to find Swedenborg's obscure analogies full of interest.[48] Presumably his search for a true Christian philosophy was a critical issue.

HOW SIGNIFICANT WAS THIS READING?

Fletcher seems to have introduced at least one of the Methodist preachers in Shropshire to mystical writers—Joseph Whittington Salmon, nephew of Matthew Salmon, a member of the Holy Club, who was connected through his sister with Elizabeth Ritchie and Hester Ann Rogers.[49] Salmon, in 1785, at the funeral service for his wife, urged the

46. Moore, *Mary Fletcher*, 351–52.

47. The earliest edition I have seen is J. W. de la Flechere, *The Portrait of St. Paul or the True Model for Christians and Pastors . . . to which is added, Some Account of the Author*, 2nd ed. corrected, (Shrewsbury: Eddowes, 1791). The ominous word *corrected* may suggest a deletion of a reference, most probably from n. 23, 220–25.

48. Ibid., 2 possibly referring to page 100 (a reference to the mystics) or 191 or 220 or perhaps the logic of answering the philosophers with the image of the sun on 229 and what sounds like correspondences on 248–49. Fletcher clearly believed that the Christian philosopher could speak of the age of the spirit as a point of vision; 262.

49. J. W. S. of Nantwich to John Wesley, 2 July 1777 in *Arminian Magazine*, 1788, 217–18; same to same, 16 March 1782 in *Arminian Magazine*, 1790, 272–73; Luke Tyerman, *The Oxford Methodists: Memoirs of the Rev. Messrs. Clayton, Gambold, Hervey and Broughton, with Biographical Notices of Others* (London: Hodder & Stoughton, 1873) 62.

Methodist congregation at Nantwich, fifty miles north of Madeley (to be distinguished from the village of Madeley much closer to Nantwich on the border of Cheshire and Staffordshire), that they needed "to go through the shadow, into the substance and reality of pure and undefiled religion."[50] Possibly this influence spread within the Methodist circuits of the region.

In 1790 Salmon described Fletcher's view of Swedenborg: "he regarded the Baron's writings as a magnificent feast, set out with many dainties, but that he had not an appetite for every dish."[51] Many years later Salmon elaborated on his last visit to Madeley "a few months before [Fletcher's] death" (so about 1784–85) in which Fletcher commented that Swedenborg's *Treatise of Heaven and Hell* would be more to Salmon's taste than his.[52] For himself Fletcher could not give it wholehearted endorsement. Salmon now claimed that Fletcher accepted the Swedenborgian doctrine by which the whole Trinity was collapsed into the person of Jesus, but his evidence on this point was no more than inferential.[53]

There were a few other people in Swedenborgian circles who were well known to Fletcher. They include William Gilbert of Antigua, who was one of the early Methodists who got to know Fletcher at West Street Chapel in 1759 but was later connected with the New Jerusalem Church.[54] His Moravian mystical acquaintance Francis Okely was much preoccupied by the ideas of Swedenborg in the late 1770s, although by 1781 he had decided against these ideas.[55] Thomas Hartley, whose writings on the mystics Fletcher recommended in his *Fourth Check*, had become a translator of Swedenborg before his death in 1784.[56] Joshua Gilpin, Fletcher's clerical neighbor and subsequently his would-be biographer,

50. J. W. Salmon, *The Robes of the Saints Washed in the Blood of the Lamb* (Leeds: Bowling, 1785) 28–29.

51. The earliest source from J. W. Salmon is in the *Magazine of Knowledge of Heaven and Hell* 1 (1790) 238–39.

52. Salmon letter of 2 July 1825 cited by Noble, *Appeal*, 253.

53. Noble, *Appeal*, 254.

54. Ibid., 21; Tyerman, *Wesley's Designated Successor*, 36.

55. See Lineham, "English Swedenborgians," 40–42. For Okely's story see Edwin Welch, ed., *The Bedford Moravian Church in the Eighteenth Century* (Bedford: Bedfordshire Historical Record Society, 1989).

56. See Lineham, "English Swedenborgians," 26–30, 43–46.

had a phase of enthusiasm for Swedenborgian ideas in 1783.[57] Fletcher's printer Robert Hindmarsh, the son of the schoolmaster at Kingswood, James Hindmarsh, was an ardent Swedenborgian.[58] Links with Ralph Mather are also interesting. The preacher Alexander Mather was one of Fletcher's correspondents. He visited Fletcher in 1765 and was recommended by him.[59] Ralph Mather was his nephew who initially impressed Wesley on his visit to Kingswood School in 1773, but was later described by the Methodist leader as "almost driven out of his senses by Mystic Divinity."[60] Ralph Mather was responsible for the list of spiritual readers with Fletcher's name on it in 1779, and in the 1780s he adopted Swedenborg as his mystical illumination. In 1785 he joined up with a Swedenborgian reading group, the Theosophical Society of London, and then in 1787 he and J. W. Salmon became the first Swedenborgian traveling preachers. Fletcher may well have been alarmed by Mather's wild enthusiasm for Swedenborg.[61]

Fletcher would have been alert to the fatal step when some advocated Swedenborgianism as an end in itself. The Swedenborgian writers explain Fletcher's public silence about Swedenborgian doctrines: "because my congregation is not in fit states to receive them."[62] It seems more likely that Fletcher prevaricated about the ideas of Swedenborg. Fletcher's thought was so profoundly Trinitarian that he was not likely to warm to a theology which condensed the whole Trinity into Jesus the divine human. He could hardly have appreciated Swedenborg's attack on the orthodox doctrine of atonement through the death of Jesus. So his liking for a spiritual reading of Scripture would surely have been tempered by his belief in the humanity of Christ. The more that

57. Robert Hindmarsh, *Rise and Progress of the New Jerusalem Church, in England, America, and Other Parts* (London: Hodson, 1861) 17–18.

58. Streiff, *Reluctant Saint*, Appendix: Sources, letter by Fletcher to Hindmarsh, 20 November 1783, Letters by Hindmarsh to Fletcher, 25 November 1783 and 1 September 1784. I am grateful to Peter Forsaith for details on one of these letters.

59. Fletcher, *Posthumous Pieces*, 156, 157; Letter to Miss Hatton on 2 June 1765 and 8 August 1765. Letter to Alexander Mather (undated), ibid, 162–63.

60. W. R. Ward and R. P. Heitzenrater, eds. *Works of John Wesley*, 22:397 [29 January 1774].

61. See Clarke Garrett, "Swedenborg and the Mystical Enlightenment in Late Eighteenth-Century England," *Journal of the History of Ideas* 45 (1984) 77–81.

62. Noble, *Appeal*, 251 cites Mrs. Walker of Bath who in turn cites Mrs. [Mevill] Horne.

Swedenborgian enthusiasts argued that these writings had a special status as revelation, the less acceptable it became to the readers of other spiritual literature. By 1786 Fletcher was dead and the link between Methodism and Swedenborgianism became more impossible when a full-blown sect—the New Jerusalem Church—was established in 1787 as a result of Salmon and Mather's preaching tour.

MARY BOSANQUET AND SPIRITUAL RELIGION

There is additional evidence suggesting that at the time Mary Fletcher had some interest in Swedenborg. Her rejection of his views was based on his odd analogies: "If he can believe there are wax-candles and feast in heaven, he must have strange ideas."[63] Yet she had long been interested in the tradition of spiritual theology. Mary Bosanquet was a strong supporter of Maxfield as he careered towards conflict with Wesley.[64] Henry Moore thought that her theology had Antinomian tendencies, and that she shared the spiritual experimentation of her husband.[65]

There is a hint of some interest in a letter by Mrs. M. Walker of Bath in 1820 which includes a rather ambiguous response by Mary Fletcher about Swedenborg. This seems consistent with her combination of spiritual exploration and caution.[66] Mrs. Walker recalled that after her husband's death Mary asked J. W. Salmon to return a book by Swedenborg, but that proves little.[67]

In later years Mary Fletcher emphatically rejected Swedenborg and denied that Swedenborg had influenced her husband. Since their marriage was in November 1781 she may not have been conversant with his earlier links with mystics. She was aroused by the indication of his Swedenborgian sympathies in Gilpin's first edition of Fletcher's *Portrait of St. Paul* to deny that he had any sympathy for the Seer. Acknowledging that Fletcher did not initially condemn the Baron's teachings, she cites his subsequent comment: "Polly, I believe Mr ＿＿＿ will be a Swedenborger, and I am very sorry for it." She insists that for

63. Moore, *Mary Fletcher*, 352.

64. Ibid., 36.

65. See Moore, *Mary Fletcher*, 228 (footnote).

66. Letter cited in Noble, *Appeal*, 251–52.

67. Ibid., 254.

him the snake in the grass was that "These books deny the atonement, and so strike at the very root of religion."[68] She was clearly defending the reputation of Fletcher for later Methodists who had very naturally come to regard Swedenborgianism as one of the heretical sects which should be avoided at all costs.

CONCLUSION

One may conclude that this rather strange footnote to the story of Fletcher casts on him an interesting light, which shows how far he endeavored to live out the spiritual openness necessary to one who believed in a third dispensation of the Spirit which completed the earlier dispensations of the Father and the Son. If Fletcher had lived longer, no doubt his views would have changed, but perhaps we should not be as indignant as his wife that Fletcher's search for a Christian philosophy led him to consider what now seem somewhat esoteric ideas.

---

68. Moore, *Mary Fletcher*, 351–52, citing her journal of 5 March [1807]. See Noble, *Appeal*, 250.

6

"Adoring the Holy Trinity in Unity"

John Fletcher's Doxological Trinitarianism[1]

Kenneth M. Loyer

INTRODUCTION: FLETCHER AS PRIEST-THEOLOGIAN

As a leading voice in the burgeoning reassessment of John Fletcher's place in eighteenth-century English church history, Peter Forsaith challenges the assertion that Fletcher should be understood above all as John Wesley's theological spokesperson, the dogmatic writer synthesizing key components of Wesley's thought and defending Wesley, and Methodism, against contrary views. Though Fletcher certainly contributed a number of theological writings that would be endorsed by Wesley, and though Wesley allegedly wished to designate him as his successor, Fletcher's importance as a subject of scholarly inquiry is by no means limited to his dogmatic output, saintly character, or presumed suitability to inherit Wesley's leadership role in the Methodist movement. Indeed, Forsaith argues that Fletcher was first and foremost an Anglican priest, staunchly devoted to his parish in Madeley.[2]

---

1. My thanks to Prof. Charles M. Wood for his feedback on a version of this essay.

2. Forsaith reaches this conclusion based on a careful reading of the primary sources (*"Unexampled Labours": Letters of the Revd John Fletcher to Leaders in the Evangelical Revival*, ed. Peter S. Forsaith [Peterborough: Epworth, 2008]). Another im-

While Forsaith is a historian, as one whose primary field is theology, I am principally interested in the theological significance of Fletcher's work. Persuaded nevertheless by Forsaith's assertion that Fletcher saw himself primarily as an Anglican clergyman, I have come to think about Fletcher not so much as Wesley's dogmatic defender but as a priest-theologian—namely, someone who was a priest first, in practice and self-understanding, and also a theologian, or a theological writer whose work emerged from and was informed by fundamentally pastoral convictions and concerns.[3]

One such set of convictions concerns the doctrine of God and its chief end. Fletcher's approach to this topic lends itself to the interpretive scheme of priest-theologian because of how he addressed a disputed theological subject—the confession of God as Trinity, its perceived rationality, and its significance for the life of faith—with explicit attention to the pastoral or priestly implications of the doctrine.

In "Remarks on the Trinity" and *A Rational Vindication of the Catholic Faith*, Fletcher referred repeatedly to the theme of doxology.[4] By doing so, he suggested that one of his deepest concerns in writing about the doctrine of the Trinity was pastoral in nature: to promote the right worship of God in the life of faith. While he certainly appealed to reason, he was not content merely repeating one standard approach

---

portant source in the recent rediscovery of Fletcher is Patrick Streiff, *Reluctant Saint?: A Theological Biography of Fletcher of Madeley*, trans. G. W. S. Knowles (Peterborough: Epworth, 2001).

3. Reading Fletcher as a priest-theologian is perhaps a way to avoid two extremes: on the one hand, inflated theological accounts conflicting with historical data, and on the other, reductively historical "correctives" overlooking the theological elements of Fletcher's work or underestimating their importance. I do not have exemplars of either perspective in mind, but describe these positions simply to delineate the boundaries within which a balanced assessment of Fletcher could be conducted.

4. "Remarks on the Trinity," in *The Works of the Reverend John Fletcher*, 7 vols. (London: Mason, 1836–1838) vol. 7, 1837, 507–15; *A Rational Vindication of the Catholic Faith; Being the first part of A Vindication of Christ's Divinity; Inscribed to the Reverend Dr. Priestley, by J. Fletcher, Vicar of Madeley, Salop* (Hull: Prince, 1790). The document titled "Remarks on the Trinity" is drawn from *La Grace et la Nature, Poëme* (*sic*). It is a compilation of two notes original to Fletcher, on *chant* X and *chant* XX. Miles Martindale translated these notes and compiled them in "Remarks on the Trinity" as pars. 1–7 and 8–16, respectively. For the purpose of comparison, I have consulted the second edition of *La Grace et la Nature* (the oldest available), published by R. Hindmarsh in 1785. Any alterations to Martindale's translation are based on my own translation of the original, and are noted as such ("alt.").

of his time, whose chief aim was to defend the doctrine of the Trinity as compatible with or confirmable by reason. Nor did he shrink from criticism coming from the other direction that the doctrine was altogether irrational. In fact, over against both alternatives, Fletcher paved a different path, one that, though not without its problems or difficulties, ultimately leads upward in praise to God. He stressed that the very purpose of Trinitarian doctrine is to convey the great mystery of God's salvation achieved in Christ, a mystery that evokes from the faithful the appropriate response of divine adoration. In Fletcher's words, "we cannot believe the whole gospel without adoring the holy Trinity in unity, as appointed by Jesus Christ and his apostles in the formula of baptism."[5] As this statement suggests, and as his overall argument confirms, the account of Trinitarian doctrine provided by the priest-theologian Fletcher is essentially doxological. As such his message offered hope, for both this world and the world to come, to men and women who knew firsthand the challenges as well as opportunities associated with England's emerging industrial society. Fletcher's doxological Trinitarianism is noteworthy in terms of both content and context, and a critical appreciation of his approach can contribute to the revival of Trinitarian doctrine in contemporary theology.

FLETCHER'S DOXOLOGICAL TRINITARIANISM: A CRITICAL READING

Although Fletcher was certainly neither the first nor the most sophisticated proponent of the doxological intention of Trinitarian doctrine,[6] he was well attuned to the importance of such doctrine for Christian faith and life. The doxological thrust of his approach is particularly evident in his "Remarks on the Trinity," a set of excerpts from La Grace et la Nature compiled and translated by the Methodist preacher Miles Martindale.[7] Despite the occasional ambiguous theological expression,

---

5. "Remarks on the Trinity," 509 (alt.). Unless otherwise noted, all italics and capitalizations are original (except capitalizations that are standard in French but not in English).

6. A much earlier and more technically advanced example is Augustine's De Trinitate.

7. I am indebted to Russell Frazier on this point.

this compilation reveals Fletcher's keen awareness of the relationship between Trinitarian doctrine and the worship of God.

Fletcher set the tone from the beginning, with a hymn glorifying the triune God:

> Sing nature's Sire, sing his redeeming Son,
> And the blest Paraclete with glory crown;
> From God, our light, life, love, divinely spring,
> His lofty praise let us incessant sing.
> Let nature, long as endless ages move,
> Of this thrice-holy God proclaim the love.[8]

After this hymn Fletcher would weave together the themes of divine adoration, holiness, and happiness in relation to the confession of God as Trinity. According to Fletcher, the doctrine of the Trinity is by nature doxological insofar as it magnifies the God who "has revealed his extraordinary essence, eternal and perfect, existing without separation under the distinctions of Father, Son, and Holy Spirit."[9] Hence an essential part of believing in the gospel is to adore the one true God—"the holy Trinity in unity"[10]—of whom Christ plainly speaks in Matthew 28:19–20, and in whose name Christian baptism is accordingly performed. Fletcher explained that the terms "Father, Son, and Holy Spirit," along with "generation" and "procession," have been handed down through Christian tradition because they convey, as well as imperfect human language allows, "ideas of a mystery altogether divine."[11] Therefore Fletcher taught that in reference to God, whatever ideas or images associated with these and other words should be evaluated on the basis of God's utter transcendence. That is, they "ought to be as much elevated above our common ideas, as the supreme Being is above imperfect and finite beings."[12] However, Fletcher insisted that the knowledge these terms convey, while imperfect, suffices for our current state, as does an infant's knowledge of its father or mother for its ongoing physical, mental, and emotional maturation. The task for Christians is not to speculate needlessly but to

---

8. "Remarks on the Trinity," 507. This hymn, written by Fletcher, comes from *La Grace et la Nature, chant* X.

9. Ibid., 509 (alt.).

10. Ibid.

11. Ibid.

12. Ibid.

desire earnestly, as newborn babes, the pure milk of the word that will nourish their souls to spiritual growth and maturity.[13]

Here the priestly convictions of Fletcher are quite evident, for he is concerned about the meaning of Trinitarian faith for the care of souls. Implicit in the relationship that he discerned between the doctrine of the Trinity and the worship of God is the understanding that the doctrine serves a vital purpose in Christian living. In his "Remarks on the Trinity," he introduced that purpose in the form of a question: "Does [this doctrine] render men more holy and happy?"[14] Fletcher attributed the question to Joseph Priestley, the Unitarian writer whose challenges to the divinity of Christ Fletcher would later respond to in *A Rational Vindication of the Catholic Faith*. The advantage of the doctrine of the Trinity, according to Fletcher, was its contribution to the cultivation of Christian virtues, including both holiness and happiness.

Keen to emphasize the essential usefulness of the doctrine, Fletcher painted a stark picture of human existence prior to the revelation of God's triunity. He posited that in such a state all nations, "not excepting the Jews, have abandoned themselves to their passions, and men in general have been neither good nor happy."[15] While some in our contemporary milieu would likely question this reading of Israel's history, Fletcher's overall purpose here was not to criticize a certain group of people, or human beings as a whole, for their perceived spiritual and moral deficiency, but rather to underscore the saving activity of the God who abundantly supplies the means necessary for the renewal of sinful human nature.

As recounted by Fletcher, God's self-revelation makes the decisive difference: "things are soon changed, when the creating God reveals himself as Immanuel in believers; as soon as God, by the manifestation of his sanctifying Spirit, has re-established his image in their souls."[16] The upshot of this revelation is divine adoration, which leads to the manifestation of holy love in Christ's disciples: "Then the Trinity being clearly revealed, God is adored in spirit and in truth, with a zeal like that which burned in the bosoms of the primitive Christians; then men begin to love

---

13. Ibid.
14. Ibid., 512.
15. Ibid.
16. Ibid., 513.

and help each other with a charity which the world never saw before."[17] Based on the Epistles and the book of Acts, Fletcher then identified happiness as another mark of the Christian life. The early Christians, having been united by faith to one another and, principally, to the one true God, were filled with joy and peace, and abounded in hope to the glory of the Trinity. "Conducted by the Son to the Father, and sustained by the Spirit of adoption, they call God their 'Father' with unshaken confidence, and praise him on the scaffolds with a transport of joy which the deists never knew."[18] Through this brief foray into Christian history, Fletcher found confirmation in Scripture and Christian experience that "the holiness and happiness of the first Christians depended on the experimental knowledge which they had of the mystery of the holy Trinity; or of God manifested in their souls, as Father, Son, and Holy Spirit; or as Creator, Redeemer, and Sanctifier."[19]

With this last phrase, along with an earlier rendering of "Creator, Saviour, and Comforter,"[20] Fletcher appears to have equated the divine persons with the offices. Yet listing either formulation is not, properly speaking, the same as naming the Trinity, for in either case that would be to reduce the persons to offices. John Wesley had warned against such a reduction in his words to Jane Catherine March on August 3, 1771: "The quaint device of styling them three offices rather than persons gives up the whole doctrine."[21] As Geoffrey Wainwright notes in his study of Wesley on the Trinity, "The appropriation of offices to persons can be done only in the context of a full trinitarian doctrine."[22] Whether with these expressions Fletcher assumed the strict equation of persons with offices or, as was more likely, simply appropriation (however loosely articulated), his emphasis was clearly on the experiential dimension of Trinitarian doctrine.[23] In this way he anticipated his next main point— that the doctrine of the Trinity lies at the heart of the Christian life.

17. Ibid.

18. Ibid.

19. Ibid. (alt.).

20. Ibid.

21. *The Letters of the Rev. John Wesley, A.M.*, ed. John Telford (London: Epworth, 1931) vol. 5, 270.

22. Geoffrey Wainwright, "Why Wesley Was a Trinitarian," in *Methodists in Dialogue* (Nashville: Kingswood, 1995) 261–74, esp. 272.

23. That Fletcher intended here to remain consistent with Trinitarian orthodoxy—

Fletcher sought to make this positive affirmation by identifying certain negative examples in a sweeping overview of church history. After admitting that the apostolic zeal of the early church was tempered over time, he interestingly interpreted this change as proof that the doctrine of the Trinity cannot be attacked "without sapping the foundation of Christian piety."[24] Over against Gnosticism, Arianism, Sabellianism, and even a stale, lifeless, purported orthodoxy more concerned about theological disputes than growth in grace, Fletcher called for a deep retrieval of the living core of the faith and a fervent application of this truth to the hearts and lives of all Christians: "The church will remain in this trifling state [of theological and moral corruption], until all the preachers announce with zeal, and the people embrace with ardour, the sound doctrine of Father, Son, and Holy Spirit, which always includes repentance toward God the Father, faith in our Lord Jesus Christ, and love poured into our hearts by the Holy Spirit—love, that mother of all good works and the distinguishing badge of true Christians."[25] According to Fletcher, just as a corruption of doctrine leads to a corruption of manners, so the clear and truthful propagation of Trinitarian doctrine in its fullness, that is, encompassing both head and heart, yields the fruit of Christian virtues that bear witness to the glory of God.

In acknowledging the link between holiness and happiness, and grounding both in the doctrine of the Trinity, Fletcher demonstrated how his theological reflection grew out of and was shaped by his pastoral concerns. According to this priest-theologian, a corollary of the doxological nature of Trinitarian doctrine is the doctrine's salubrious advantage in promoting Christian piety and morality.

As intimated earlier, however, Fletcher's reflections are significant not simply for what he says positively about the doxological intention

---

and thus assumed the doctrine of appropriations rather than a strict equation of the divine persons with the offices—seems probable given the zeal for defending traditional church teaching against dissenters and unbelievers that he often showed. E.g., on November 22, 1764, he held a meeting of parishioners to answer objections against the Church of England's teaching, in which he expounded and defended the doctrine of the Trinity based on the Athanasian Creed. When Abiah Darby, a Quaker, asserted that the Creed contained false statements about God, Fletcher responded by questioning her in person and later defending the Creed in a written reply (Streiff, *Reluctant Saint?* 121–22).

24. "Remarks on the Trinity," 514.
25. Ibid. (alt.).

of Trinitarian doctrine. In order to appreciate Fletcher's approach for what it truly is, we must also understand what it is not. On this score, an admittedly brief consideration of the context in which Fletcher was writing can be instructive.

FLETCHER AND TWO ALTERNATIVES: ENGLISH UNITARIANISM AND ENGLISH RATIONAL THEOLOGY

The kind of doxological Trinitarianism propagated by Fletcher was by no means the only option at the time. In eighteenth-century English Protestant theology, there was arguably no more contested doctrine than that of the Trinity, concerning which there had developed numerous interpretations, some attacking the doctrine and others defending it. In short, there was a continuation of the controversy over the doctrine of the Trinity that had begun a century before among the likes of Ralph Cudworth (1617–1688),[26] John Locke (1632–1704),[27] and Edward Stillingfleet (1635–1699).[28] Because of its complexity, the story of this controversy far exceeds the scope of the present inquiry.[29] Yet what

26. E.g., *The True Intellectual System of the Universe* (1678), in which Cudworth argued that Christianity provided the only source of real knowledge.

27. E.g., *Essay concerning Human Understanding* ("1690," but actually published in 1689), in which Locke challenged the Platonic notion of innate ideas as well as traditional metaphysics and asserted that the existence of God could be discovered with certainty by reason; and *The Reasonableness of Christianity* (1695), in which Locke maintained that the only secure basis of Christianity was its reasonableness.

28. E.g., *A Discourse in Vindication of the Doctrine of the Trinity* (1697), in which Stillingfleet attempted to show that his understanding of the immanent Trinity was compatible with a Lockean conception of personhood and a Lockean account of reason.

29. Jason Vickers provides an overview of two salient features of the debate, the nearly exclusive concern with the immanent Trinity and the preoccupation with reason and rationality as a basis for theological reflection ("Charles Wesley and the Revival of the Doctrine of the Trinity: A Methodist Contribution to Modern Theology," in Kenneth G. C. Newport and Ted A. Campbell, eds., *Charles Wesley: Life, Literature and Legacy* [Peterborough: Epworth, 2007] 278–98, in particular 279–82). For a more comprehensive analysis of the Trinitarian controversy in seventeenth-century England, see Philip Dixon, *"Nice and Hot Disputes": The Doctrine of the Trinity in the Seventeenth Century* (London: T. & T. Clark, 2003). On Anglicans, reason, and Scripture in the latter part of the same century, see Gerard Reedy, *The Bible and Reason: Anglicans and Scripture in Late Seventeenth Century England* (Philadelphia: University of Pennsylvania Press, 1985). For a discussion of the prevalence of doubts about the Trinity as well as outright anti-Trinitarianism during the eighteenth century in England, see R. N. Stromberg,

stands out for our purposes here is the assumption shared by virtually all parties involved that the principal task of theology was to exhibit the rationality of Christian beliefs. Broadly speaking, according to this outlook, a doctrine deemed in accord with the dictates of reason was acceptable, whereas one that was not must be rejected. Thus the ultimate question for assessing the doctrine of the Trinity, or any other doctrine for that matter, was whether that doctrine could be compatible with or confirmable by reason. While some writers, including those influenced by Socinian or Unitarian principles, outright rejected the doctrine of the Trinity on allegedly rational grounds, others—the rational theologians—sought primarily to demonstrate its rational coherence. In other words, ultimately the controversy gave rise to at least two common views, English Unitarianism and English rational theology.

Compared to these positions, however, Fletcher's approach to the doctrine of the Trinity was distinctive. He distanced himself from both alternatives, though in different ways and for different reasons. He was openly critical of English Unitarianism, as in his response to Priestley. In *An History of the Corruptions of Christianity*, Priestley had asserted the doctrine of the Trinity to be irrational, and that of Christ's divinity to have no scriptural basis.[30] Fletcher, staunchly opposed to both claims, responded in *A Vindication of Christ's Divinity*, the first part of which is *A Rational Vindication of the Catholic Faith* concerning the Trinity and the divinity of Christ. The work, unfinished at the time of Fletcher's death, was revised and finished in the spirit of Fletcher by the Methodist preacher Joseph Benson, at Mary Bosanquet Fletcher's request. Notwithstanding Benson's revisions and additions, the sections authentic to Fletcher provide ample evidence of the theological substance of his response to Priestley. Therefore this discussion will be limited primarily to those parts that come from Fletcher's pen: the introduction, the expostulatory letter, and the first four chapters.[31] In characteristic fashion, here Fletcher addressed a controversial issue in an irenic spirit. At the

Religious Liberalism in Eighteenth-Century England (London: Oxford University Press, 1954) ch. 4. On the English Enlightenment more broadly speaking, see Frederick Beiser, *The Sovereignty of Reason: The Defense of Rationality in the Early English Enlightenment* (Princeton: Princeton University Press, 1996).

30. *An History of the Corruptions of Christianity*, 2 vols. (London: Printed for J. Johnson, 1782).

31. Chapters 3 and 4 were incomplete and finished by Benson, as he noted in his preface.

end of the introduction, for example, he stated his overall intent in the following way: "May it be the sincere wish of the reader, as it is of the author, that all who name the name of Christ, may soon agree in such an evangelical confession; and that the names of *Unitarian* and *Trinitarian*, may for ever be lost in the sweeter names of *Christian* and *Brother!*"[32] Yet Fletcher believed that much was at stake here, and this self-styled "poor *country-vicar*" was keen to "break a spear" with Priestley "on the very ground" where he thought himself "invincible—*philosophy, reason*, and *common sense*."[33] Over against Priestley's assertions that the doctrine of the Trinity was irrational and that the divinity of Christ had no sufficient scriptural foundation, Fletcher defended the doctrines of Christ's divinity and of the Trinity on both rational and scriptural grounds.

In the first four chapters of the treatise, Fletcher proceeded in systematic fashion by appealing primarily to reason in chapters 1 and 2 and to Scripture in chapters 3 and 4. He began by affirming that the world itself declares *that* God exists, although the precise manner of God's existence is "far above our reach": "Of this, we only know what [God] plainly reveals to us, and what we may infer, from what he hath plainly revealed."[34] This insight leads Fletcher into an overview of catholic faith in the Trinity, a teaching made known through divine revelation. With emphasis on the unity of the Godhead, he observes that insofar as God is one, "true Christians are all *Unitarians*."[35] In a strict sense, however, the name "Trinitarian" is preferable because "the *one* divine essence manifests itself to us in *three* divine subsistences most intimately joined and absolutely inseparable."[36] The main question in the debate between catholic Christians and deists of every description concerns "the two precipices"—idolatry and impiety—"between which the Christian's road lies all the way to heaven."[37] Regarding the present debate, then, either catholic Christians committed idolatry in worshiping Christ who by

---

32. *A Rational Vindication*, introduction, par. 9.

33. "An Expostulatory Letter to the Rev. Dr. Priestley, Occasioned by his History of the Corruptions of Christianity," introduction.

34. *A Rational Vindication*, ch. 1.

35. Ibid. Streiff notes that the unity of the Godhead is a common characteristic of Fletcher's later writings on the doctrine of God (Streiff, 259–60). Fletcher's use of the theme here is consistent with this tendency.

36. *A Rational Vindication*, ch. 1.

37. Ibid.

nature is not divine or Socinians were impious for refusing to worship the Son of God and actually worshiping "a mangled notion of Deity" rather than the God revealed in Scripture.[38]

Not content merely to distinguish Trinitarians from tritheists, ditheists, deists, and Socinian Unitarians as in chapter 1, Fletcher would go on to criticize Priestley in the second chapter for being inconsistent and himself irrational through a comparison of two of his works: *Disquisitions Relating to Matter and Spirit* and *An History of the Corruptions of Christianity*.[39] In his *Disquisitions Relating to Matter and Spirit*, Priestley had maintained that "we have no idea at all" about the divine substance and that, therefore, "all that we can conceive, or pronounce concerning it, must be merely hypothetical."[40] Yet Fletcher asked how, if pronouncements concerning God's substance were only hypothetical, Priestley could absolutely declare in *An History of the Corruptions of Christianity* that the divine substance, of which he had "no idea at all," was "incompatible with the three divine subsistences, which the scripture calls *the Father, the Word*, and *the Holy Ghost*."[41] Fletcher also found Priestley's logic inconsistent in that Priestley, who had insisted that we have no clear conception of God's nature, that God's mode of existence is unknown, and that speculation about God's nature is incredibly complex and difficult, was attempting "to argue the catholic Church out of the belief of the TRINITY, *because we have no (clear) conception of its nature*, because it *has* NO KNOWN *mode of existence*, and because, (in our present state,) the *speculation of it is attended with* some INSUPERABLE *difficulties*."[42] As additional evidence for the unreasonableness of the position of this alleged defender of reason, Fletcher could point to the incomprehensibility of God and the essential difference between God and all else, two points affirmed by Priestley: "a philosopher . . . who publicly grants this, must be one of the most prejudiced of all men, if he reject the sacred Trinity, into whose name he was baptized, because the Trinity is in some sense *incomprehensible*, and because he insists that three *divine* persons must be *divided* and *separated* like three

---

38. Ibid.

39. *Disquisitions Relating to Matter and Spirit* (London: Printed for J. Johnson, 1777).

40. Ibid., 109–10.

41. *A Rational Vindication*, ch. 2.

42. Ibid.

human persons; just as if he did not himself maintain, that the divine essence, or personality, *hath properties most essentially different from men, angels, and every thing else."*[43] Simply put, Priestley could not overthrow the doctrine of the Trinity by arguments from his avowed ignorance of the divine nature. If we know so little about the nature of God, then how can we absolutely dismiss the confession of God's triunity?

Fletcher would turn more directly to the light of revelation in order to demonstrate the scriptural basis for belief in the divinity of Christ, and thereby the doctrine of the Trinity, in chapter 3. He began this section by naming the "capital truth" conveyed in Scripture, namely, "that God, considered as Father, has an only begotten Son, called the *Logos*, or the *Word*, whom he 'loved before the foundation of the world' . . . ; 'who is the express image of his person' . . . ; 'by whom he made the worlds, who was in the beginning with God, and was God.'"[44] Indeed the very name "Father," which is applied to God in numerous biblical passages,[45] implies that there is another within the Godhead who may be called God's Son—a Son not merely by creation, like Adam, nor by adoption, as taught concerning human beings by St. Paul, nor still by the resurrection, but a Son by nature. To this Son Scripture bears ample witness, according to Fletcher.[46]

The fourth chapter of *A Rational Vindication*, which is the final chapter original to Fletcher, follows from the third. In particular, Fletcher focused here on Christ claiming the honor of being the proper Son of God the Father, as evinced in his passion and resurrection. Fletcher cited a number of verses, especially excerpts from the Gospel of John, to that effect.

In this way, Fletcher's criticism of Priestley involved an appeal to both reason and revelation.[47] After criticizing Priestley on the basis of philosophy, reason, and logic—the primary grounds on which Priestley

43. Ibid.

44. Ibid., ch. 3. The biblical quotations are from John 17:24, Heb 1:3, and John 1:1, respectively.

45. Of course, Scripture contains feminine imagery for the divine as well (e.g., Matt 23:37).

46. *A Rational Vindication*, ch. 3.

47. Fletcher called reason and revelation the "two lights" that providence has given human beings (*A Rational Vindication*, introduction, par. 9).

had attacked the faith—Fletcher employed the language of Scripture in a concise defense of the doctrine of the Trinity and the divinity of Christ.

Although Fletcher's criticism of Priestley and Unitarianism was direct even if generally irenic, in response to Priestley's claims against classical Christian faith, Fletcher set himself apart from English rational theology in more nuanced fashion. While he reached the same basic conclusion as the rational theologians of his day about the complementary relationship between faith and reason, he differed from them and ultimately went beyond them in an important way. Again, Fletcher also argued on the basis of reason against the charge that the doctrine of the Trinity was irrational. Yet rather than attempt to demonstrate the compatibility of, for example, an understanding of the persons of the Trinity with a Lockean notion of personhood or with its Cartesian counterpart, in the manner of Stillingfleet[48] and William Sherlock,[49] respectively, Fletcher took a different approach.

Wishing to offer more than an exposition of God's triunity in primarily philosophical terms, Fletcher first expanded the scope of the discussion to include catechetical and doxological concerns, and then shifted the focus accordingly. His primary aim was not to give a rational account of the nature and attributes of God (the "immanent" Trinity) but to reflect on God's actions in salvation history (the "economic" Trinity) and the implications of those actions for Christian living. Thus he suggested that what was truly at stake in the debate was the question of the doctrine's function in promoting in its adherents the life of God and, in turn, in evoking from them the worship of God. Either God is worshiped rightly on the basis of what God has done in covenant with Israel and especially in the person of Jesus Christ—actions whose effects become realized in the lives of the faithful as they experience and respond to God's grace—or people run the risk of worshiping something other than the living God, of devoting themselves to something else in a way that is not directly conducive to salvation. In one of his more forthright statements, Fletcher asserted on scriptural grounds that "the deists and their associates," who do not acknowledge the whole Trinity, "worship a

---

48. *A Discourse in Vindication of the Doctrine of the Trinity.*

49. *A Vindication of the Doctrine of the Holy and Ever Blessed Trinity, and the Incarnation of the Son of God, Occasioned by the Brief Notes on the Creed of St. Athanasius, and the Brief History of the Unitarians, or Socinians; and Containing an Answer to Both* (London, 1690).

being created by their superb reason, rather than the only living God."[50] Lacking the Spirit of Christ, they do not believe in the Son,[51] and denying the Son they reject the Father.[52] Positively, however, because God is triune as self-revealed in salvation history, worship of Christ and of the Holy Spirit ensures the proper worship of the Father, whose majesty the deists and Socinians allegedly wished to uphold.[53]

In response to the criticism that the doctrine of the Trinity is irrational, some appeal to reason is certainly necessary in order to meet the criticism head on. Whereas the rational theologians generally emphasized reason to such an extent that they ended up reformulating the doctrine of the Trinity in more explicitly rational terms, Fletcher, in an attempt to show the rationality of the purportedly irrational doctrine, argued on more explicitly theological grounds, with a particular sensitivity to the implications of Trinitarian doctrine for the worship of God and the formation of Christian character. Thus, while acknowledging the force of reason in the discussion (hence his title *A Rational Vindication*), Fletcher did not see reason as an end in itself but, more precisely, put reason to the service of faith in priestly fashion. His basic approach was to ground the doctrine in the divine economy, as conveyed in Scripture, and thereby to locate it in the context of vital, experiential religion. According to Fletcher, the actual benefit of sound teaching on God's triunity is neither abstract, overly speculative conjectures, nor the ability to prove that this doctrine is in fact reasonable and thus worthy of our faith, but rather is transformation through our participation, by grace, in God's own life. More than providing a clear and detailed exposition of the nature and attributes of God and the distinctions in the divine essence, and more than recasting Trinitarian doctrine to reflect the regnant philosophical schools of thought, what mattered most for Fletcher was that we come to know and worship God the Father, whom we call "Abba" by the grace of adoption;[54] God the Son, who is "the way, the truth, and the life";[55] and God the Spirit, through whom "the love of God

---

50. "Remarks on the Trinity," 511 (alt.; cf. Martindale's translation of *Raison superbe* as "proud reason").

51. Cf. Rom 8:9.

52. Cf. 1 John 2:23. "Remarks on the Trinity," 511

53. Cf. Fletcher's expostulatory letter in *A Rational Vindication*, fourth expostulation.

54. Rom 8:15.

55. John 14:6.

has been shed abroad in our hearts"[56]—that is how we truly understand and can thus best account for the Christian doctrine of the Trinity.[57]

So although Fletcher appeared far more sympathetic to English rational theology than to its Unitarian counterpart, he was not content with merely attempting to establish the Christian confession of God as Trinity as being consistent with or confirmable by reason. Given his priestly convictions, he clearly had in view a still higher goal: the praise of the triune God in Christian faith and life. What Fletcher was after took him to the intersection of doctrine and doxology.

Understood in its historical context, Fletcher's message of genuine happiness and holiness in God was especially timely for people in the emerging industrial society of which Madeley, home to the world's first cast iron bridge, was very much a part. During a time of great industrial and societal change, this gospel of universal redemption conveyed good news for men and women regardless of social location. It would have resonated particularly well among persons on the outskirts of society who had been displaced by the social and economic forces of Hanoverian England, including miners and other common laborers.[58] Indeed, one reason for its appeal, then and now, is that Fletcher's teaching on the Trinity and the Christian life speaks to the true dignity and potential of all human beings in God.

FOLLOWING FLETCHER: THE PROMISE OF DOXOLOGICAL TRINITARIANISM

In "Remarks on the Trinity" and *A Rational Vindication of the Catholic Faith*, Fletcher has elucidated the implications of belief in the Trinity from a doxological perspective. In the process, he provides a helpful reorientation in focus with regard to understanding the nature and purpose of the doctrine of the Trinity. According to Fletcher, while reason has a certain place in reflection on this doctrine, the doctrine itself is about something far more than what the human mind can comprehend or show to be reasonable. It has to do, at root, with God and with the

56. Rom 5:5.

57. Cf. Benson's preface to *A Rational Vindication*, pars. 5–7.

58. Cf. George Rudé, "The 'Other' London," in *Hanoverian London, 1714–1808* (London: Secker & Warburg, 1971) 82–99.

human communion with God that is made possible by God's activity in the economy of salvation. Therefore, whereas in one sense the defense of the rationality of Trinitarian doctrine is an understandable response to the Socinian-influenced criticism of irrationality, in a deeper sense, if the response is based primarily on philosophical grounds, and nothing more, then something decisive is missing. As Fletcher shows, the doctrine of the Trinity demands more from those who hold to it than rational confirmation and assent alone; it calls for the praise of the very God who is the subject of this cardinal doctrine—for the hearts and voices of all Christians as well as their minds.

In conclusion, I would like to suggest that the importance of this reorientation toward doxological Trinitarianism transcends Fletcher's own context and should not therefore be limited to the study of figures and debates from a bygone era. A critical retrieval of this approach, reclaiming its essential core, holds promise for contemporary theology because it can contribute to the ongoing revival of Trinitarian doctrine. It can do so precisely by highlighting the crucial connection between the doctrine of the Trinity and the worship of God in the life of faith. Thanks in large part to the work of Karl Barth and Karl Rahner, the late twentieth and early twenty-first centuries have seen a renaissance of scholarly interest in the Trinity, leading many theologians to give more consideration, for example, to the relationship between the doctrine of God and the doctrine of salvation.[59] Within Methodism and the broader Anglican tradition, Geoffrey Wainwright and Jason Vickers have already suggested that John and Charles Wesley, respectively, are noteworthy for grasping the doxological and catechetical significance of Trinitarian doctrine.[60] The complexities of his relationship to the Wesleys and to early Methodism as a whole notwithstanding, in his own right the Anglican clergyman John Fletcher can certainly be added to that list as well.[61] What this priest-theologian understood and attempted to convey

59. E.g., Catherine Mowry LaCugna, *God for Us: The Trinity and Christian Life* (San Francisco: HarperSanFrancisco, 1991).

60. Wainwright, "Why Wesley Was a Trinitarian." Vickers, "Charles Wesley and the Revival of the Doctrine of the Trinity," and "'And We the Life of God Shall Know': Appreciating Charles Wesley as Theologian at the Tercentenary of His Birth," in *Anglican Theological Review* 90:2 (2008) 329–44.

61. For a reassessment of Fletcher's associations with the Wesley brothers and with early Methodism overall that challenges existing understandings, see Forsaith's introduction in *Unexampled Labours*, esp. 9–33.

is a vital lesson for the church across the ages: the doctrine of the Trinity is best understood not as a dry, intellectual assertion aimed at mere rational assent, but rather as a genuinely life-giving doctrine that evokes from faithful hearts the adoration of the saving God—Father, Son, and Holy Spirit.

7

Women, Work, and Worship in the Trefeca Family 1752–1773[1]

Eryn M. White

THE TREFECA FAMILY WAS a religious community set up by Howel Harris, one of the main leaders of early Welsh Methodism, following his expulsion from the movement in 1750. Ostensibly, the division between Harris and Daniel Rowland and the other leading Methodists arose out of concerns that he espoused heretical beliefs, in particular that he preached that God had died on the cross, which was contrary to orthodox doctrine. They had good grounds for these misgivings, as Harris freely owned on several occasions that he preached of "a dying God."[2] Added to these concerns were suspicions regarding his relationship with Mrs. Sidney Griffith, a married woman whom Harris had converted and whom he took with him on his preaching tours, hailing her as a prophetess. Although his closest colleagues do not seem to have given

1. "Trefeca" is the correct Welsh spelling of the name, but a number of alternative spellings have appeared in the past. Lady Huntingdon's College adopted "Trevecca," and the manuscript collection at the National Library of Wales, Aberystwyth, has inherited the anglicized form, "Trevecka."

2. For the Division and its causes, see Eryn M. White, "'A Breach in God's house': The Division in Welsh Calvinistic Methodism 1750–63," in Nigel Yates, ed., *Bishop Burgess and his World: Culture, Religion and Society in Britain, Europe and North America in the Eighteenth and Nineteenth Centuries* (Cardiff: University of Wales Press, 2007) 85–102.

credence to the rumors that this was an adulterous relationship, the fact that such gossip arose led them to advise Harris to be more circumspect in his behavior, advice which he refused to countenance, protesting his innocence. By 1752 Harris had retreated to his home at Trefeca, in the parish of Talgarth in Breconshire, where he fulfilled a longstanding desire to establish a community or "Family" of believers who would live, work, and worship together, sharing what they owned and earned.

The connection between Madeley, John Fletcher, and Trefeca, arose in 1768 when Fletcher was asked by the Countess of Huntingdon to become "President" of the college that she had established at Trefeca in order to train ministers.[3] As a result, from time to time he visited Trefeca, where Howel Harris heard him preach "with great life" and "very home and searching."[4] The college and the Family were actually in separate locations (the Family lived at Harris' home at Trefeca Fach, and the college was built at Trefeca Isaf), but they were very close at hand and Fletcher could not have escaped hearing all about the Family when he visited and spent time with Harris. That he also came into contact with local evangelicals when at Trefeca is evident from the fact that he was able to provide the Countess of Huntingdon with a shrewd assessment of the abilities of Thomas Davies, curate of the nearby parish of Llangors.[5] Harris and Fletcher were part of the same network of evangelical contacts and would inevitably have heard news of each other in addition. Harris always mentioned Fletcher with great respect, and Fletcher in turn believed Harris to be "an extraordinary man, I would not know to whom to compare him more aptly than to Lady H[untingdon], he is an exceptional character as she is, and the path they lead seems to be laid out on the same principles."[6] The Countess spent a considerable proportion of her time at Trefeca during the 1770s and 1780s, using it as a base from which to organize her students' preaching missions, so that it became something of a center for evangelical activity during that time.[7]

3. See Boyd S. Schlenther, *Queen of the Methodists: The Countess of Huntingdon and the Eighteenth-Century Crisis of Faith and Society* (Bishop Auckland: Durham Academic Press, 1997) 68–82.

4. National Library of Wales (NLW), Calvinistic Methodist Archive, Diaries of Howel Harris, 254, September 20, 1759, January 6, 1760.

5. Peter S. Forsaith, ed. *"Unexampled Labours": Letters of the Revd John Fletcher to Leaders in the Evangelical Revival* (Peterborough: Epworth, 2008) 238.

6. Ibid., 202.

7. Schlenther, *Queen of the Methodists*, 113–14; Stephen Orchard, "Selina, Countess

Despite its associations with leading evangelical figures, the Trefeca community has attracted little scholarly interest, both within Wales and beyond. Since many of the key primary sources are written in Welsh, non-Welsh-medium historians have quite naturally felt ill-equipped to research the subject. Biographies of Harris have invariably included some account of the Family, although there is a general tendency to skim over Harris' activities post-1750.[8] Denominational histories, largely written by Methodist ministers, have in the past tended to omit any substantial discussion of the Family, regarding the community as a somewhat eccentric departure from the mainstream movement and thus of only marginal relevance to Methodist history.[9] The tradition of regarding it at best as an interesting interlude, but usually very much as a whimsical offshoot of mainstream Welsh Methodism, can be traced back to William Williams' elegy to Harris, in which he questions why his old comrade bothered to build himself a monastery, when Henry VIII had gone to so much trouble to demolish them all.[10]

Comparisons to monasteries notwithstanding, the initial inspiration for the foundation of the Family seems to have come to Harris late in 1736 when he read about August Hermann Francke's work at Halle in Prussia and recorded in his diary his desire to sell all he had to build an almshouse and a schoolhouse, emulating Francke's example.[11] He was also impressed by George Whitefield's orphanage in Georgia, for which he collected money on some of his preaching tours. There has

---

of Huntingdon," *Journal of United Reformed Church History Society* 8:2 (2008) 77.

8. For instance, Griffith T. Roberts, *Howell Harris* (London: Epworth, 1951) 63–71; Gomer M. Roberts, *Portread o Ddiwygiwr* (Caernarfon: Llyfrfa'r Methodistiaid Calfinaidd, 1969) 129–39; Eifion Evans, *Howel Harris, Evangelist 1714–1773* (Cardiff: University of Wales Press, 1974) 58–59. The most recent biography by Geraint Tudur, *Howell Harris: From Conversion to Separation, 1735–1750* (Cardiff: University of Wales Press, 2000) concentrates on the period up to 1750 and therefore does not discuss the Family in any detail.

9. See, for instance, Rev. John Hughes, *Methodistiaeth Cymru Cyfrol I* (Wrexham: R. Hughes a'i Fab, 1851) 390–95. More recently, an MA thesis by Alun Wyn Owen in 1957 concentrated on the history of the Family up to 1760, and in 1973 Monica Davies contributed a chapter on the Family to the first volume of the official history of the Welsh Methodist movement: K. Monica Davies, "Teulu Trefeca," in G. M. Roberts, *Hanes Methodistiaeth Galfinaidd Cymru Cyfrol I: Y Deffroad Mawr* (Caernarfon: Llyfrfa'r Methodistiaid Calfinaidd, 1973) 356–77.

10. N. Cynhafal Jones, *Gweithiau Williams Pantycelyn Cyfrol I* (Holywell: Evans, 1887) 494.

11. Diaries of Howel Harris, 18, January 10, 1737.

been some speculation that Harris might also have been influenced by an industrial community set up by Rowland Vaughan in the Golden Valley in Herefordshire in the early seventeenth century,[12] but there is no evidence that Harris was aware of this venture, and it would appear that his influences were rather more contemporary, deriving chiefly from Pietism and Moravianism. The Trefeca community has often been compared to Moravian settlements such as those established at Fulneck in Yorkshire and Ockbrook in Derbyshire,[13] and R. T. Jenkins may well have been right to suggest that such similarities arose from the common inspiration supplied by Francke and Pietism.[14] Harris did indeed visit Fulneck, where he was afforded a most cordial welcome, but that was in 1766, well after he had established his own community. Given, however, that Harris had been in contact with the Moravians from quite early on in the Evangelical Revival and would have learnt of their religious communities, at Herrnhut and Herrnhaag as well as in England, it would hardly be surprising that their example was a possible influence. The impetus towards forming religious communities was by no means confined to the Moravians, however. For instance, in 1755 the Countess of Huntingdon decided to form a short-lived community of select women at Clifton who would spend their time in prayer and contemplation.[15] Her "Colony" was not obliged to engage in manual labor, unlike the "Family" set up by Mary Bosanquet at Leytonstone in 1763 to care for needy women and children.[16] The community moved to Cross Hall near

---

12. M. H. Jones, *The Trevecka Letters* (Caernarfon: Llyfrfa'r Methodistiaid Calfinaidd, 1932) 190; Alun Wyn Owen, "A study of Howell Harris and the Trevecka 'family' (1752–60), based upon the Trevecka letters and diaries and other Methodist archives at the National Library of Wales," MA thesis, University of Wales, 1957, 13–14.

13. See Colin Podmore, *The Moravian Church in England, 1728–1760* (Oxford: Oxford University Press, 1998).

14. R. T. Jenkins, "The Moravian Brethren in North Wales," *Cymmrodor* 45 (1938) 14; Geoffrey Nuttall, *Howel Harris 1714–1773: The Last Enthusiast* (Cardiff: University of Wales Press, 1965) 24–27; J. C. S. Mason, *The Moravian Church and the Missionary Awakening in England 1760–1800* (Woodbridge: Boydell, 2001) 50.

15. Edwin Welch, *Spiritual Pilgrim: A Reassessment of the Life of the Countess of Huntingdon* (Cardiff: University of Wales Press, 1995) 84–85; Schlenther, *Queen of the Methodists*, 49–50.

16. Phyllis Mack, *Heart Religion in the British Enlightenment: Gender and Emotion in Early Methodism* (Cambridge: Cambridge University Press, 2008) 159–60. See also J. Burge, *Women Preachers in Community: Sarah Ryan, Sarah Crosby, Mary Bosanquet* (Peterborough: Epworth, 1997).

Leeds in Yorkshire in 1768, where Bosanquet managed the running of the dairy farm, school, and orphanage until she married John Fletcher in 1781. Like Trefeca, it seems to have been inspired largely by the active Pietism advocated by Francke and also reflected the not unnatural desire of some evangelicals to withdraw from their surroundings and find solace and support in the company of those who had undergone similar spiritual experiences. Trefeca was therefore by no means a unique undertaking within the context of the Evangelical Revival, however unusual it might have seemed to many observers within Wales at the time.

John Walsh has discussed the extent to which John Wesley was influenced by the notion of a "community of goods,"[17] which may have engendered a similar desire to establish orphanages and charity schools, but it was Harris, out of the early leaders of the Evangelical Revival in England and Wales, who was to do most to implement such ideas. To begin with, twenty-nine individuals were drawn to the new venture, but by 1756 there were over one hundred. There seemed to be an almost unending process of building work to house the expanding numbers, and it soon became necessary to rent nearby farms to accommodate some of them. By 1763 the place was impressive enough for John Wesley to describe it in his diary as "one of the most elegant places which I have seen in Wales. The little chapel, and all things round it are finished in an uncommon taste; and the gardens, orchards, fish-ponds, and mount adjoining make the place a little paradise . . . About six score people are now in the Family—all diligent, all constantly employed, all fearing God and working righteousness."[18]

Those who were attracted in the first instance tended to be diehard supporters of Howel Harris, who were not content to remain members of the Methodist movement without him. Harris was frequently told by adherents that they gained significantly from his visits and guidance, so it comes as no surprise that some of his supporters felt that being continually in his presence would benefit them spiritually. Very few recruits hailed from the southwest and none from Cardiganshire, which was Daniel Rowland's county. There the mainstream Methodist movement

17. John Walsh, "John Wesley and the community of goods," in Keith Robbins, ed., *Protestant Evangelicalism: Britain, Ireland, Germany and America, c.1750–1950: Essays in Honour of W. R. Ward*, Studies in Church History, Subsidia 7 (Oxford: Blackwell, 1990).

18. A. H. Williams, ed. *John Wesley in Wales 1739–1790* (Cardiff: University of Wales Press, 1971) 63–64.

remained active and, almost from the moment of separation, Harris had resigned himself to the reality that as far as he was concerned, that area of Wales was a lost cause.[19] Most of the members of the Family were drawn from north and mid Wales, where they had often been the most active members in their own localities, helping to organize meetings and visiting preachers, so that the Methodist cause suffered for a period as a result of their withdrawal. The Family continued to draw new members from these areas, largely through sporadic preaching tours by Evan Moses, one of Harris' most loyal lieutenants at Trefeca, who proved a very effective recruiter.[20]

It is difficult to calculate accurately the precise membership of the Family or to know for certain the proportion of men and women. It is estimated that around 374 individuals were attracted during the Family's ninety-year history. Harris would note the total number from time to time in his diary, and Evan Moses kept a journal recording those who died at Trefeca, but of course this did not include those who came and went, so it is difficult to come up with an accurate list of the members. John Wesley noted that there were 120 inhabitants in 1763, and throughout its existence the numbers do not seem to have exceeded 150. Between 1752 and 1773, Evan Moses recorded the deaths of forty-six men and sixty-five women, which probably gives us a fair indication of the gender balance.[21] Certainly, all available evidence suggests that women probably formed roughly half of the population most of the time.

Despite that, as one might expect, it was very much a patriarchal community, with Harris as the patriarch; the members of the Family, over whom he exercised a quite rigorous discipline, commonly called him "Father Harris." This patriarchal authority was bolstered by Harris' chief assistants, Evan Moses, James Pritchard, and Evan Roberts, who shouldered a considerable proportion of responsibility for the Family and its affairs, particularly during the three years between 1759 and 1762 when Harris served as a captain in the Breconshire militia and was largely absent. However, there was a matriarchal dimension to authority within the Family from the very start. At the outset, Harris had intended that Mrs. Sidney Griffith would act as "Mother" to the Family, alongside his

19. White, "A Breach in God's House," 85–102.

20. See R. T. Jenkins, "Evan Moses o Drefeca," *Cylchgrawn Cymdeithas Hanes y Methodistiaid Calfinaidd* 47 (1962) 5–10.

21. NLW, Calvinistic Methodist Archive, Trevecka MS 3151.

role as Father. He did not, by the way, consider his wife for this position, and she was probably rather too retiring for such a role. Unfortunately for his plans, Mrs. Griffith died on May 31, 1752, just as the Family was being established. Yet, with so many women as part of the Family, it was considered appropriate to have a woman act as a sort of matron who would oversee any particular difficulties arising among them. The women in Trefeca were divided into married and unmarried, with the single women sleeping in the same dormitory. The new building for the Family had been designed to include a loft with three separate sections, each with its own stairway to ensure these divisions according to gender and marital status. Early on, following Sidney Griffith's death, Harris had apparently envisaged a substitute matron in the form of Bridget Glynne, who belonged to a minor gentry family from the Newtown area and married the squire of Glyn Clywedog.[22] She had come to know Harris through her connections with the Montgomeryshire Methodists, before she moved to Pride Hill, Shrewsbury. At first, she was receptive to his suggestions that she should come to Trefeca,[23] but when she agreed to visit for a sort of trial period, in 1753, they barely lasted a day before disagreeing violently. She departed within the week, never to return, although Harris continued to write to her for the remainder of the decade to try to cajole, shame, or coerce her into changing her mind, with a conspicuous lack of success.[24]

Harris was not always lucky with his choice of matriarchs, largely because if they had the right sort of character and aptitude for that position, then they might also be inclined to speak their minds in a way that might seem to constitute a challenge to Harris' patriarchal position. That certainly seemed to be the case with Sarah Bowen. The Bowens were a well-to-do family who were longtime supporters of Methodism in Montgomeryshire, and Harris was a frequent guest at their home in Tyddyn, Llandinam. The two daughters, Sarah and Hannah, and their grandmother, Ann Swancott, joined the Family in its early years, the girls bringing with them all their worldly wealth, which amounted to £280, a sum that helped finance the initial building work to house the

22. She was the daughter of Edward Lloyd of Aberbechan. Richard Bennett, *Methodistiaeth Trefaldwyn Uchaf Cyfrol I: Hanes Cyfnod Howel Harris, 1738–1752* (Bala: Evans, 1929) 169–70, 230–31, 244.

23. Trevecka MSS 2052, 2247, 2249, 2250.

24. Trevecka MSS 2092, 2100, 2109, 2120, 2157, 2831.

Family. Sarah acted as matron for a while, but clashed with Harris and made her escape by marrying Simon Lloyd of Bala in 1755. She and her husband spent years trying to reclaim the money she had contributed to Trefeca, Harris arguing that what had been given freely to God should not be asked for again.[25] Despite Sarah's disagreements with Harris, her sister Hannah later presided in her place, acting as general housekeeper, overseeing the women at their spinning, and supervising the daily school for the younger children. Richard Bennett, the historian of Methodism in Montgomeryshire, suggested that Hannah was "wiser and more flexible" than her sister,[26] which is how she managed to retain her position for over twelve years, becoming an authoritative figure at Trefeca, especially during Harris' absence. Few decisions were made without her being consulted. Yet, she too ultimately chafed against the regime and moved to the Countess of Huntingdon's College to act as housekeeper there in 1768, before eventually leaving to get married.[27]

Some women, therefore, obviously acquired considerable authority in the Family, but even the less prominent members made a crucial contribution to the Family's economic success. The wealthier women, like the Bowen sisters, brought a respectable financial investment with them, but others brought their skills, which helped generate income for the community as a whole. The idea was that the Family should be self-sufficient and should be able to sustain themselves through the food they could produce and the goods and services they sold and provided. Trefeca attracted a large number of craftsmen who worked on the house and its buildings, but who also brought in money by the work they undertook elsewhere. Most of their income came from their building work and the sale of woolen goods, with farming also playing an important part. They owed a good deal of their financial success to the arrival of Evan Roberts, who had previously been manager of a lead mine in Minera, near Wrexham, before joining the Family in 1754.[28] At that time, it was northeast Wales that seemed to be leading the way in terms of industrialization rather than the south, to a large extent because of the proximity to Shropshire and the expertise that could be drawn on

25. Trevecka MS 2224, May 20, 1758.

26. Bennett, *Methodistiaeth Trefaldwyn Uchaf*, 246.

27. Trevecka MS 2635, Countess of Huntingdon to Howel Harris, December 17, 1767; Schlenther, *Queen of the Methodists*, 137–38.

28. Roberts, *Howell Harris*, 65.

in that area. Prior to Roberts' arrival, the Family's approach to business had been somewhat disorganized, and his experience obviously introduced greater efficiency, although, even so, their finances were always quite uncertain and they were frequently in considerable debt. In 1763, Harris noted in his diary that there was "nothing to spare" after eleven years of work and spending over £1,000 annually on rent for the surrounding farms and household expenses, and that they were "living by faith wholly, wanting nothing and saving nothing."[29]

One of their most important ventures was their sale of woolen cloth, and it was here that the women made their most obvious contribution, along with their work in the dairy and with the housekeeping. It is probably worth noting that a large number of members were recruited from parts of mid Wales, including Montgomeryshire, which was a center of the woolen industry. They had experienced spinners as a result who could be set to work following the same model of domestic industry that had been used in mid Wales for generations. With Breconshire's location near the border, many of the most natural trading links were with English towns like Gloucester and Bristol, where they could hope to reach wider markets and receive better payment. The fact that Harris' brother, Thomas, ran a successful tailoring business in London also boosted their trade. By the end of the 1750s, they were selling cloth in Chester, Manchester, Bristol, Gloucester, London, Coventry, and Kidderminster.[30]

Many of the factors that attracted women to join the Family were much the same as those that attracted women to join the Methodist movement in general, including access to fervent preaching and the sense of belonging to a close-knit society of supporters. Many gained new skills and crafts by learning from others in the Family, so that some of those who left were better equipped to make a living. A number of women also gained by learning to read and write in the Family. When he had first established the Family, Harris had asked the vicar of the parish for permission to excuse the children from lessons in the local school.[31] It was arranged that they be taught at home by other members of the Family, which was probably the most practical arrangement as the

29. Diaries of Howel Harris, 241, May 12, 1763.

30. See, for instance, Trevecka MSS 2208, September 26, 1757, and 2210, October 6, 1757.

31. Trevecka MS 2044, HH to Pryce Davies, January 29, 1753.

numbers grew. Older members of the Family were also given instruction by their better educated colleagues, which meant that literacy levels were probably well above the norm for society in general, especially among the women.[32]

However, there were a number of deficiencies, some of which became apparent to the members only after they joined. During Harris' absence between 1759 and 1762, Evan Moses and his helpers increasingly struggled to maintain order and to prevent members from deserting, and it was the women in particular who were the major source of unrest. Moses' letters to Harris during this period contain a catalogue of women who left or attempted to leave, whether temporarily or permanently. In 1760, Moses wrote to Harris complaining that Robert Hughes' wife condemned everything connected with the place and that Nancy Smith of Pembrokeshire had left, as had "the girl from Bala," who departed "blaspheming" heartily.[33] In June 1761 he reported that Margaret Woosnam, one of three sisters from Montgomeryshire who had joined the Family, had left them, apparently without warning, since Hannah had set out to search for her.[34] By January 1762, Moses found himself outside trying to persuade a woman called Grace not to leave when he caught sight of another of the women heading for the road, trying to make her escape while he was preoccupied.[35] Mary Roberts apparently left for her old home in Minera while her husband Benjamin was away in Devon serving with Harris in the Breconshire militia and received a severely reproving letter from her husband warning her that she might be called to account in the next life for thus dishonoring God's name.[36] The absence of Harris and the other Trefeca men serving in the militia over such an extended period of time seems to have weakened patriarchal authority and the community ethos within the group, but even in more normal times, departures were not uncommon. Life in the Trefeca Family may have seemed like a "little paradise" to the occasional visitor,

32. Eryn M. White, "Women, Religion and Education in Eighteenth-Century Wales," in M. Roberts and S. Clarke, eds., *Women and Gender in Early Modern Wales* (Cardiff: University of Wales Press, 2000) 210–33

33. Trevecka MS 2291, August 24, 1760.

34. Trevecka MS 2349, June 26, 1761.

35. Trevecka MS 2438, January 15, 1762. "Grace" may refer to either Grace Richard or Grace Roberts.

36. Trevecka MS 2388, October 4, 1761.

but the reality was constant hard labor and strict discipline. Members of the Family worked a fourteen-hour day and were allowed six hours sleep, everyone having to be in bed by ten at night, with the remaining four hours spent eating and listening to the word. The adults had to be up at four in the morning and at work by six, at which time the children were called to breakfast. Harris, when present, preached twice a day, and conducted a private society in the evenings for the spiritual elite of the community, with one of the other preachers in the community providing the sermon over breakfast. There was no leisure time and no time or space to be by oneself since Family members worked, ate, slept, and prayed alongside each other. Trefeca became renowned for its rigorous discipline, and some people hired its workers on the basis of this strong work ethic, including Sir Edward Williams of Llangoed Hall, who employed them on several occasions and praised their diligence.[37] One local couple dispatched their daughter to Trefeca when she was caught pilfering so that she might reform her ways under the influence of the strict discipline that prevailed there. Harris pledged "to make her usefull, subordinate & industrious," and refused to accept payment for the service.[38] Harris felt the need to maintain a paternal discipline over all the members and to reprove the women for their "clacking," which he felt often arose because of their fondness for tea drinking and gossip.

For some, this existence proved intolerable, especially since one lacked the freedom to make one's own decisions, even on the most personal of matters. As in the Methodist community at large, the question of courtship and marriage caused many complications, and no member was allowed to marry without the consent of Howel Harris and the rest of the Family. Moses was occasionally troubled that the Devil was trying "to bring the flesh among them" through such relationships.[39] Abigail Woosnam, Margaret Woosnam's sister, fell in love with one of the Family's young men, but was said to have realized that her feelings were based on the flesh, although she found it a heavy trial to have to part from him. The young man left Trefeca, and Abigail died unmarried in 1758 at the age of 31.[40] Another who fell foul of the rules regarding marriage was Hannah Bowen, who was found to have been secretly courting

37. Trevecka MSS 2106, September 8, 1754, and 2470, May 16, 1762.

38. Trevecka MSS 2222, March 13, 1758; 2226, June 5, 1758; and 2227, June 5, 1758.

39. Trevecka MS 2327, November 30, 1760.

40. Trevecka MS 3141, 19.

Edward Oliver and was turned out of the house on a rainy night by Harris, who ordered her bed and clothes also to be deposited outside in the rain.[41] When he found her seeking shelter in a barn at midnight, he drove her out of there as well. Although she was later forgiven, she was never allowed to pursue her relationship with Oliver. Harris had hoped to arrange a marriage between her and Evan Moses, possibly in order to ensure that the Family would have a Father and Mother to continue the work after his death, but they were disobliging enough not to fall in with his plans in this instance. Even Hannah occasionally felt the need to flee from what could be an intense and claustrophobic atmosphere, seeking sanctuary for a period in 1759 among the Bristol Moravians, until retrieved by Harris and Moses.[42]

Several of the married women who came to Trefeca found that membership of the Family could cause untold strain to relations inside the family units within the community, especially when one spouse was a less enthusiastic recruit than the other. Some families compromised by leasing one of the properties near to Trefeca, enabling those who were eager to join to have ready access to the Family, while allowing their more reluctant relatives their liberty. For some this might serve as a trial period before embarking on full membership. William Roberts of Denbighshire leased the nearby eighty-acre farm of Geuffordd[43] in order to reunite his son and daughter-in-law who had separated when Mary Roberts had accompanied her father-in-law to Trefeca.[44] Mary's husband, Thomas, had no desire to join the Family but his wife refused to leave, despite being pregnant with her first child, who was subsequently born there, in her husband's absence. The relocation to Geuffordd must have seemed to be the only solution to their situation that did not involve a permanent separation. William Roberts was already the owner of a farm in Denbighshire, which he had passed on to his eldest son, and was evidently in a position to secure the lease of the farm in Breconshire. Not all strained relationships could be healed in this way, however, and in some

41. Diaries of Howel Harris, July 15, 1753.

42. R. T. Jenkins, "Bryste a Threfeca," in *Yng Nghysgod Trefeca: Ysgrifau ar Hanes Crefydd a Chymdeithas yng Nghymru yn y ddeunawfed ganrif* (Caernarfon: Llyfrfa'r Methodistiaid Calfinaidd, 1968) 58.

43. John Davies, "Howell Harris and the Trevecka Settlement," *Brycheiniog* 60 (1963) 105.

44. Trevecka MS 3140, 27–28, 56–57; Trevecka MS 3141, 37.

instances, husband and wife ended up separating because one spouse could not endure either the prospect or the reality of life in the Family. This happened in the case of Anne Morris of Crafnant, Caernarfonshire, who was left alone at Trefeca after her husband failed to adapt to their new life there and departed, taking their daughter with him.[45] It is notable how often it was the women in the family who seemed to be most committed to life in the community, although this was not always the case. By way of contrast, Janet Griffith wrote to her husband, Griffith Price, in 1756, informing him that she had no intention of returning to him at Trefeca where she had experienced neither health nor happiness, demanding that he return her belongings, including her Bible, and hoping that he do his duty by providing for her financially.[46]

In the light of these examples, and the fact that many of the members made substantial financial contributions to the community, it is hardly surprising that rumor and suspicion abounded regarding the Trefeca Family. Harris was frequently accused of taking advantage of the gullible by persuading them to sell their property to join the Family but refusing to reimburse them should they subsequently choose to leave.[47] Critics mocked the venture, calling it the "New Jerusalem," which Harris maintained was in truth an accurate description.[48] Many of the women recruits, in choosing to subsume their individuality by joining the Family, seem to have been fulfilling the suggested definition of agency for the Methodist as a self-negation that entailed "subduing at least some of one's own habits, desires, and impulses."[49] There is no record of any of the women being allowed to exhort, although they took part in discussions in society meetings, so they were permitted no greater freedom than ordinary Welsh Methodist women.[50] Although the Family evidently provided support and spiritual fulfillment for many members, for others it was too restrictive. Even so, many members found great comfort there

45. Trevecka MS 3141, 7.

46. Trevecka MS 2187, November 15, 1756.

47. Robert Jones, *Drych yr Amseroedd*, ed. G. M. Ashton (Cardiff: University of Wales Press, 1958) 82–83.

48. Diaries of Howel Harris, March 29, 1753.

49. Mack, *Heart Religion*, 9. See also Phyllis Mack, "Religion, Feminism, and the Problem of Agency: Reflections on Eighteenth-Century Quakerism," *Signs: Journal of Women in Culture and Society* 29:1 (2003) 149–77.

50. Eryn M. White, "Women in the Early Methodist Societies in Wales," *Journal of Welsh Religious History* 7 (1999) 103–8.

and were happy to remain for the rest of their lives. When Harris himself died in 1773, he left the Family in the care of his most trusted helpers, Evan Moses, James Pritchard and Evan Roberts, who acted as trustees for the community. Yet as they died off at the beginning of the nineteenth century, there did not seem to emerge a new generation of leaders able and willing to take on the responsibility for the Family, so ownership of Trefeca was ultimately transferred to the Methodist Connexion, bringing Harris' vision for his self-contained community to an end.

8

Mothers in Christ

Mary Fletcher and the Women of Early Methodism[1]

Brett C. McInelly

WRITING TO MARY FLETCHER in 1809, Joseph Cross, "being pretty far advanced in life," reflected on the role that Fletcher's *An Aunt's Advice to a Niece* (1780) played in his religious awakening: "That work was the instrument in God's hand of my conversion. So if you wrote that book, as my dear mother assured me you did, it follows, that you are my mother in Christ."[2] Writing more than a decade earlier, Anne Conibear told Fletcher, "I look up to you, as [a] Minister of God for good to me."[3] Such comments suggest the influential position Fletcher occupied among early Methodists and point to an even more significant fact: many of the women of early Methodism seized the opportunity for public ministry afforded by the Methodist revival. As mothers in Christ, Fletcher and her Methodist sisters took on leadership roles within the

1. Parts of this essay have been previously published in Brett C. McInelly, "'I had rather be obscure. But I dare not': Women and Methodism in the Eighteenth Century," in Diane E. Boyd and Marta Kvande, eds., *Everyday Revolutions: Eighteenth-Century Women Transforming Public and Private* (Newark: University of Delaware Press, 2008) 135–58. Used by permission.

2. Joseph Cross to Mary Fletcher, May 15, 1809, The John Rylands University Library, Fletcher-Tooth Collection, 2.1/30.

3. Anne Conibear to Mary Fletcher, November 12, 1792, Fletcher-Tooth Collection, 2.1/15.

Methodist societies, organized charitable enterprises, administered to the sick and to condemned felons, lobbied for the abolition of slavery, and even preached and exhorted in public. While eighteenth-century social convention attempted to compartmentalize the private and the public in relegating women to the domestic sphere,[4] Methodism defied the division.

But in defying this division, John Wesley, who encouraged women's involvement in the movement, and his followers inadvertently invited criticism from contemporaries who worried that Methodism's appeal to women could potentially undermine the fabric of eighteenth-century society. Rather than accept the faith of these women on its own terms, as a sincere expression of their innermost beliefs, critics dismissed Methodist spiritual experience as mere enthusiasm. Much modern scholarship has similarly paid a great deal of attention to the sociopolitical outcomes of women's involvement in early Methodism while ignoring the depth and complexities of spiritual experience.[5] In attending to the religious as religious, my aim in this essay is to show how personal spiritual experience, a touchstone of eighteenth-century Methodist theology, clouded for many women the distinction between the private and the public, whereas the anti-Methodist literature demonstrates how public activity motivated by faith could be easily politicized by writers wanting to discredit Methodism.

Given the high profile of women in early Methodism and the range of their activities, it is tempting to call attention to the sociopolitical ramifications of their involvement. Gail Malmgreen's introduction to *Religion in the Lives of English Women, 1760–1930* effectively defines the scope of those studies that privilege the politics of religion: "Perhaps the most important task confronting the historian of women's spirituality is to keep alive the central paradox, the complex tension between religion as 'opiate' and as an embodiment of ideological and institutional sexism, and religion as transcendent and liberating force."[6] But regarding

---

4. This claim has been challenged and debated by historians over the last several decades, a point to which I return later in this essay.

5. See, for example, Gail Malmgreen, "Domestic discords: Women and family in East Cheshire Methodism," in Jim Obelkevich, Lyndal Roper, and Rahael Samuel, eds., *Disciplines of Faith: Studies in Religion, Politics and Patriarchy* (London: Routledge & Kegan Paul, 1987) 55–70, and Henry Abelove, *The Evangelist of Desire: John Wesley and the Methodists* (Stanford: Stanford University Press, 1990).

6. Gail Malmgreen, "Introduction," in Gail Malmgreen, ed., *Religion in the Lives of*

religion as "institutional sexism" or "liberating force" may cause us to lose sight of religious activity as just that, religious activity, a sincere expression of faith that, from the point of view of the religiously devout, overshadowed the political.

Ken Jackson and Arthur Marotti suggest that contemporary critics and historians, whose work is often informed by New Historicism and cultural materialism, are apt to recast "religious issues . . . into social, economic, and political language . . . assuming that religion itself is a form of 'false consciousness.'" Jackson and Marotti go on to argue that "there is often a relentless 'presentism' in political readings of early modern culture. The otherness of early modern religious agents and culture(s) is translated into (for us) more acceptable modern forms conformable to our own cultural assumptions."[7] Accordingly, women preachers become proto-feminists, a designation that likely would have seemed alien to the very women to whom it is applied. For Mary Fletcher and the women of early Methodism, the spiritual implications of their activities eclipsed the potential political consequences of their actions; that is, while Fletcher recognized that her society and family disapproved of her involvement in the Methodist societies, she was much more concerned with answering a divine call than with turning the social order on its head. Moreover, the desire of Fletcher and these women to obey their spiritual impressions enabled them to overcome the anxieties that naturally accompanied the impulse to behave in ways that seemingly ran counter to social expectation; that is, these women were acutely aware that many observers disapproved of their activities, yet the desire to follow God's command proved an ultimate trump card, at least in their own minds, a point to which I return later in this essay.

I do not mean to suggest here that religious motives limited the effects of the actions of these women in the public domain, nor do such motives extricate religious activity from sociopolitical critique. As I acknowledge throughout this essay, women's involvement in the Methodist movement *did* have political consequences, and although the women of early Methodism likely did not intend nor anticipate all of these consequences, our assessments of their activities should not lose sight of this fact. However, my primary objection to the kind of scholarship

English Women, 1760–1930 (London: Croom Helm, 1986) 6–7.

7. Ken Jackson and Arthur F. Marotti, "The Turn to Religion in Early Modern Studies," *Criticism* 46 (2004) 167–68.

Malmgreen describes is that scholars, in attending to women's religious experience, ironically pay little attention to the spiritual. A more responsible way of evaluating women's involvement in religion would account for the spiritual complexities of religious experience, in addition to the sociopolitical repercussions of religious activity. As I argue in this essay, to fully appreciate the experiences of early Methodist women and the ways they challenged the status quo, we must first come to realize the central role faith played in their lives and how faith, not some kind of sociopolitical agenda, motivated public religious expression for many of these women.[8]

In contrast to the more politically nuanced readings of womens' religious involvement, there are several studies that give almost exclusive attention to the roles these women played in the revival, with little regard to sociopolitical implications. Paul Chilcote's work tends to be mostly descriptive and at times even devotional in its account and praise of early Methodist women, and he is much less interested in theorizing and analyzing the ways that the religious and sociopolitical intersect.[9]

The avenues Methodism provided women for day-to-day public activity opened at the historical moment when women, as Nancy Armstrong has argued, were "disappearing into the woodwork to watch over the household."[10] According to Armstrong, the process that led to the development of modern notions of domestic womanhood gained momentum throughout the eighteenth century and was fully realized in the nineteenth century,[11] and she grounds her thesis in the prolifera-

8. For a notable exception to the trend typified in Malmgreen's comment, see Phyllis Mack, *Heart Religion in the British Enlightenment: Gender and Emotion in Early Methodism* (Cambridge: Cambridge University Press, 2008). Mack probes faith and Methodist religious experience on their own terms and with critical acumen.

9. See Paul Chilcote, *John Wesley and the Women Preachers of Early Methodism*, ATLA Monograph Series, no. 25 (Metuchen, NJ: The American Theological Library Association and the Scarecrow Press, 1991); *She Offered Them Christ: The Legacy of Women Preachers in Early Methodism* (Eugene, OR: Wipf & Stock, 2001); *Her Own Story: Autobiographical Portraits of Early Methodist Women* (Nashville: Kingswood, 2001); and *Early Methodist Spirituality: Selected Women's Writing* (Nashville: Kingswood, 2007).

10. Nancy Armstrong, *Desire and Domestic Fiction: A Political History of the Novel* (New York: Oxford University Press, 1987) 80.

11. Catherine Hall and Leonore Davidoff have similarly argued that, during the later part of the eighteenth century and the early nineteenth century, gendered divisions between the public and private spheres developed in England, with women being confined to the home as men went into the workplace and politics. See *Family Fortunes: Men and*

tion of conduct literature for women during the period. This literature defined the ideal female as unassuming and suited to private as opposed to public life. Moreover, the ideal was largely constructed on a religious foundation as women assumed the responsibility of propagating religious and moral standards through their work in the home. With the decline of the government's backing of the established Church, the attacks on orthodox Christianity by the deists and others, and a growing apathy toward religion in society,[12] women, Dale A. Johnson argues, played a primary role in preserving Christianity in Great Britain.[13] Ruth H. Bloch similarly observes that "fictional and religious literature began attributing to women not only a commendable piety but also the primary power to enforce religious and moral standards."[14]

The so-called rise of the domestic woman, or what Lawrence Klein has termed the "domestic thesis,"[15] has not gone unquestioned. As Leonore Davidoff explains, "the main sources of contention have been its chronology, location, and actual practice."[16] Historians have debated whether the domestic woman is an eighteenth- or nineteenth-century phenomenon, or whether generalizations regarding femininity can accurately be applied as we move from one locale to another; historians

Women of the English Middle Class, 1780–1850, 2nd ed. (London: Routledge, 2002).

12. The suggestion that the Church's influence diminished during the period and that religiosity similarly declined has been challenged in more recent studies. See J. C. D. Clark, *English Society, 1660–1832*, 2nd ed. (Cambridge: Cambridge University Press, 2000); Jeremy Gregory, *Restoration, Reformation and Reform, 1660–1828* (Oxford: Clarendon, 2000); and William Gibson, *The Church of England, 1688–1832: Unity and Accord* (London: Routledge, 2001). All of these studies assert, in varying ways, that the role the Church played in eighteenth-century society was much more consequential than Johnson suggests. Nonetheless, whether the feminization of piety was spurred by the decline of the Church's influence and/or other forces is, within the context of my argument, a relatively extraneous point. The more pressing concern is whether we can say with some confidence that eighteenth-century culture invested femininity with the power to affect religious and moral reform, a point I address in the next few pages.

13. Dale A. Johnson, *Women in English Religion, 1700–1925*, Studies in Women and Religion, vol. 10 (New York: Edwin Mellen, 1983) 13.

14. Ruth H. Bloch, *Gender and Morality in Anglo-American Culture, 1650–1800* (Berkley: University of California Press, 2003) 52.

15. Lawrence E. Klein, "Gender and the Public/Private Distinction in the Eighteenth Century: Some Questions About Evidence and Analytic Procedure," *Eighteenth-Century Studies* 29:1 (1995) 97.

16. Leonore Davidoff, "Gender and the 'Great Divide': Public and Private in British Gender History," *Journal of Women's History* 15:1 (2003) 11.

have also noted incongruities between theory and practice. "At least in some sense," Klein observes, "women had extensive public lives in the eighteenth century," while Amanda Vickery claims that Victorian women were surprisingly more active than social theories or historical accounts sometimes suggest.[17] The feminization of piety has similarly been scrutinized. Noting the feminization of angels in religious iconography in early nineteenth-century British art, as seraphic beings came to be depicted as feminine instead of masculine, which was the more traditional technique, Callum Brown has argued that the feminization of British religiosity was a nineteenth-century development, with Victorian women and their piety becoming "central to the life of not just the churches but of the nation."[18]

To thoroughly engage these debates is beyond the scope of this essay. Suffice it to say that notions of an unassuming femininity comfortably situated in a domestic ideal and endowed with a reforming virtue or piety were features of both the eighteenth- and nineteenth-century cultural landscapes. As Jane Rendall has argued, "To anyone who has even sampled British prescriptive literature in the eighteenth and nineteenth centuries, the contrast between private and public worlds, . . . the language of separate spheres, assigned to women and men, is immediately familiar."[19] Joseph Addison stressed the notion of separate spheres in 1711 in an issue of *The Spectator*. After criticizing the "showy and superficial" nature of French women, Addison extolled the virtues of a reticent lifestyle: "True Happiness is of a retired Nature, and an Enemy to Pomp and Noise . . . false happiness loves to be in a Crowd, and to draw the Eyes of the World upon her." The ideal woman "delights in the Privacy of a Country Life" and, with her husband, quietly manages an

17. Klein, "Gender and the Public/Private Distinction," 100; Amanda Vickery, "Golden Age of Separate Spheres? A Review of the Categories and Chronology of English Women's History," *The Historical Journal* 36 (1993) 390. Klein further reminds us that the terms *private* and *public* shifted in meaning during the period (99); Davidoff similarly suggests that notions of private and public must be studied in particular contexts (22). In response, a forthcoming study by Joanna Cruickshank examines the ways Methodist women used and understood the terms. See Joanna Cruickshank, "'If God . . . see fit to call you out': 'Public' and 'Private' in the Writings of Methodist Women, 1760–1840," in Brett C. McInelly, ed., *Religion in the Age of Enlightenment*, vol. 2 (New York: AMS, 2010).

18. Callum C. Brown, *The Death of Christian Britain* (London: Routledge, 2001) 61.

19. Jane Rendall, "Women and the Public Sphere," *Gender and History* 11:3 (1999) 476.

efficient household: "Their Family is under so regular an Oeconomy, in its Hours of Devotion and Repast, Employment and Diversion, that it looks like a little Common-wealth within it self." Addison's colleague, Richard Steele, argued a similar point: "We have indeed carried Women's Characters too much into publick life . . . the utmost of a Woman's Character is contained in domestick life . . . All she has to do in this World, is contained within the Duties of a Daughter, a Sister, a Wife, and a Mother."[20] Moreover, the reforming power of feminine virtue and religiosity is as equally evident in Richardson's *Pamela* as it is in Brontë's *Jane Eyre*.

Within the context of the Methodist revival, women were generally admired for their exceptional piety, and their anxieties regarding public ministry suggest that social convention, throughout the period, restricted such activity. Wesley, in particular, placed a premium on women's religiosity: "It is certain that Mr. Wesley had a predilection for the female character; partly, because he had a mind ever alive to amiability, and partly from his generally finding in females a quicker and fuller responsiveness to his own ideas of interior piety and affectionate devotion."[21] Wesley eagerly involved these women in the revival, even if it meant breaking with social convention. In a letter discouraging one young woman from marrying, Wesley exclaimed, "I thought [God] was preparing you for a large sphere of action. Surely you was [*sic*] not . . . designed to be shut up in a little cottage and fully taken up with domestic cares." To another woman he declared, "I believe the one thing which has hurt you is . . . silence . . . Learn to speak for God without either fear or shame."[22] Methodism thus allowed many of these women to transform the maternal role they "naturally" assumed as nurturers and moral authorities within the domestic realm into a more public role of religious ministers, or mothers in Christ.

Even with strong encouragement from the movement's leader, the women of early Methodism were keenly aware that their actions cut against the grain of accepted feminine behavior, and in answering

20. Joseph Addison and Richard Steele, *The Spectator*, ed. Gregory Smith (London: Everyman's Library, 1964) 1:48–49, 3:70.

21. Alexander Knox, "Remarks on the Life and Character of John Wesley," in Robert Southey, *The Life of Wesley and the Rise and Progress of Methodism* (New York: Harper, 1874) 2:340.

22. John Telford, ed., *The Letters of John Wesley, A.M.* (London: Epworth, 1931) 8:248 and 6:88.

God's call, women Methodists felt the weight of social expectations as well as the forms of the Church, which disapproved of women speaking in church. Methodist women were particularly anxious when speaking before large audiences, whether in cottage meetings or the open air, in a manner that resembled preaching. Sarah Crosby entered into her ministry rather reluctantly. Following her first public exhortation, she wrote, "I was not sure whether it was right for me to exhort in so public a manner."[23] Bathsheba Hall similarly felt the tension between her status as a woman and her desire to share the gospel: "I had rather be obscure. But I dare not."[24] Mary Fletcher experienced the same anxieties: "The other day one [man] told me, 'He was sure I must be an impudent woman; no modest woman, he was sure, could proceed thus!' Ah! How glad would nature be to find out,—Thou, Lord, dost not require it!"[25]

The high profile of women in Methodism indicates, as Klein and Vickery suggest, that our historicizing of the domestic woman should account for both the subtle and dramatic ways that these women's stories resist a monolithic formulation of femininity in the eighteenth century. Their experiences push against notions of history that seem as eager to isolate womanhood to the domestic sphere as eighteenth-century social convention. Perhaps more importantly, these women's involvement in the revival reveals how permeable the private-public divide was in the lives of women motivated by spiritual faith.

The women themselves found it difficult to "withstand God," and Bathsheba Hall's statement—"I had rather be obscure. But I dare not"—vividly demonstrates the force a divine mandate carried in the minds of these women. In addition, Hall's comment reveals a curious paradox relating to Methodist women and public expression. Most women who assumed a public voice during the eighteenth century generally did so apologetically; they were reluctant to speak up, at times even self-effacing when entering into public discourse. The prefaces to countless novels written by women, for example, begin with apologetic

---

23. Zechariah Taft, *Biographical Sketches of the Lives and Public Ministry of Various Holy Women* (Leeds: Cullingworth, 1828) 2:42.

24. Bathsheba Hall, *The Diary of Bathsheba Hall*, in Paul W. Chilcote, ed., *Her Own Story: Autobiographical Portraits of Early Methodist Women* (Nashville: Kingswood, 2001) 105.

25. Quoted in Chilcote, *She Offered Them Christ*, 87–88.

and self-deprecating language.[26] Hall's comment, however, puts an interesting spin on these more traditional and formulaic introductions to women's public speaking and writing. Unlike women novelists, who were anxious about assuming a public voice, Methodist women worried more about the consequences of *not* speaking. To not speak was to ignore the commands of God. The spiritual pretext of religious expression assumes a preexisting authority that supersedes all others in the mind of the believer and in the minds of faithful auditors. Those who entertained what women of faith had to say legitimized their religious authority simply by listening, and Wesley reinforced their clout as much as any Methodist leader. It was to Wesley that Fletcher addressed what Chilcote refers to as "the first serious defense of women preaching in Methodism,"[27] to which Wesley responded with approval. But those who either could not or were unwilling to accept the religious pretext of the words and actions of these women inevitably construed their activities as subversive of the social order.

This takes us to the core of the problem faced by Methodist women in the eighteenth century. Personal spiritual conviction in the mind of the believer was one thing; convincing others of one's private witness was quite another. Even Wesley subjected those who claimed a divine call to rigorous examination before authorizing their activities, and several of Wesley's male preachers strongly opposed the public ministry of women, despite the women's claims of inspired authority.[28] The liminal nature of spiritual experience, then, is both its greatest asset and its greatest liability. Because the spiritual assumes ultimate authority for the believer, those women who claimed a divine call could assert their private experience as a means of overcoming social expectations that confined their activities to the home and family, and as a way of assuaging their own anxieties regarding public ministry. But because this type of experience could not be explained to nor understood by the skeptical observer, it could not serve as a viable basis for dismantling social codes outside the mind of the believer. Those who questioned or were skeptical of the convictions and motives of these women thus interpreted the

26. See Mary Davys, *The Reform'd Coquet*, ed. Martha F. Bowden (Lexington: University of Kentucky Press, 1999) 5.

27. Chilcote, *She Offered Them Christ*, 78.

28. See Joseph Benson, Appendix E: A Joseph Benson Letter, in Chilcote, *John Wesley and the Women Preachers*, 308.

activities of early Methodist women as socially subversive and as steps towards female emancipation. It is not so much a matter of whether Methodist women really received a divine call; for them, the experience was real enough.

Convincing themselves of the reality of their experiences and acting on spiritual promptings was, in some cases, as formidable a challenge for women Methodists as overcoming restrictive social codes. Fletcher recorded, "I even feared that the Lord did not approve of my calling the people together, when there was no one but me to speak to them. Yet I knew well that 'all the good done upon the earth is the Lord's doing,' and that he can work by the meanest instrument. However, this was the conclusion, I must ask and wrestle for every meeting, public and private, and hang by faith on Christ alone, believing that word: 'It is not you that speak, but the Spirit of your Father which speaketh in you.'"[29] Fletcher's authority to speak in public was supported by the conviction that she was a mere conduit through which God spoke. In surrendering herself and her voice to God, Fletcher, like other Methodist women, paradoxically forged and maintained a public presence and identity that helped neutralize her own anxieties and shielded her from the contempt of those who objected to women's public engagement.

Methodist women in the eighteenth century, however, faced a perplexing situation. By exercising their spiritual gifts beyond the walls of their own homes, these women placed themselves in a vulnerable position in that the very same society that commended them for their piety and moral fortitude was quick to censor religious activity that seemingly overstepped the bounds of feminine propriety. Ironically, social commentators who invested femininity with religious and moral authority helped open the door to the kinds of public activities practiced by early Methodist women, but some of these commentators eventually came to worry about the ramifications of their own positions.

Examining the topical scope of *The Weekly Miscellany* just prior to and immediately after the advent of Methodism in the late 1730s, Cynthia J. Cupples observed a peculiar shift in the periodical's focus. The *Miscellany*, produced by William Webster from 1732 to 1741 and initially printed by Samuel Richardson, looks like many newspapers and magazines printed during the period, though it is somewhat unique in its almost exclusive focus on religious matters. The *Miscellany* devoted

29. Quoted in Chilcote, *John Wesley and the Women Preachers*, 244.

particular attention to women's education during the early part of the
1730s and repeatedly encouraged women's religious involvement, particularly in the "work of moral reform." But such commentary—generally in the form of letter correspondences between a series of real and
imagined readers—"disappeared after 1738[30] as Webster recognized the
growing threat posed by the largely female Methodist movement."[31] By
encouraging female piety, conservatives like Webster "empower[ed]
women to claim a greater scope of action in the religious sphere," but
when faced with the rise of Methodism, these writers "retreated from
the implications of their ideal of the pious woman or worked out various
ways of protecting her from the taint of heterodoxy."[32]

As Cupples' study demonstrates, concerns regarding Methodism's
appeal to women began to surface from the outset of the revival, and
they continued throughout the eighteenth century. Not surprisingly,
women, much more than men, were criticized for their involvement
in the Methodist societies and its effect on the home front.[33] Common
charges included disregard of wifely and maternal responsibilities, and
the misuse of family funds. Of course, such accusations were surely
exaggerated. Methodism received its share of negative press during the
eighteenth century, and detractors were anxious to discredit Methodism

30. Given that John Wesley did not start his evangelistic ministry in England until
1739, this date may seem problematic. However, Wesley's friend and colleague, George
Whitefield, had taken to the open air by 1737, attracting large crowds and public attention. From the outset of the revival, Whitefield, and later Wesley, was accused of attracting predominantly female followers. The year 1739 represents one of several high-water
marks in the anti-Methodist campaign to discredit Methodism via the press, and critics immediately accused Methodism of attracting predominately female followers.
The first dramatic attack on Methodism, published in 1739, drew explicit attention to
Methodism's appeal to women and its supposed effects on the home front. In the play,
a Cobbler explains to his wife-turned-Methodist, "And so you must dance about after
this Mock-Preacher [Whitefield], must you? and leave me to nurse your children? (*The
Mock-Preacher* [London: C. Corbett, 1739], 15). In short, the high profile of women in
Methodism was recognized and criticized from the outset of the revival. *The Weekly
Miscellany* was particularly well known for its attacks on Methodism. Webster thus
would not have seen the advent of Methodism as a viable vehicle for encouraging the
reform he sought.

31. Cynthia J. Cupples, "Pious Ladies and Methodist Madams: Sex and Gender in
Anti-Methodist Writings of the Eighteenth Century," *Critical Matrix* 5 (1990) 41.

32. Ibid., 52 and 60.

33. See Donald Henry Kirkham, "Pamphlet Opposition to the Rise of Methodism:
The Eighteenth-Century English Evangelical Revival Under Attack," PhD diss., Duke
University, 1973, 214.

in any way possible.[34] But more important than the truth or falsity of the accusations leveled against Methodist women is the extent to which the anti-Methodist literature translated religious matters into political terms and reasserted a patriarchal order and the passivity of women. Women's involvement in Methodism was generally portrayed as domestic rebellion—and, by extension, social rebellion—as women resisted the authority of their husbands.[35] Contemporary accounts of the Wednesbury Riots (1743) blame the incident, which resulted in the looting of Methodist homes and abuse of members of Wesley's societies, on a woman who had reportedly abandoned her husband and children and was found at a Methodist meeting.[36]

Much of the anti-Methodist literature drew attention to the ways women supposedly played the religious card in dictating the dynamics of their relationships with their spouses. The ex-Methodist James Lackington reported that some Methodist women would, after conversion, refuse to have sex with their husbands. After three years of marriage one "husband [was] not sure as to the sex of his wife; and on every attempt of the husband for that purpose, the servants [were] alarmed with the screams of the pious lady, who would not permit such carnal communication for the world."[37] Such accounts effectively discredited Methodist women by recasting religious faith as an expression of an emotionally unstable and overzealous mind. The screams that accompanied a husband's attempts to exercise his conjugal rights in Lackington's account hint at an enthusiasm that bordered on hysteria. Enthusiasm was the most common charge leveled against Methodists generally, but in the case of women, the charge carried extra weight, since women were generally perceived as more emotional than men and more susceptible to religious delusion.[38]

---

34. See Clive D. Field, "Anti-Methodist Publications of the Eighteenth Century: A Revised Bibliography," *Bulletin of the John Rylands University Library of Manchester* 73 (1991) 159–280. See also Albert M. Lyles, *Methodism Mocked: The Satiric Reaction to Methodism in the Eighteenth Century* (London: Epworth, 1960). Lyles provides a comprehensive survey of the motives and methods of the anti-Methodist satire.

35. See, for example, *The Story of the Methodist Lady: Or the Injur'd Husband's Revenge* (London: Strahan, 1745).

36. See *Some Papers Giving an Account of the Rise and Progress of Methodism at Wednesbury in Straffordshire* (London: Roberts, 1744) 21–22.

37. James Lackington, *Memoirs of the Forty-Five First Years of James Lackington* (London: Whittaker, Treacher & Arnot, 1830) 139–41.

38. See Lyles, *Methodism Mocked*, 97.

Perhaps nothing discredited the charges of enthusiasm more, however, than the introspection that typically accompanied the experiences of these women. Not merely carried away by enthusiastic flights, they relentlessly interrogated and analyzed their feelings before asserting themselves in ways that challenged the social conventions of the day. Their anxieties about speaking in public checked their emotions and ensured that spiritual promptings were submitted to reflective examination. On one occasion, Mary Fletcher was so overwhelmed at the prospect of public speaking that she devoted an entire day to praying and considering the validity of the impulse to preach.[39] As Phyllis Mack convincingly argues in *Heart Religion in the British Enlightenment*, the Methodist revival, while promoting emotional excess in many cases, simultaneously encouraged its participants to analyze and "make sense" of their feelings.[40] For women, in particular, social convention and stereotypes provided additional motivation to cautiously act on spiritual impulses.

To some degree, recent scholarship has treated the religious component of women's experience in ways similar to the anti-Methodist literature by giving almost exclusive attention to the politics of women's religious involvement. As already noted, our interest in the experience of these women stems, in part, from the fact that Methodism did empower women. "It is clear," Malmgreen states, "that for some women . . . religion became a means of avoiding or delaying marriage, and even after marriage the call to preaching or missionary or philanthropic work could become the excuse for long separations and other unconventional domestic arrangements."[41] Henry Abelove similarly discusses the ways Wesley's pro-celibacy stance could become a rationale for "the devaluing and breaking of family ties, same-sex eroticism, [and] the refusal at the wife's insistence of marital sex."[42]

But in assessing the ways that Methodism provided a basis for female self-assertion, Malmgreen and Abelove rearticulate, in part, the same attitude that underlies much of the anti-Methodist literature. While giving attention to the outcomes of women's religious involvement, the question of sincerity goes virtually unexplored. Their work seems to imply that women's interest in Methodism derived more from

39. Chilcote, *She Offered Them Christ*, 87.

40. Mack, *Heart Religion*, 7.

41. Malmgreen, "Domestic discords," 61.

42. Abelove, *Evangelist of Desire*, 63.

a desire to free themselves from oppressive relationships and restrictive social codes than it did from a desire to obey the commands of God. Abelove states, "His [Wesley's] followers understood him as they wished, as they needed to, and they heard his implied assent far more distinctly than his explicit condemnation [of socially questionable behavior]."[43] Abelove does not consider for a moment that Wesley's followers were motivated primarily, or even partially, by spiritual conviction. Some women may well have found in Methodism a convenient way of resisting social convention, but this way of appraising women's religious experience undervalues the extent to which the behavior of these women may have been motivated by faith, and it recasts religious experience as a mere pretext for self-liberating behavior.

Though the women of early Methodism were not nearly as radical in their thinking as such feminists as Mary Astell and Mary Wollstonecraft, their activities may well have been as subversive of an oppressive social order that restricted female activity as any of Wollstonecraft's pleas for women's rights. But juxtaposing Mary Fletcher with Mary Wollstonecraft presents some serious problems, since these women were motivated by radically different principles. Moreover, the gains made by women's involvement in the revival were ultimately experienced on a relatively private scale; that is, the opportunities afforded by Methodism probably meant more to each individual woman than it did to women generally. Few women enjoyed the freedom Fletcher eventually found among the people of Madeley: "My call is . . . so clear, and I have such liberty in the work, and such sweet encouragement among the people."[44] It would thus be a mistake to see Methodism as a women's movement, at least in an overtly political sense like, say, the suffrage movement.[45] While our scholarship should, as Malmgreen suggests, pay careful attention to the politics of religion, we should also keep in mind the central role that faith played in the lives of these women. Though the current critical climate would privilege the political, the women whose experiences provide the material for our enquiries undoubtedly privileged the spiritual.

43. Ibid., 63.

44. Quoted in Chilcote, *John Wesley and the Women Preachers*, 184.

45. David Hempton refers to Methodism as a women's movement in an effort to draw attention to the numerical preponderance of women in early Methodism and to acknowledge their influence on the movement, not in the more politically nuanced sense I describe here. See David Hempton, *Methodism: Empire of the Spirit* (New Haven: Yale University Press, 2006) 149–50 and 137 ff.

9

Support Groups for Methodist Women Preachers 1803–1851

John H. Lenton

ARL KENT BROWN described in detail how support groups worked for Methodist women in the late eighteenth century.[1] He showed how preachers but also class leaders and visitors corresponded regularly, visited each other, and generally gave mutual support. I shall chart similar groups which existed among Wesleyan[2] Methodist women preachers in England between 1803 and 1851, using surviving papers or printed sources such as Zechariah Taft's *Holy Women*.[3] I shall describe how support operated and assess the importance of key participants, as Brown did for the earlier period.

1. Earl Kent Brown, *Women of Mr. Wesley's Methodism* (New York: Edwin Mellen, 1983).

2. There were many other Methodist women preachers, some itinerant, especially among the Primitive Methodists and Bible Christians.

3. Zechariah Taft, *Biographical Sketches of the Lives and Public Ministry of Various Holy Women: Whose Eminent Usefulness and Successful Labours in the Church of Christ Have Entitled Them to Be Enrolled Among the Great Benefactors of Mankind: In Which Are Included Several Letters from the Rev. J. Wesley Never Before Published*, 2 vols. (London: Kershaw, 1825). For further biographical information on most of the main figures described in this essay, see the *Dictionary of Methodism in Britain and Ireland* (hereafter, *DMBI*), available at: http://www.wesleyhistoricalsociety.org.uk.

In 1803 the British Wesleyan Conference forbade any woman to preach except "with an extraordinary call from God" and declared "that she should, in general, address her own sex, and those only."[4] In this new situation existing women preachers feared they might be excluded from membership if they persisted and therefore those such as Mary Taft and Mary Fletcher linked together more for self-preservation. Yet Conference regulations were not necessarily enforced in circuits, so many women preached just as they had before. By 1851 relatively few women preachers are known to have remained in the British Wesleyan Methodist connexion.[5] The three principal preachers of this later period, Mary Taft, Mary Tooth, and Sarah Boyce,[6] died between 1843 and 1851.

The three main groups are shown in diagrams: the first shows the Madeley circle, using evidence from the Fletcher-Tooth papers,[7] as it existed before Mary Fletcher's death in 1815. It illustrates links to other preachers, all of whom either visited Madeley or corresponded with Mary Fletcher in this period (or both), which activities Mary Tooth continued. She invited them to Madeley and encouraged them to preach, visit, pray publicly, and lead classes. The second group was in communication with Mary and Zechariah Taft, mainly in the north of England. The third was the East Anglian network centered around Sarah Boyce in Norfolk and Charlotte Berger in Essex. Madeley was thus central to women preaching in Wesleyan Methodism in this period.

---

4. An extract from the response of the 1803 Conference to Question 19 ("Should women be permitted to preach among us?") reads: "1 Because the vast majority of our people are opposed to [women preaching]" "2 Because their preaching does not seem to be at all necessary, there being a sufficiency of Preachers . . . to supply all the places in our connexion with regular preaching." Wesleyan Methodist Church, *Minutes of the Methodist Conference from the First, Held in London, by the Late Rev. John Wesley, A.M. in the Year 1744*, vol. 2 (London: Cordeux, 1813) 188–89. The Irish Conference in 1802 declared "it contrary to both scripture and prudence that women should preach in public" and excluded Alice Cambridge from membership when she continued to preach. D. L. Cooney, *The Methodists in Ireland: A Short History* (Dublin: Columba, 2001) 121.

5. John H. Lenton, "Labouring for the Lord: Women Preachers in Wesleyan Methodism 1802–1932: A Revisionist View," in *Beyond the Boundaries: Preaching in the Wesleyan Tradition*, ed. Richard Sykes (Oxford: Applied Theological, 1998) 58–86.

6. See David East, *My Dear Sally: The Life of Sarah Mallet one of John Wesley's Preachers* (Emsworth: WMHS, 2003).

7. The Fletcher-Tooth papers at Methodist Archives and Research Centre, John Rylands Library, comprise 43 boxes of letters, journals, diaries, and other papers, cited hereafter as MAM Fl. --/--/--.

Barrie Trinder wrote how Mary Fletcher, Sally Lawrence and Mary Tooth were the "leaders of a religious order drawn together by the charisma of John Fletcher" and described their sub-circuit and flock.[8] Part of their ethos was an insistence that women were called to preach, to "labour publicly" as they expressed it. They welcomed women preachers and male Methodist leaders, largely sustained by Mary Fletcher's and Mary Tooth's capacity for correspondence, networking, and visitation. At Madeley women preachers were persuaded to speak in the tithe barn after which they returned home emboldened, comforted that they were being prayed for and upheld by further letters. This was true for well-known women preachers from further afield than the West Midlands like Mary Taft who (as Mary Barritt) had converted many in Yorkshire and elsewhere across northern England in the 1790s.[9] Driven by the 1803 ban to widen her network of friends from merely those in the north, Mary Taft first wrote to Mary Fletcher[10] that year and began a close correspondence with her and later with Mary Tooth.

After 1803, though a few Wesleyan women preachers ceased to preach,[11] most, like Taft and Fletcher, continued as they had done before, and with the consent of the local Superintendent. (There is a parallel in the United States where women continued to preach throughout the nineteenth century in the African Episcopal Church, Zion, despite official prohibition.[12]) In the 1809 Sheffield District meeting Jabez Bunting proposed to strengthen the ban and the penalties.[13] Before the 1809 Conference Zechariah Taft sent a printed circular to many ministerial friends, and to

8. B. S. Trinder, *The Industrial Revolution in Shropshire*, 3rd ed. (Chichester: Phillimore, 2000) 179.

9. Before her marriage, Barritt preached in every northern circuit except Liverpool, Sunderland, and Newcastle.

10. This letter was printed in Taft, *Holy Women*, 1:19–21. P. W. Chilcote, *Early Methodist Spirituality: Selected Women's Writings* (Nashville: Kingswood, 2007) 293–94.

11. See Lenton, "Labouring for the Lord," 64. The only person who stopped around this period was Elizabeth Collet Tonkin in Cornwall in 1804.

12. Julyanne Dodson "Nineteenth-Century A.M.E. Preaching Women: Cutting Edge of Women's Inclusion in Church Policy," in *Women in New Worlds: Historical Perspectives on the Wesleyan Tradition*, vol. 1, ed. Hilah Thomas and Rosemary Keller (Nashville: Abingdon, 1981) 276–89.

13. "The Minutes of the Sheffield District were drawn up by himself [Bunting] . . . 'We express our opinion that the practice [of female preaching] is unscriptural, disgraceful to our Connexion . . . and that it ought to be discountenanced.'" T. P. Bunting, *The Life of Jabez Bunting* (London: Longmans, 1859) 331–32.

Fletcher because he cited her example: "If you were sent into the circuit where Mrs Fletcher has laboured for so long . . . would you expel her from the Society for this?"[14] The Tafts received several supportive replies, and the Sheffield District proposal was stopped for the moment.[15]

The Tafts first visited Madeley in 1810. Mary Taft recorded in her manuscript Journal: "(Mrs. Fletcher) rejoiced to see us. We spent this week I think next door to heaven."[16] Mrs. Fletcher then wrote to Joseph Benson, whom she knew well as a friend of her husband and his biographer, defending Mary Taft. "She really speaks sensibly and with much unction. Blessed be the Lord for raising up helpers among his people."[17]

THE MADELEY GROUP

Mary Fletcher (1739–1815) and Mary Tooth (1778–1843) and their "romantic friendship" are dealt with in more detail elsewhere in this volume.[18] Growing research into the Fletcher-Tooth papers shows that Mary Tooth's friendship with Mary Fletcher started earlier than once thought.[19] In 1796 Mary Tooth described Sarah Lawrence (1759–1800), Mary Fletcher's adopted daughter, as her friend who told her that she was being "called to come forward in a more active manner."[20] Tooth then apparently became a teacher in Shifnal, three miles east of Madeley, where from the beginning she spent weekends at Madeley Vicarage, leaving on Monday mornings what she described as the "Castle Beautiful."[21]

14. Zechariah Taft to Mrs. Fletcher, 27 June 1809, MAM Fl. 104/5/3.

15. See letters from Samuel Bradburn, Bath, 10 July 1809, MARC: MAM PLP 14/8/8; Henry Longden, Sheffield, 18 July 1809, MARC: card PLP; Robert Harrison, Ripon, 27 July 1809, MAM PLP 50/33/6; and George Thompson, Ramsey, 19 July 1809, Duke University, Frank Baker Collection, Box 7, 23–I, Taft Folder.

16. Mrs. Taft's MS Diary at Birmingham Central Library, MS 977, p. 221.

17. MS Letter to Joseph Benson 20 July 1810, Duke University, Baker Collection, Benson papers.

18. See also Phyllis Mack, *Heart Religion in the British Enlightenment: Gender and Emotion in Early Methodism* (Cambridge: Cambridge University Press, 2008) 153.

19. Gareth Lloyd suggested the move of Mary Tooth to Madeley was "about 1809." *The Fletcher-Tooth Collection*, vol. 1 (Manchester: JRULM, 1997) ii.

20. MAM Fl. 14 Mary Tooth "MS Account of Her Life and Journal, 13 September 1796 to 30 December 1797," 51–52 (18 September 1796).

21. Mary Tooth's Pocket Book, 1799, MAM Fl. 25/2, entry for Monday, 9 Sept. "Castle Beautiful" is a reference to Bunyan's *Pilgrims Progress*.

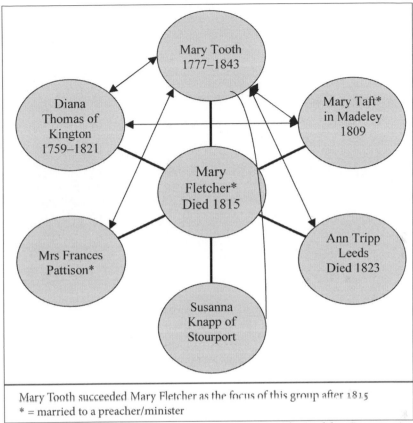

Mary Tooth succeeded Mary Fletcher as the focus of this group after 1815
* = married to a preacher/minister

Diagram 1. The Madeley Group to 1815

It is clear that, well before Sarah Lawrence's death, Mary Fletcher was preparing Mary Tooth to succeed her. In October 1800 Mary Tooth had given notice to her employer, Miss Lutton in Shifnal, and moved into the Madeley Vicarage permanently.[22] In her will Mary Fletcher described Mary Tooth as "my useful right hand."[23]

After Mary Fletcher's death in 1815 support for Mary Tooth came from various quarters, not least her older sister Rosamond. "Rose" or "Rosie"[24] first came to Madeley to supply her younger sister's place at

22. Tooth Journal for 18 Oct. 1800, MAM Fl. 14/17.

23. Mary Fletcher's Will in "Papers of Mary and John William Fletcher," Drew University Methodist Library 1306–5–3:05.

24. MAM Fl. 1/12/4 spelled "Rossee" by Sarah Boyce in 1830 or in MAM Fl. 4/16/3 the other Tooth sister calls her "Rose."

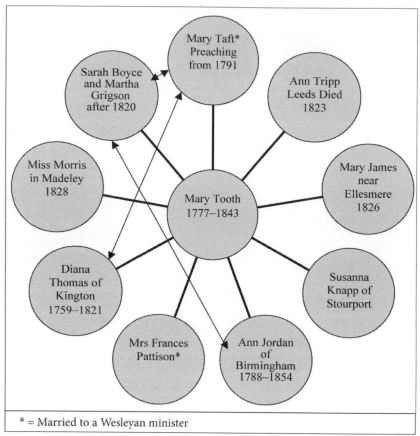

* = Married to a Wesleyan minister

Diagram 2. The Madeley Group after 1815

the Micklewright's school in 1797.[25] In 1808 she was invited by Mary Fletcher to join them in the Vicarage permanently and remained in Madeley after Mary Fletcher's death, continuing to live with Mary Tooth until her own death in 1832. After 1815 Rosamond's companionship provided Mary Tooth with support similar to that Mary Fletcher had received from Sally Lawrence and Mary Tooth.

Diana Thomas (1759–1821) of Kington, Herefordshire,[26] does not seem to have preached before she first visited Madeley in March 1806. She wrote to Fletcher "[I] heard you expound on the word Candlestick.[27] While you were speaking I experienced the Lord conveying light into

25. Tooth, "MS Account," 33.

26. See obituary of R. Thomas in *Wesleyan Methodist Magazine* (1830) 646, (hereafter, *WMM*); *Proceedings of the Wesley Historical Society* 14 (1924) 110–11; *DMBI*.

27. Mrs. Fletcher's Watchwords, MAM Fl. 27–29.

my Soul."[28] Diana Thomas was encouraged by Fletcher to speak, and subsequently she travelled over much of mid Wales, preaching both in the open air[29] and in Wesleyan chapels. She returned to Madeley in 1808 and twice after 1815, encouraging Mary Tooth to continue preaching after Mary Fletcher's death.[30] She was authorized to preach by the Kington Quarterly Meeting in 1809 in the wide border territory of the circuit, covering much of mid Wales, where there were many small congregations and few preachers.

Mrs. Ann Jordan (1788–1852) was a businessman's wife of Withall Street, Birmingham, who stayed with Tooth first in 1824,[31] and visited Norfolk at least twice in the 1830s, preaching in both areas.[32] Miss Susanna Knapp (1770–1856) was a former correspondent and protégée of Wesley, living in Stourport, Worcestershire,[33] who first visited Madeley in 1811. There at the Coalport chapel she was "enabled to speak a little under the instruction of that extraordinary woman"[34] as her biographer referred to Fletcher. Knapp then preached around Stourport at least until 1831. Little is known of Miss Morris except that in 1828 she preached at Madeley (on Isaiah 40:11) and also at Dawley Green, Coalbrookdale, and two other places where "her labours won her a troop of converts."[35] She may or may not have been the Miss Morris of Eastbourne who preached between at least 1825 and 1841.[36] There were also other preachers, often distant, with whom Mary Fletcher and Mary

28. Edith Rowley, *Fruits of Righteousness in the Life of Susanna Knapp* (Worcester: Osborn, 1866) 67–70.

29. Mary Fletcher (as Mary Bosanquet) preached outside in Yorkshire in 1776. See P. W. Chilcote, *John Wesley and the Women Preachers of Early Methodism* (Lanham: Scarecrow, 1992) 166–69. For other examples of Diana Thomas' period, see ibid., 227.

30. John Lenton "More Information on Diana Thomas," *Proceedings of the Wesley Historical Society* 51 (2000) 178–79.

31. MAM Fl. 4/7/2–7 (with a reference to a conversation about dress showing Mary Tooth's influence).

32. Obituary in *WMM* (1855) 662–64.

33. For Stourport, see *DMBI*.

34. Rowley, *Fruits of Righteousness*, 67–70.

35. See letters from J. Evans, John Gething, and Rosamund Tooth in MAM Fl. 2/14/5; 3/1/6; 3/1/7. Quotation from J. Evans of Madeley in MAM Fl. 2/14/4. Coalbrookdale was in Madeley parish; Dawley Green is immediately to the north.

36. See Carlos Crisford, *A Golden Candlestick or Methodism in Eastbourne* (Eastbourne: Crisford, 1913) 32–33, 35, 37. I am indebted to Michael Hickman for this reference.

Tooth corresponded in this period, such as Elizabeth Collet in Cornwall to whom Fletcher wrote in 1807.[37]

MARY TAFT (1772–1851) AND ZECHARIAH TAFT (1772–1848)

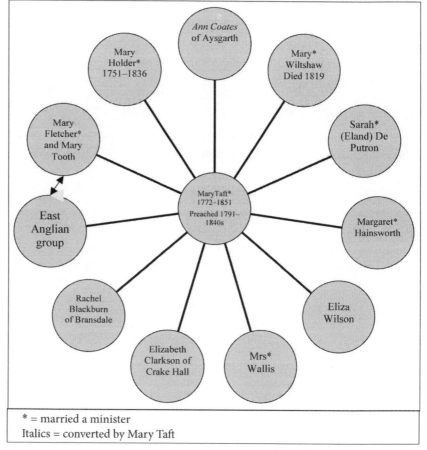

Ann Coates of Aysgarth

Mary Holder* 1751–1836

Mary* Wiltshaw Died 1819

Mary Fletcher* and Mary Tooth

Sarah* (Eland) De Putron

East Anglian group

MaryTaft* 1772–1851 Preached 1791– 1840s

Margaret* Hainsworth

Rachel Blackburn of Bransdale

Eliza Wilson

Elizabeth Clarkson of Crake Hall

Mrs* Wallis

* = married a minister
Italics = converted by Mary Taft

Diagram 3. Members of Mrs. Mary Taft's Circle

If Madeley was the focal place for circles of women preachers, the Tafts must be seen as the powerhouse behind the organization of a pressure-group to protect women preachers. When Mary Barritt married Zechariah Taft in 1802, they were immediately sent to Kent,

37. *Arminian Magazine* (Bible Christian) (1823) 286–88. The Bible Christians (see *DMBI*) strongly supported women preachers. Chilcote, *Early Methodist Spirituality*, 298–300.

outside the area where they were known. The Chairman of the District, where they were accused of dividing the society, was Joseph Benson. The Tafts were afraid the District decision would go against them, so they persuaded the aged John Pawson to write twice in support; however, the District meeting found in their favor.[38] After a successful year they were sent back north to Epworth, close to Taft's first circuit. In 1803 Mary Taft wrote to Zechariah while he was at Conference and his stationing was undecided, that "if an Irish minute should take place . . . I feel fully willing to wash my hands of Methodism. I have ever been willing to be turned out for Labouring for God."[39] Mary Taft did not leave but continued inside Wesleyan Methodism, determined to continue preaching, and with her husband to publicize the cause of women's preaching. From 1803 they moved around circuits in the north of England, most of whom had invited Mary Barritt to preach in the 1790s. They superannuated[40] to Ilkeston (Zechariah Taft's home circuit) in 1828 where they both continued to preach, but in general only locally. He died in 1848 and she in 1851.

In 1825 Zechariah Taft published the first volume of *Holy Women* about women preachers, largely but not all Methodists, most with northern connections and many still alive when he wrote it; four, like Mary, had married active ministers. The second volume appeared in 1828. *Holy Women* was a means of expressing support for women preaching, and reflects much correspondence, some quoted by Taft, of which almost no manuscripts survive.[41] It shows the Tafts in touch with a wide variety of areas and women preachers—some had been Mary's converts in the 1790s. She saw herself as the spiritual mother of many (not only preachers), both male and female.[42] In 1827 Zechariah published his wife's *Memoirs*.[43] He saw his publications and correspondence

---

38. See Mary Taft, *Memoirs of the Life of Mrs Mary Taft formerly Miss Barritt Written by Herself*, 2 vols., ed. Zechariah Taft (Ripon: Printed for the author, 1827) 2:39–95, concluding with a letter from the Kent stewards and trustees asking for the Tafts to be sent back by Conference. For Pawson's letters, see ibid., 2:55–57 and 77–79.

39. Dated Colne, 5 July 1803. MAM Fl. 104/4/15. For the Irish Conference Minute see note 4 above.

40. For Supernumerary see *DMBI*.

41. See Taft, *Holy Women*, passim.

42. Mack, *Heart Religion*, 212–15.

43. Up to 1805. Taft, *Memoirs*.

as polemical, protecting and encouraging the place of women preachers within Wesleyan Methodism.

Mary Wiltshaw (née Chapman, 1763–1819) from Spalding, Lincolnshire, was married in 1797 to the Reverend John Wiltshaw. He superannuated in 1809 to his native Elkstones near Leek in north Staffordshire, in the southern Pennines, and died in 1818.[44] She became a preacher as a result of Mary Barritt staying with them in 1799.[45] "[Mary Wiltshaw] began to hold meetings in order to expound the word of God and exhort sinners to turn to him for mercy and salvation. God made her the instrument in the conversion of very many . . . She used occasionally to supply the place of her husband and at other times assist him in his work . . . Her talents for preaching were very good and her sermons not only showed that she had received a good education but that she was in possession of that salvation which she recommended to others."[46]

Sarah Eland (born *c.* 1770s) was from Hutton Rudby near Stokesley, on the edge of the North Yorkshire moors. Her brother Richard entered the Methodist ministry.[47] Converted in 1802 by the former missionary William Warrener, Sarah left Wesleyanism after 1818 and was associated first with the Primitive Methodists and then the Leeds Revivalists.[48] When she married another former missionary, Rev. John De Putron (a correspondent of Zechariah Taft), in 1824,[49] she returned to the Wesleyans.

Margaret Hainsworth (née Hargreaves, 1775–1848) married Rev. William Hainsworth at Newchurch in Rossendale in 1793. He superannuated in 1818 and died in 1823. She continued to preach occasionally after his death, living at Rakefoot near Bacup in the Rossendale Valley.[50]

44. *Methodist Magazine* (1818) 705.

45. See Taft, *Memoirs*, 1:89.

46. Taft, *Holy Women*, 2:184–93.

47. Richard Eland entered 1813, died 1866. Hutton Rudby was an important Methodist center.

48. D. C. Dews, "Ann Carr and the Female Revivalists of Leeds," in *From Mow Cop to Peake*, ed. D. C. Dews, WHS Yorkshire Branch Occasional Paper no. 4 (Leeds, 1982) 18–22.

49. Taft, *Holy Women*, 2:194–201. For De Putron, see *WMM* (1861) 961–68. Sarah (dates of birth and death unknown) was still alive at his death.

50. William Jessop, *Methodism in Rossendale and the Neighbourhood* (Manchester: Stubbs, Brook & Chrystal, 1880) 292–93; Chilcote, *John Wesley and the Women*

Mrs. Mary ("Polly") Holder (1751–1836) was the daughter of Isaac Woodhouse, a Master Mariner in Whitby (a prosperous coaling port), in whose house the Methodist preachers stayed, including at different times John Wesley and the famous woman preacher of the earlier period, Sarah Crosby.[51] Mary became a member under William Brammah[52] in 1767, then a class leader and preacher under the influence of Mary Bosanquet, Sarah Crosby, Elizabeth Hurrell, and others. She married the locally born preacher George Holder[53] in 1788, and travelled with him, exhorting after he had preached in his circuits, especially in country places.[54] He spent nine years on the Isle of Man and eventually superannuated in 1818 to her parents' house in Whitby. They were childless and he was relatively well off due to his inheritance from his wife, leaving £400 to connexional funds and more to local trusts.[55]

Mrs. Rachel Blackburn (née Ware, 1777–?) was born at Farndale in the remote and rugged North York Moors, where Methodist women preachers like Sarah Crosby were active in the late eighteenth century, and remained in the area all her life. She was converted at seventeen (almost certainly by the young Mary Barritt). Then a domestic servant, she moved to work for the Methodist Robert Venis of Fryupdale[56] in the Esk valley, becoming a Methodist member. In November 1799 she married James Blackburn,[57] joining a class led by J. Wood. Her experience exemplifies Phyllis Mack's idea of "agency"[58] with Rachel attempting to understand and control her emotions at the prospect of speaking for God, where she had previously been silent.

> One Sunday morning as she was going to the meeting, it was powerfully impressed upon Rachel's mind "thou must speak for

Preachers, 268–69; Taft, *Holy Women*, 2:224–26.

51. For Sarah Crosby see *DMBI*. For earlier women preachers, see Chilcote, *John Wesley and the Women Preachers*, Appendix A.

52. William Brammah (c. 1732–1780) from Sheffield entered the ministry around 1762.

53. See John Lenton, *John Wesley's Preachers* (Carlisle: Paternoster, 2009) 106–7.

54. Taft, *Holy Women*, 1:100–128. Taft had been given a copy of her journal.

55. *WMM* (1836) 967.

56. Robert Venis, James Blackburn, and J. Wood (below) are only known through *Holy Women*, and the next note. "Venis" may be a form of the more common local name "Ventress." The Esk valley drains the northern side of the Moors.

57. 23 November at Danby Parish church; International Genealogical Index.

58. Mack, *Heart Religion*, 12–18.

God." She felt a spirit of resistance within and suddenly her mind was covered with darkness and distress. She thought "I must try the spirits, to see which is of God." As soon as she "submitted to the divine teachings, she felt immediately a willingness to do whatever the Lord required of her; and heavenly light shone upon her mind, and unutterable peace filled her heart. She spoke to the people that morning from a verse of a hymn: she was at liberty and some of her hearers were affected even unto tears. Her leader . . . encouraged her in this labour of love, and she spoke a second time; after which she went to a meeting near Helmsley, and addressed the congregation on "thou shalt love the Lord thy God with all thy heart, etc."[59]

Other women known from Taft's publications to have preached included Mrs. Wallis of Ockbrook, who was preaching in Hemington near Derby in 1810,[60] Eliza Wilson, the daughter of Francis Wilson of Wharton Lodge near Wetherby (and niece of the late Isabella Wilson of Sinnethwaite),[61] Ann Thompson Coates,[62] and Mrs. Elizabeth Clarkson from Crake Hall near Easingwold in the North Riding of Yorkshire.[63]

59. Taft, *Holy Women*, 1:297. Her preaching commenced around 1806.

60. Mary Taft's MS Diary, 223. Mrs. Wallis visited Madeley in 1810. Probably not Mrs. Wallis in East Anglia, see below.

61. Taft, *Holy Women*, 2:227–29. *Methodist Magazine* (1808) 372–75, 410–15, 461–69, 516–18, 562–67, 595–605. For Isabella Wilson see Chilcote, *John Wesley and the Women Preachers*, 93; Chilcote, *Her Own Story: Autobiographical Portraits of Early Methodist Women* (Nashville: Kingswood, 2001) 59–64.

62. Her husband, who was a Local Preacher, was the postmaster at Reeth. Taft, *Holy Women*, 2: 218–19.

63. Ibid., 2:181–83.

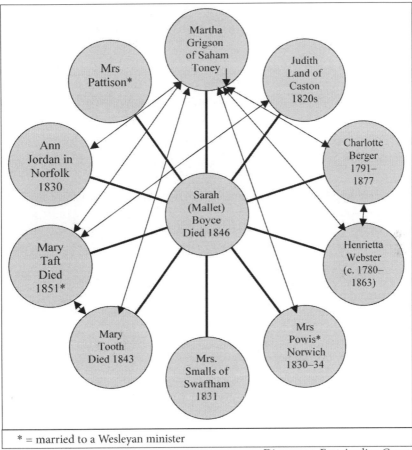

* = married to a Wesleyan minister

Diagram 4. East Anglian Group

THE EAST ANGLIAN GROUP[64]

In East Anglia two pairs of women preachers in this period lived and preached together. The first were Sarah Boyce and Martha Grigson. Sarah Boyce (née Mallet, 1764–1846)[65] had been encouraged to continue preaching by John Wesley in the 1780s. By the 1820s she was a widow living with her friend Mrs. Martha Grigson (née Twells, 1777–1839)[66] at

64. See John Lenton, "East Anglian Women Wesleyan Preachers to 1910," in *Bulletin of the WHS East Anglia District* 112 (2008) 1–10.

65. David East shows that Sarah had at least six children, of whom three died young and one at eighteen. *My Dear Sally.* See also *Arminian Magazine* (1788) 91–93, 238–42.

66. Grigson (sometimes spelled "Gregson") was a clergyman's daughter, who married in 1799 and began to preach between 1818 and 1825. Her name appeared on the plan of both the Swaffham and Attleborough circuits.

Saham Toney,[67] and together they preached over a wide area of Norfolk. They met Mary Tooth in London and were then invited to Madeley. In March 1830 Boyce wrote of preaching in Norwich: "our way is to go out together and speak short, one after the other, as it is too much for our strength to go through the whole of the work alone, nor can we preach more than twice a week, once on the Sunday and once on the weekday. We go by the rule our dear father Wesley gave me: 'Let the voice of the people be to us the voice of God.' He said 'where the people invite and receive you, there God call(s) you, go, and he will be with you.'"[68] This typifies how women preachers justified themselves against criticism from within Methodism, although by 1830 only the aging Boyce could use Wesley as a defense.

The younger pair were Miss Charlotte Sophia Berger (1791–1877),[69] and her friend Mrs. Henrietta Elizabeth Webster (c. 1780–1863).[70] They began their ministry near Leytonstone, home of Mary Bosanquet to 1768, but by the 1820s had moved to Saffron Walden, possibly because opportunities to preach near London were becoming more restricted. From their new base they ranged widely northwards into East Anglia, preaching at Ely, Cambridge, and Newmarket and making contact with Sarah Boyce.

CONCLUSIONS

Networking

Wesleyan Methodist women preachers in the late eighteenth and early nineteenth century created a network to provide mutual assistance and what has been described as "spiritual companionship"[71] for each other by writing letters, visiting, passing on news, publishing, travelling and preaching together. They also encouraged, persuaded, and trained

67. Saham Toney is a village in West Norfolk, six miles southeast of Swaffham.

68. Lloyd, *Fletcher-Tooth Collection*, vol. 1, 111–20; see also Lloyd, vol. 3 (Manchester: JRULM, 1999) 82–101. See letters at MAM Fl. 1/12/1, and 1/12/6 with the quotation in 1/12/2. "Vox populi vox Dei" is a quotation from Alcuin, who disapproved.

69. J. Holland Brown, *Memoir of Miss Charlotte Berger* (London: Wesleyan Conference Office, 1879).

70. Ibid. and *WMM* (1864) 761–62, with her obituary by Berger.

71. V. T. Burton, *Spiritual Literacy in John Wesley's Methodism* (Waco: Baylor, 2007) 175–96.

possible recruits, introducing them to places where they were able to preach, and taking them out with them. In Madeley or in East Anglia a home or monetary support might be offered. They made links with sympathetic itinerants and provided information for those who would defend women's preaching.

Women preachers had common interests and sometimes lived communally. They did not form a religious order though many remained single, often with a friend or relative living with them. They were usually class leaders, devoted to those in their charge, but their chief loyalty was to the Methodist Society. Some, like Mary Barritt, made a conscious effort to attend Conference, partly to be able to hear and meet the leading preachers. It is clear that women preachers flourished, especially in the countryside and wherever Methodism was strong, such as the north, midlands, and East Anglia. They were scarce in London and the South; exceptions like Mrs. Webster and Miss Berger soon moved a little farther north.

Gendered Relationships

In addition to female support groups there were also men who supported and encouraged them, including itinerant ministers, some of whom were husbands,[72] other relatives,[73] Superintendents who invited women preachers to their circuits,[74] correspondents who encouraged women to continue to preach,[75] and preachers who preached in favor of women preaching.[76] At least one Anglican clergyman supported individual women preachers.[77] Many lay men (often local preachers) and

72. For example, Zechariah Taft, John de Putron, William Hainsworth, John Wiltshaw, Henry Powis, and George Holder.

73. For example, for Mary Taft, John Barritt (d. 1841), Robert Melson, and Henry Taft.

74. For example, William Bramwell (d. 1818), Philip Hardcastle, Thomas Vasey, William Blagborne (d. 1816), James Wood, Jonathan Brown, Michael Emmott, Richard Elliott, George Deverell (d. 1825), John Hodgson, John Barritt, and Isaac Brown (d. 1815).

75. For example, Philip Hardcastle, Thomas Vasey, William Bramwell, James Wood, Jonathan Brown, Michael Emmott, Richard Elliott, John Pawson (d. 1806), R. C. Brackenbury (d. 1818), and John Radford (d. 1844).

76. For example, Thomas Scott, William Bramwell, and R. C. Brackenbury.

77. The Evangelical Vicar of Wellington, John Eyton (d. 1823), who sent Mary Tooth his book of sermons for Mary Fletcher's comments. MAM Fl. 2/14/6.

women also supported them, some becoming increasingly hostile to the Wesleyan hierarchy, which was in turn suspicious of women preachers. These male supporters often belonged to the group of "evangelical laity which devoted its emotional and intellectual life to religious activity, but did not want to accept clerical leadership without question."[78]

The (male) Wesleyan hierarchy in the early nineteenth century moved to become strongly opposed to women preachers. Under Wesley, leading preachers who opposed women preachers usually held their peace, though their views might be expressed verbally or in letters to each other.[79] After Wesley, and with the threat of revolution polarizing politics, Methodist leaders had new priorities, one being to avoid antagonizing the government. By 1802 important preachers as diverse as Benson and Entwisle[80] were writing to demand that women not be allowed to preach in circuits because this was seen as demeaning to the male preachers' effectiveness and a reversal of proper social order. By the 1820s the leading itinerants who had supported women preachers, men like John Pawson, Alexander Mather, William Bramwell, and Thomas Vasey, and leading laymen, like Richard Carr Brackenbury, were all dead.

The Wesleyan hegemony led by Bunting and his friends was united against women preachers and happy to confine them to rural areas, deny them publicity, and see them decrease through death. Vicki Tolar Collins showed how Methodism after Wesley tried to silence women preachers by removing the oxygen of publicity and elevating the deceased Hester Ann Rogers instead.[81] Margaret Jones has pointed out how women's access to speaking through the Magazine was drastically reduced.[82] Benson and his fellow editors hid and disguised the fact

---

78. J. H. S. Kent, *Holding the Fort: Studies in Victorian Revivalism* (London: Epworth, 1978) 363.

79. For example, John Poole in Norwich in 1788. See N. Virgoe, *A Season Highly Profitable: The Travels of an Itinerant Methodist Preacher in Norfolk and Suffolk 1788–9* (Wymondham: WHS East Anglian Branch, 2007) 8.

80. For Joseph Entwisle see *DMBI* and Burton, *Spiritual Literacy*, 172.

81. Vicki Tolar Collins, "Perfecting a Woman's Life: Methodist Rhetoric and Politics in the Account of Hester Ann Rogers," PhD diss., Auburn University, 1992; Collins, "Walking in Light, Walking in Darkness: The Story of Women's Changing Rhetorical Space in Early Methodism," *Rhetoric Review* 14 (1996) 336–54; Burton, *Spiritual Literacy*, 171–75.

82. M. P. Jones, "Whose Characterisation? Which Perfection? Women's History and Christian Reflection," *Epworth Review* 20:2 (1993) 96–103; Jones, "From 'the State of My Soul' to 'Exalted Piety': Women's Voices in the *Arminian/Methodist Magazine*

that women preached: their diaries and journals were not printed, and references to their preaching were deleted. Successive editors of the Magazine made sure their obituaries were omitted, or amended to remove references to preaching.[83] What is not always realized is that the evidence from the women's own sources, including the Fletcher-Tooth correspondence and Taft's *Holy Women*, is also not complete. Very few letters from Mary Tooth to women preachers have survived. Some of her journals are no longer extant. In Mary Taft's journal there are references to Methodist women preachers who are not represented in *Holy Women*, such as Mrs. Wallis of Ockbrook. Few letters from women preachers to the Tafts survive.[84]

The absence of much primary source material is a continuing obstacle to research. The letters of women preachers were, in general, not preserved. If they preached, often it was not recorded on the circuit preaching plan.[85] Identification on plans is difficult because they were frequently not listed or were listed only by surname with perhaps an initial. The services they took were often "specials" for missions, children, Sunday School Anniversaries, or filling vacant appointments. Their portraits rarely survive. Often all that is known is the surname.

The attitude of Methodist ministers toward female preaching changed in this period. Arguably the late 1820s marked a point where women preachers suddenly found life more difficult in Wesleyanism.[86] In 1828, for instance, one minister, John Sumner,[87] made life difficult for

1778–1822," in *Gender and Christian Religion*, Studies in Church History 34, ed. R. N. Swanson (Woodbridge: Boydell, 1998) 273–85; and Jones, "'Her Claim to Public Notice': The Historiography of Women in British Methodism" (unpublished lecture given at Westminster College, 12 Nov. 1999).

83. For example, the obituary of Mrs. Margaret Hainsworth in *WMM* (1848) 1031, has no mention of her preaching, though she appears as a preacher in Taft, *Holy Women*. See also Chilcote, *Her Own Story*, 16–17, and Mack, *Heart Religion*, 293.

84. See Taft, *Holy Women*, 2:200: "a letter that now lies before me," but no longer survives.

85. For "Preaching Plans" see *DMBI*; Lenton, "Labouring for the Lord," 68–69; E. A. Rose, "The Evolution of the Circuit Plan," *Proceedings of the Wesley Historical Society* 37 (1969) 50–54.

86. Possible reasons for this include Taft's retirement and the increasing power of the Buntingites following the secession of the Leeds Protestant Methodists in 1827–28.

87. John Sumner had been a correspondent of Bunting. See W. R. Ward, *The Early Correspondence of Jabez Bunting 1820–1829*, Camden Fourth Series 11 (London: Royal Historical Society, 1972) 146. The second minister was the second named in the min-

Evans[88] and others who had asked Mary Tooth to take their services, a very common practice until that point.[89] The Tafts' decision to publish, between 1825 and 1828, more substantial books than previously on the theme of women preaching may well mark their reaction to this.

Zechariah Taft was particularly significant, for other preachers wrote to him to show their support.[90] His publishing in favor of women preaching began with his *Thoughts on Women Preaching* (1803), which was enlarged in 1820 as *The Scripture Doctrine of Women's Preaching*. In the later 1820s, as he came close to superannuation, he published *Holy Women* and Mary Taft's *Memoirs* with local presses, not the Wesleyan Methodist Bookroom which had consistently opposed women preaching, so that the cause he and Mary Taft had pioneered for so long by preaching would continue and the record of it could not be completely hidden.

Most women preachers were married (exceptions tended to be those with independent means or, among the Madeley circle, Mary and Rosamond Tooth, Susanna Knapp, and also Charlotte Berger and Judith Land). Women preachers who married often wed clergymen, ministers or local preachers. Although doubtless not their main motives, this increased their preaching opportunities while also affording some protection from opposition. Children and domestic responsibilities could make preaching more difficult. Those without children certainly preached more (though both Sarah Boyce and Mary Taft are exceptions to this). Mary Taft, however, was thirty before she married, and, by delaying marriage, she reduced her potential childbearing period. When she travelled home from distant Kent to her mother's in Colne for her first confinement, she preached on the way.[91] Sarah Boyce seems to have preached less when her children were young.[92]

---

utes for the year for that circuit, assisting the first minister named who was in charge as the Superintendent.

88. J. Evans, otherwise unidentified, was one of the Local Preachers in the Madeley Circuit in 1828. See MAM Fl. 2/14/4–5.

89. Trinder, *The Industrial Revolution in Shropshire*, 180, quoting MAM Fl. 2/14/4 (J. Evans, 31 July 1828).

90. See, for example, MAM PLP 102/12/8 (Sykes); 9/33/5 (Blanshard); 80/46/16 (Ouseley).

91. Taft, *Memoir*, 2:87–92. She preached 8 June 1803 at Long Eaton near Nottingham. Mary (Ann) Taft was born 25 June 1803, near Colne.

92. East, *My Dear Sally*, 66–74.

Joan Thirsk suggested in a paper in 1993 that women were able to play an important part in the early stages of movements, before male controls were later reimposed.[93] Certainly new structures within Wesleyanism were making it more difficult for women preachers in this period, just as they did for both Primitive Methodist and Bible Christian itinerant women ministers slightly later in the century.[94] Despite this the support groups which this essay has described enabled women preachers to continue to preach throughout the first half of the nineteenth century in many parts of British Wesleyan Methodism. Mary Fletcher and Mary Tooth at Madeley, the Tafts, and the presence of several determined preachers in East Anglia all helped new women preachers, encouraged others to imitate them, and maintained a consistent witness to their cause. By the second half of the century it became possible for Thomas Champneys to send female evangelists into villages and T. B. Stephenson to found a deaconess order, which included Deaconess Evangelists. This led to the recovery of women's preaching in the whole of British Methodism in the twentieth century.[95]

93. Cited by David Hempton, *Methodism: Empire of the Spirit* (New Haven: Yale University Press, 2005) 138 n. 16.

94. Jennifer Lloyd, *Women and the Shaping of British Methodism: Persistent Preachers 1807–1907* (Manchester: Manchester University Press, 2009).

95. See Lenton, "Labouring for the Lord," 68–79; E. Dorothy Graham, *Saved to Serve: The Story of the Wesley Deaconess Order, 1890–1978* (Peterborough: Methodist Publishing House, 2002).

10

"Oh That the Mantle May Rest on Me!"

The Ministry of Mary Tooth

Carol Blessing

WHILE JOHN WESLEY NEVER came out wholeheartedly in favor of women's preaching—he erred on the side of caution, skirting the issue rhetorically by terming their oral proclamations exhorting, expounding, prophesying, and leading class rather than preaching or ministry—he did create an environment favorable to women in many ways. By privileging the subjective and emotional through encouraging followers to develop introspection by keeping journals, writing and sharing conversion accounts, narratives of happy deaths, accounts of dreams, and letters, all of which emphasized personal experience over education and theological prowess, he opened the door for women to play a leading role. He published many of their conversion and "happy death" narratives—serene and sanctified deathbed accounts—in *The Arminian Magazine*, and they continued to be published in the renamed publication *The Methodist Magazine* after his death. Indeed, although Wesley's intentions might not have been to legitimize female ministry, he provided fertile ground for women to flourish in leadership and proclamation by encouraging them to write their stories, which lead them to speaking their stories. Susie Stanley has asserted that females were able to transcend gender roles through appeal to the work of the Holy Spirit in their lives.[1] David Hempton has gone as far as to state: "Methodism was without question a woman's movement."[2]

Women's public speaking within Methodism received notice, acclaim, and disdain in the eighteenth century, and is a subject of many studies today. Earl Kent Brown's and Paul Chilcote's research have traced Wesley's attitudes toward women in ministry as it evolved throughout his work.[3] Chilcote sees the change in Wesley's attitude toward using women in his work as shaped by several factors. At first, he was influenced by and tied to the Anglican Church, which he wanted to reform, not overturn; there was no preaching by women within the Church. Wesley's initial conservatism toward women was linked to his desire to avoid creating dissension in this area. As his ministry grew, Wesley was less worried about maintaining this decorum. Wesley was also influenced by Moravian practices that allowed women active roles in the Church, as well as by his mother Susanna Wesley.[4] Chilcote also emphasizes Wesley's focus on "personal, religious experience and its power to transform both the individual and the society . . . He would utilize almost any method to accomplish this divine mission," including allowing women leaders.[5] Nonetheless, Chilcote seems a bit too optimistic in his assessment of Wesley's acceptance of women's speaking; although guardedly allowing certain women to preach, including the first female Methodist preacher, Sarah Crosby, Wesley never flatly condoned

1. Susie C. Stanley, *Holy Boldness: Women Preachers' Autobiographies and the Sanctified Self* (New York: Palgrave MacMillan, 2006) 195.

2. David Hempton, *Methodism: Empire of the Spirit* (New Haven: Yale University Press, 2005) 145.

3. See Earl Kent Brown's discussions in "Women of the Word: Selected Leadership Roles of Women in Mr. Wesley's Methodism," in *Women in New Worlds: Historical Perspectives on the Wesleyan Tradition*, vol.1, ed. Hilah Thomas and Rosemary Keller (Nashville: Abingdon, 1981) 69–87, and *Women of Mr. Wesley's Methodism* (New York: Edwin Mellen, 1983). Paul Wesley Chilcote has written four books on women in early Methodism; for detailed coverage, see his *John Wesley and the Women Preachers of Early Methodism* (Metuchen, NJ: Scarecrow, 1991); *She Offered Them Christ: The Legacy of Women Preachers in Early Methodism* (Nashville: Abingdon, 1993); *Her Own Story: Autobiographical Portraits of Early Methodist Women* (Nashville: Kingswood, 2001); and *Early Methodist Spirituality: Selected Women's Writings* (Nashville: Kingswood, 2007).

4. Chilcote, *John Wesley and the Women Preachers*, 18–23, 141–42, 237–40.

5. Ibid., 46.

the regular presence of women in the pulpit, and even condemned the Quaker practice of allowing both sexes to preach.[6]

Nonetheless, Methodism did set in place a movement that created space for women. Wesley allowed women to participate actively within the Methodist class meeting structure, including leading meetings. He and his ministry were supported financially through women, including the wealthy and influential Countess of Huntingdon. His work embraced all economic classes and both sexes, albeit not always equally. The movement Wesley put into place evolved to the point in which some women in practice, if not in official position, were functioning as preachers and/or ministers of their local congregation.

For over forty years within late eighteenth-century and early nineteenth-century Shropshire, Mary Fletcher and Mary Tooth played important roles in the Methodist movement. Mary Bosanquet Fletcher, the wealthy, independent, and outspoken woman, worked within Methodist circles before, during, and after her three-year marriage to John Fletcher until her own death in 1815. Mary Tooth, who resided with Mary Fletcher until her death, and continued in Madeley for twenty-eight years following, is often remembered only in terms of being Mary Fletcher's assistant. What is true, however, is that Tooth continued to work in her own version of Methodist ministry until her 1843 death. This is her story, one which cut across the grain of what was meant by Methodism, ministry, and female roles in early to mid-nineteenth-century Shropshire, England. Through the influence of Mary Fletcher and beyond, Mary Tooth rewrote ministry into a female mode, seeking out and emulating female mentors, filling speaking roles traditionally occupied by males, and embracing the authority to minister through her perception of the Holy Spirit's working.

Phyllis Mack's recent volume discusses the female circle of Mary Fletcher and Mary Tooth, as well as Fletcher's helper and adopted daughter Sarah Ryan, using many primary sources within the Methodist Archives. Her work illuminates the life of Mary Fletcher in particular, focusing on the ways her dreams and suffering helped shape her conception of self and spirituality.[7] Vicki Tolar Burton focuses more rhetorically

6. John Telford, ed. *The Letters of the Rev. John Wesley, A. M.*, vol. 2 (London: Epworth, 1960), Letter to Thomas Whitehead, February 10, 1748, p. 119.

7. Phyllis Mack, *Heart Religion in the British Enlightenment: Gender and Emotion in Early Methodism* (Cambridge: Cambridge University Press, 2008) esp. 171–218.

upon Mary Fletcher's letter writing, teaching, and speaking and the ways in which they stretched the definitions of preaching, but deals only in passing with Tooth.[8] This essay deals more specifically with the work of Mary Tooth as ministry, also drawing from archival materials that have been previously unused in reconstructing the female world of late eighteenth- and early nineteenth-century Methodism.

Mary Tooth without question felt called by God to service, seeing herself as working firmly within Methodist parameters, whether or not posterity would view her in the same way. Dale Johnson notes that Tooth's work, though not classified as preaching, "reflected a resistance as well as a determination to carry the message and advance the cause, with or without denominational recognition or support."[9] When recording her thoughts on the death of Mrs. Fletcher, in 1815, Tooth viewed herself as a successive prophet to fill the role of her mentor and spiritual adviser. Tooth began:

> Knowing that it is your desire to have something respecting the close of the life of my invaluable friend Mrs Fletcher now in Glory. & being well assured that none but myself can undertake the work as I alone was her constant companion without being separated scarcely a day for more than 15 years; I have endeavoured, while my mind has been exercised with the most painful feelings of heart-felt sorrow for the loss of the best of friends; the wisest of Counsellors, & the tenderest of parents, to set down a few circumstances related to the close of a life surpassing in usefulness most of her fellow mortals.
>
> It was upon the 9th [of December] of 1815, a day never to be forgotten by me that my Elijah was taken to heaven. O that the mantle might rest on me![10]

Tooth endeavored to assume that mantle, fulfilling and perhaps exceeding Mary Fletcher's workload, as she served for another twenty-eight years following the latter's death. Her journals reveal a high degree of self-consciousness as a woman in a religious movement that was sometimes controversial, who was the mentee of another strong, famous, and

8. Vicki Tolar Burton, *Spiritual Literacy in John Wesley's Methodism* (Waco, TX: Baylor University Press, 2008).

9. Dale A. Johnson, "Gender and the Construction of Models of Christian Activity: A Case Study," *Church History* 73 (2004) 261.

10. Mary Tooth, Commonplace book of Mary Tooth, undated, Methodist Archives Research Centre, John Rylands Library (MARC): MAM Fl. 26/14/1.

anomalous woman, and who herself was engaged in work that might provoke censure as well as praise.

Tooth was, in fact, so aware of herself and her unique role that her journals were at times written in retrospect, for posterity, rather than at the actual date of events, particularly throughout her earlier life in Madeley. Though no physical evidence exists, it is conceivable that Tooth rewrote her journals from previously written daily diary accounts, as had John Wesley. Although the consistently humble Mary Tooth claimed no such aspiration, she may have envisioned posthumous publication of her journals, similar to the *Life of Mary Fletcher* based on source material that Tooth helped Henry Moore gather from Fletcher's journals. She clearly desired her life to be interpreted correctly, as her 1796 entries open with her pronouncement that she wants to set right a "silly tale" about her life, "now I am come almost to the end of it now." She recounts "The Erroneous tale" as follows:

> 'Miss Tooth of Madeley said they was a foundling picked up by Mr Fletcher at his door she had one tooth & so he called her Mary Tooth.' Now as it respects the Rev. J. W., or Fletcher of Madeley, he never saw me nor I him, when he died at Madeley I was 7 years old in my Fathers house at Birmingham where I was Born by St Marys Chapel about the middle of Marys Row . . . it was ten years after Mr Fletchers death before I even saw Madeley, it was in the Dec. of 1795 that I came to Mrs Micklewright of Madeley, then I was turned 17th. My father had a sister of the name of Mary after her I had the name of Mary given to me.[11]

Her disclaimer which followed this information negated the idea that she wrote for publication, although it ignored the example of Mary Fletcher, whose biography, heavily edited by Henry Moore from Fletcher's journals, was printed in numerous editions, and still remains the major work on Mary Fletcher's life. "With regard to writing any thing respecting myself for Publication I have never been willing to spend my time in that way, I once knew one that spent much time in that way & thought her experience would be rendered a great blessing, but when she was gone I never heard that one word of all she had written was made of any use in private, & I well know none of it was ever published, nor was there even a funeral sermon or a line written on her death."[12]

11. Journal of Mary Tooth, Undated, MARC: MAM Fl. 14/B/i–ii.

12. Ibid., iv.

Born in 1778, Mary Tooth first visited Madeley vicarage in 1796, beginning a relationship with Mary Fletcher that shaped both women and Madeley parish for years to come. As a teenage girl of an apparently middle-class family, Tooth was sent by her mother to work as a helpmate to Mrs. Micklewright of Madeley. In her free time, Tooth went frequently to hear Mary Fletcher speak. In glowing, almost revelatory terms, Tooth described the place set apart for Fletcher, an alternative sacred space that allowed for a woman's speaking. Mary Fletcher held her meetings in the Tithe Barn, the place where parishioners had formerly brought their grain and other dues. Through Tooth's eyes, it became a glorious, luminous space to spotlight the woman to whom she would devote the rest of her life. The passage's tone shows the preeminence of this special place in Tooth's life, as it contained a powerful spiritual experience for her. On December 11, 1796, Tooth reflected: "In a review of the past year I feel deeply indebted to God for his great goodness in bringing me to Madeley I feel fully persuaded it will ever be recorded by me as one of the happiest events of my life."[13]

Continuing in her December 20 entry, she conveyed the image of Mary Fletcher's meeting place, transforming the mundane into a sacred space carved out for the female speaker:

> At this time all the protestant worship of God, that was in the Town or Village of Madeley was all held in what was called Mrs Fletcher's Room. Which I do not think I can describe in better words than her own. When writing to a friend the story of it, 'It is not very fine, yet it is not as plain as the Stable at Bethlehem. Some Slabs make a good dry wooden floor. A thatched top keeps out the rain & paper shades the cold & dust. The sides & top are lined with Lead & washed with White, so that seven large candles reminds us of the Light & Perfection wich the Spirit hath promised to Baptize us with, when our Robes shall be made Whiter than our Walls.'[14]

Tooth's coverage of the religious landscape continued a few days later, as she outlined the unorthodox coverage of the Anglican services. While not an ordained Anglican priest or a Methodist preacher, Mary Fletcher functioned unofficially as a shepherd to her flock. Female leadership seems to have been favorably perceived by the parishioners, as Tooth records:

13. Journal of Mary Tooth, 11 December 1796, MARC: MAM Fl. 14/B/73.
14. Ibid., 20 December 1796, MARC: MAM Fl. 14/B/85–86.

> I have now been just one year in Madeley & have found here a people with whom I wish to live & die, the means of grace here are truly sweet to my taste, the church service is only once in three weeks & then held in Mrs Fletchers Room, the other two Lords Days Mr Walters is at either Coalbrookedale or Madeley-wood. While he is at those places Mrs Fletcher speaks to the people in her own Room. This has been the case ever since Sept. 21st 1794 & the people are so well pleased with the arrangement that they are wishing the building of the Church did not go on so fast they do so well without it.[15]

Tooth herself seems to have come from a Baptist background; her conversion to Methodism and joining the Methodist Society caused her mother consternation. Negative depictions of Calvinism and Calvinistic religious meetings are contrasted with her delight with the Madeley Methodist circle. Tooth writes of her worship experiences in several journal entries in April, 1798:

> April 1st Lord's day, the Baptist Chapel & the church are all the places of worship in Shipperal nor is there a Methodist in the Town but myself, the Church has in it such a minister that I could not think of sitting under, & at the Chapel they are Calvenests [sic] of the most rigid kind, so ther is no pleasant food for my soul in this place, however I see it right to be at the public worship of God I therefore went this morning with Miss Luten . . . O! how cold & dead, what contrast between this & last Tuesday at Madeley.[16]
>
> April 2d Monday was at the Baptist chapel again tonight at another cold dead prayer meeting.[17]

She disagreed at other points with her mother, who apparently wanted her to accept a marriage proposal from Mrs. Micklewright's son. This dissent caused Tooth to break her relationship with her mother, regarding Mary Fletcher as a surrogate to fill the maternal role. Fletcher's flock had termed her "a mother in Israel" after the Judge Deborah, and Tooth seems to have truly regarded Mary Fletcher as both a spiritual and a literal nurturing mother. Tooth expressed throughout her journals a calling to Madeley, a strong connection to both the Methodist meetings there and Mrs. Fletcher herself, returning to the town as

15. Ibid., 31 December 1796, MARC: MAM Fl. 14/B/95.

16. Ibid., 1 April 1798, MARC: MAM Fl. 14/C/33.

17. Ibid., 2 April 1798, MARC: MAM Fl. 14/C/33.

often as she could; the journal records many visits and listening to Mrs. Fletcher's preaching. On April 27, 1798, Mary Tooth recorded her increasing dissatisfaction with her home town: "Here I am in this town quite alone, I am called the Quaker because of my dress, & of that persuasion there is none here, nor is there a Methodist any where nearer then Madeley, so that I stand alone, those that make any profession of serious Godliness are Calvenests of the highest order & look upon all the Wesleyans as a deluded people, one of them the other day told me that Mr Wesley was 'frying in Hell.' but I avoid arguing with them as it can answer no valuable end."[18]

Mary Tooth shaped her identity around her difference; that is, she accepted the fact that her religious beliefs and practices made her unlike her family and acquaintances. The disapproval she felt from her mother motivated her attraction to another mother figure, Mrs. Fletcher. Fletcher, when single, had published a tract titled *Jesus Altogether Lovely*, admonishing young women to focus on their devotion to Christ rather than on their beauty, dress, and attracting men. The work paralleled Mary Astell's *A Serious Proposal to the Ladies* (1688), in which Astell hypothesized a female Anglican educational community. Distancing herself from Calvinism and from social practices of dressing well and desiring to attract a husband, Tooth was attracted to the idea of religious vocation, located intentionally within a female community.

Tooth refused several marriage proposals throughout her life, seeing them as impediments to her service to God, and regarding the counsel of Mary Fletcher as her deciding factor. By 1802, Tooth had settled permanently in Madeley with Fletcher, who had been allowed to remain in the parsonage following her husband's death. Tooth filled the void left by the death of Sarah Lawrence, helper and adopted daughter of Mary Fletcher. According to Tooth's journals and correspondence, she functioned as a secretary, helping with Mrs. Fletcher's correspondence, and then moving into a speaking role at class meetings. Fletcher's own manuscript journal, published in an edited version by Henry Moore following her death, with the help of Tooth, who provided the manuscripts, contains at least two references to Tooth that were in fact deleted, either by Tooth or Moore:

---

18. Ibid., 27 April 1798, MARC: MAM Fl. 14/C/41.

> Aug 1 1802 I find Miss Tooth a very great help & a faithful dili-
> gent assistant. She is truly a gift of God that I could not do with-
> out – how true is that now 'no manner of thing that is good shall
> be with held.'
>
> Nov 13 1802 True, I have a good deal to do, much writing on
> my hand, & many things to attend too for the poor . . . this would
> be difficult without my dear Sally who was as my right hand on
> all these occasions, but I was not permitted to feel this want, as
> the Lord who never fails me gave Mary Tooth to me as an as-
> sistant, & her a capacity to take off several burdens.[19]

By the time of Mary Fletcher's death in 1815, Tooth was well en-
sconced in the meeting circuit, as her carefully documented speaking
records attest. She was travelling to many Shropshire locales, speaking
primarily on Sunday and Wednesday evenings, writing her sermons in
assorted bound booklets, and listing the date and location at which each
message was given. She viewed her ministry as a call from God, retro-
spectively recording, in 1837:

> I was very young when I resolved by the grace of God that I
> would never take a step in life with out a beck from God. It has
> proved to me a good rule to walk by, & while I have been watch-
> ing providence I have never lacked a providence to guide, but
> have had my way as clearly marked out before me as if I had actu-
> ally seen a visible cloud & pillar diverting at every turn which
> path I should walk in. Many have wished to persuade me I should
> be more useful in another station of life, but in this I could never
> see in their light, so clear has my conviction been respecting my
> call to abide in Madeley that I have never for one moment had a
> doubt upon that subject.[20]

Tooth continued meeting as well in Mary Fletcher's Tithe Barn
for a number of years, preserving the sacred space of her foremother.
Writing to Rev. Joseph Benson, at the City Road Methodist Chapel,
London, in 1819, she lays out the religious landscape in her environs,
concluding by stating that she is still holding service in the Tithe Barn
four years after Mary Fletcher's death: "Madeley is in the Broseley circuit, Mr Squarebridge is our Superintendant but poor man he as [sic]
never preached at Madeley since the Conference . . . Two chapels are
being built in our circuit one at Much-Wenlock about 6 or 7 miles from

19. Manuscript of Henry Moore's *Life of Mary Bosanquet-Fletcher*, MARC: MAM.
20. Journal of Mary Tooth, 18 March 1837, MARC: MAM Fl. 14/L/2.

Madeley, the other at Dawley-green about 2 or 3 miles from Madeley . . . We still go on with the Vicarage Barn no man saying anything to hinder us. I will now only detain you to beg an interest in your prayers for the little flock of Christ in these parts."[21]

Another 1819 letter in draft form, for which the addressee is unknown, conveys Tooth's staunch commitment to continue speaking at the Tithe Barn. "There being no prospect of the vicarage Barn being taken from us I have had it repaired & cleaned, the whole expense has been fifty shilling a sum that would go a small way in repairing any of your fine chapels yet it has made a difference much for the better in our poor Barn, but what is best of all, the Lord owns & blesses his own word preached therein, we seldom if ever meet in it without feeling a sweet influence from above."[22]

Although Tooth had to deal with the controversy over women's public speaking or preaching, she never made it central to her work. She was, however, vehement in a letter to Henry Moore, while helping him prepare Mary Fletcher's biography, that John Wesley's letter legitimizing Mary Fletcher's work should be included. Moore had omitted the 1771 correspondence between Wesley and the then single Mary Bosanquet, regarding the latter's call to preach. Wesley had answered that such was permitted for those women who had "an extraordinary call."[23] The letter was important to Tooth because, in allowing Mary Fletcher's work, it also validated Tooth's speaking. Despite Tooth's pleading, the letter received only a brief mention by Henry Moore in the published *Life of Mrs Fletcher*, rather than a transcription of the whole.

There is some epistolary evidence of those who questioned or expressed strong disapproval of Mary Tooth's public speaking or preaching. Among the most outspoken in his correspondence was Joseph Peake of Newcastle, whose 1822 letter seems to question Tooth's call to minister as a female, hinting at egotism as her motivation. "Your acting in public involves a delicacy which nothing can shelter except a very extraordinary call of that God to the work who 'sends by whom he will send'. That your call hereunto is as dear and satisfactory as was that of Mrs F is

21. Mary Tooth to Joseph Benson, 12 November 1819, MARC: PLP 34/1/2.

22. Mary Tooth draft letter, addressee unknown, 22 April 1819, MARC: PLP 34/9/14.

23. John Telford, ed. *The Letters of the Rev. John Wesley, A. M.*, vol. 5 (London: Epworth, 1960) 257.

not my task to enquire into—I neither doubt nor affirm . . ."[24] Later correspondence from Peake indicates a concern for Tooth and her ministry, and shows more support for her speaking, while still questioning the unique position of Tooth as a female speaker: "I feel extremely anxious to know how you fare at the old Barn. Are you allowed to hold quiet meetings there as formerly? Or does the offence of the cross revive? . . . Does the Lord still uphold and support you my dear sister in speaking a word for him? I know that in the eye of faith all things are (scripturally) possible it is therefore possible that you may cut off occasion from such as seek occasion and put to silence the ignorance of foolish men, and (by the bye) of foolish women too."[25]

Instead of seeking male validation, Tooth looked to other preaching women in order to help justify her own work. In an 1828 letter to her sister Rosamund, written during a stay in London, Tooth relates details of the Methodist conference meetings that she was attending, showing both her continued connection to organized Methodism and her desire for female role models. Tooth especially focused on going to hear "three of the Travelling preachers & one woman was one that was a public speaker in Mr Wesleys time & one that he approved of. She is 68 years of age." An additional woman speaker, whose ministry outshone her husband's, provided for Tooth a further example of women divinely called to participate in Methodist preaching:

> Another female that spoke was the clergyman's wife that her husband has been in the habit of driving in the carriage to the Chapel where he has left her to preach while he has wheeled off to preach in his own church but has been lately convinced that he was never called to preach & has given up his church preaching but she continues her in the chapels. He says it is his wife's conduct that has convinced him that he is wrong. This subject often last evening induced Mr Moore to give his sentiments on women preaching which he did in the following manner: 'I do declare I am a Coward'. On saying 'how so Sir?' he replied, 'I have not hindered them if their lives agreed. Nothing but a wicked life could make me oppose.' & then added, 'Mr Wesley could never get any further then [sic], It is an extraordinary call & so is the whole work of Methodism.'[26]

24. Joseph Peake to Mary Tooth, 21 November 1822, MARC: PLP 5/12/1.
25. Joseph Peake to Mary Tooth, 2 December 1823, MARC: PLP 5/12/4.
26. Mary Tooth to Rosamund Tooth, 12 August 1828, MARC: PLP 34/8/10.

Tooth never seemed to confront directly the issue of women's preaching, preferring to carry on her work and calling, rather than argue for her rights; while not in a position to change widespread cultural and institutional practices, she focused instead on the local. An 1840 journal entry records having to deal with an unseasoned preacher; showing restraint that belied her strong sense of mission, Tooth refrained from defending her own work.

> This afternoon a young Preacher on the list of reserve who resides in Birmingham that has been preaching here for a short time in Mr Watsons place with Mrs Morris Miss Fowlar & R Guman all took tea with me. He wished to see my upper room which when I shew'd him he appeared greatly surprised & much pleased, & said had I ever asked the Preachers to give me regular preaching in it? I only replied in the negative not caring to enter in the subject with a Stranger. I am naturally too communicative but I am striving to avoid that error: Lord, teach me <u>when</u>, <u>how</u> — & <u>what</u> to speak that my speech may be with grace seasoned with salt & meat to minister grace to them that I am called to converse with.[27]

Here, Tooth was clearly offended by the suggestion that her own speaking would not be considered "regular preaching," but chose not to debate the issue. She allowed her practice alone to stand as her defense, no doubt realizing as well that there were still few apologists for women preachers. The discrepancy between males who were able to gain higher education and become ordained and women who could speak primarily from their experiences and the leading of the Holy Spirit was well entrenched.

Other journals and letters provide evidence, however, that Tooth was well received within the Methodist milieu following Mrs. Fletcher's death. While attending the Methodist conferences and other special events, Tooth was asked to pray and even to preach. Apparently, she had gained a positive reputation among many. Her letter to her sister Rosamund, labeled Dudley July 25, 1828, records her popularity while speaking in Dudley: "The house was exceedingly crowded & the Lord was in our midst. The next day (Wednesday) they had friends to dine with me & in the evening I had a meeting at Bethel a place fitted up for preaching & it was the night for it. but Bethel so overflowed with hearers that my seat was obliged to be moved out into the air or it would

---

27. Journal of Mary Tooth, 27 November 1840, MARC: MAM Fl. 14/N/12.

not have been possible for half the people to have heard. The people both within & without where deeply attentive & many afterwards expressed how much their Souls was blest."[28] In fact, Tooth seemed to be so popular that people were vying for her presence in their meetings, as she recorded later in the same letter: "I had a meeting in a Chapel at Dixons Green on Coventry [Cowery?] hill . . . There had been some degree of contest respecting my coming here because they wished me that night to be at the Schoolroom in Dudley where a prayer meeting is held by all the local preachers & Leaders in Dudley & the other had not generally so honourable a congregation but when I heard the debate I decided in favour of the small congregation & the poorer people."[29] A few days later, she wrote from London:

> I had engaged to hold a meeting at Dudley Chapel . . . & when we got home there was fresh solicitations for me to take then an appointment of Mr Goward[?] at Dudley Chapel the next evening this I repeatedly refused but at length Mr Goward said if I would only do what I find I cou'd at the time he wou'd be with me & I shou'd give it up wither at the beginning, in the middle or at the close & he wou'd do more or less just as I pleased. He declared he never asked a female in his life before to take his work & when he had had opportunity to do so never felt in the least inclined to it in this Mr Neath joined him saying I have gone beyond you Brother Goward for I have been an opposer of women speaking. However I did not at last consent only sayed I wou'd pray that the Lord wou'd shew me the thing proceeded from himself & if he wou'd be with me I shou'd satisfy me of my call to it. They prayed & I prayed & in the morning I awoke with a commission from the Lord. Viz. Go in this they might have not I sent thee.
>
> I felt from that moment a willingness to go to that great Chapel which is twice the size of Madeley Church . . . The Pulpit I would not go into before the time they took down the brass rod & red curtains before the Organ. As I set on the high stool the organist sets in I got then to speak to him to give up the playing of that Need nought for that night. The Lord very graciously strengthened me for the work & I now believed I did right in complying with the request. Many of them got about me most earnestly desiring of me that I would return thro' Dudley but I thought I ought to refuse that as I had said I wou'd go to Birm

28. Mary Tooth to Rosamund Tooth, 25 July 1828, MARC: PLP 34/8/6.

29. Ibid.

& had sent that message there it would have been a breach of promise which I couldn't do.[30]

Nine years later, Mary Tooth recorded being asked to pray at Wesley Chapel in Birmingham: "at night we all went to the circuit prayer-meeting at the Wesley Chapel Constitution-Hill. All their Preachers was there & each of them spoke & prayed their exhortations & prayers was all accompanied with the influence of the Spirit indeed such was the feelings of my soul that when Mr Naylor called upon me to pray I found as much freedom at the throne of grace, as I do in my own upper room among my own people."[31]

Despite her travels, Tooth always expressed joy in returning home and ministering specifically to the working-class people in her locale. Consistently, she emphasized her desire to remain in Madeley, refusing any suggestions of relocation to another geographical area, always preferring to remain where she had been spiritually nurtured, as she writes in her journal:

> After being from home I always feel a peculiarly sweet feeling on entering my own house I seem to come where peace abides . . . When I was about leaving the Vicarage & purchasing this House my friend Mr Puritan said to me 'was I in your place I would take Lodgings'. I replied so would I if I had only myself to consider, but the people where would they have to meet if I have no house of my own? 'O! let them go to Madeleywood many walk farther then that for the gospel'. But I could not see it right to act in this way, his light was not my light.[32]

The times of providing spiritual leadership from the Tithe Barn, however, were to end seventeen years after Mary Fletcher's death. A letter dated January 13, 1831, and addressed to "Dear Brother" (addressee unknown), lays out the demise of the era, as a new chapel was being built to replace her tithe barn.[33] The new chapel scheduled services at the same time she was holding them. Unwilling to alter her meeting times to suit the new chapel, Tooth received "advice" from

---

30. Mary Tooth to Rosamund Tooth, 31 July 1828, MARC: PLP 34/8/7.

31. Journal of Mary Tooth, 30 September 1837, MARC: MAM Fl. 14/L/23.

32. Ibid., 8 September 1838, MARC: MAM Fl. 14/L/201.

33. Mary Tooth to unknown addressee, draft letter, 13 January 1831, MARC: MAM Fl. 34/1/10.

circuit preacher John Radford on 5 November 1833 that she should change her meeting time.[34]

However, there were ten more years until Tooth's death, and her writings indicate that she continued with her speaking ministry almost until her death. Her house functioned as a substitute for the tithe barn, as she held services in what she termed her "upper room," which she had discussed earlier in a journal entry from 1824:

> This evening the Lovefeast was held in my upper room neither of our Preachers could make it convenient to attend but glory be to a Triune God Jesus was present to break the bread of life to all our waiting souls, the sweet the farest unction of this Holy Spirit was most powerfully felt, the cleanness of the peoples experience & the simplicity with which they related it made hours pass away as moment. I do see a fulfilment of my glorified friends words, 'The residue of the spirit is with the Lord & he will pour it out'. Yes, glory be to God he does![35]

Eight years later, Tooth was still working in her upper room, serving again as sole overseer at the love feast, or communion service:

> This was the day appointed for our quarterly Love feast but for various reasons neither of our preachers was expected to attend, & knowing that in that case I should be looked up too to lead it, notwithstanding the Lords past loving kindness in former cases, I was sorely harassed by the enemy all the day, but it drove me to the footstool of divine Mercy, Glory forever be to his adorable name from the moment the service commenced I found Satan was a liar, instead of the Death that he suggested would be in the meeting, the people was all alive & their mouths opened to magnify the Lord.[36]

In another five years, Tooth was in declining health, but still held forth in the Upper Room. She reflected at length upon her life on New Year's Day, 1837, concluding that she was called to a particular place and a particular work. Tooth's single-minded determination in the face of societal pressures, criticism, and well-meaning advice shaped her life and work,

---

34. John Radford to Mary Tooth, 5 November 1833, MARC: PLP Fl. 6/2/19.

35. Journal of Mary Tooth, 7 December 1824, MARC: MAM Fl. 14/H/folder of journal fragments.

36. Ibid., 9 January 1832, MARC: MAM Fl. 12/I/14.

and showed her belief that she had been set apart as a prophet of God, one who inherited Mary Fletcher's divine anointing:

> Many times I have gone to the Upper-room so ill I have felt unable to utter a single sentence without great sufferings, but have no sooner begun to meet the people then my strength of mind & body have been so renewed that I have neither felt suffering or pain of any kind, the joy of the Lord being my strength I have returned from my Room refreshed both Soul & Body . . . It is now upward of twenty one years since my beloved friend & Spiritual Mother entered glory, I was then incompassed with many difficulties respecting the work of the Lord, & many was the calls that I had to go to various places while some . . . would have urged my removal & my dear Mrs Fletcher had said, 'not withstanding all I have said respecting your remaining in the work of the Lord <u>here</u>, after I am taken away, I leave you intirely at your own liberty to stay or go, believing you will have Divine guidance . . . Had I removed from Madeley I had certainly been saved from many trials I have been exercised with in it. But however great or many my crosses might be in abiding among the people I felt the cloud abide there, & there I must take up my abode & when at several distinct periods of time I have had arguments used with me to persuade me to chose another line of life to walk in, I have invariably found the light shine upon my path, with a conscienous sense that I was in the way of duty & acting under the approval of my God, a conscienous sense of being in the Divine Order.[37]

In her last years, Tooth, in declining health, noted in her journal that she was frequently feeling violent pains in her head. Nonetheless, she led as many meetings as she could, including class meetings, missionary meetings, the teetotaler society, and sewing circle meetings. She counseled the many people who came to visit her, was active in writing correspondence, and recorded the following observation: "Time flies very rapidly along, & my mind ever being in presenting work to be done makes me see the necessity of adhering as closely as possibly I can to that excellent rule of Mr Wesleys '<u>Never Be Idle</u>.'"[38] Her last entry discussed working at the parish bazaar.

Mary Tooth's obituary in the December 1843 *Methodist Magazine* encapsulated much of what is still thought of her. Memorialized in print

37. Ibid., 1 January 1837, MARC: MAM Fl. 14/K/3–6.

38. Ibid., 16 February 1841, MARC: MAM Fl. 14/N/41; cf. John Wesley's "Twelve Rules for a Helper."

primarily for her connections to the Fletchers, she is associated as well with the more controversial beliefs of Mary Fletcher, such as communication with spirits and the interest in dream revelations. The column does cover some of her vigorous service for more than forty years, but does not do full justice to the ways in which her life has provoked rethinking women's roles in the Methodist movement. The obituary's conclusion reflects and perhaps even shapes Tooth's reputation, as her account is included primarily for her connection with John Fletcher's legacy, but there was much more significance to her life.[39]

Whether those who knew of Tooth in the past or those who study her in the present choose to term what she did as preaching, it was certainly proclamation and ministry. Both Earl Brown and Paul Chilcote have classified the stages of women's speaking within Methodism as including public prayer, testimony, and exhortation; Brown extends those forms in Mary Fletcher's case to include expounding and preaching.[40] The latter categories would describe Mary Tooth's work as well. She continued to term herself a Methodist throughout her days, referring often to John Wesley and his writings, but bore the indelible imprint of Mary Fletcher as her mentor. In examining her life and work, it is clear that Tooth expanded in some senses the boundaries of women's work in early nineteenth-century religion and made an impact on the Methodist world in Shropshire, as she accepted the mantle of Mary Fletcher. Her 28 October 1841 journal entry expressed her wish to emulate the Fletchers beyond time, especially Mary Fletcher, as she prayed: "The desire of my Lord is, to live her life, & die her death, then shall I be one with them in glory."[41]

39. *Methodist Magazine*, December 1843, 1036–37.

40. Chilcote, *John Wesley and the Women Preachers*, 92–107; Brown, *Women of Mr. Wesley's Methodism*, 19–25.

41. Journal of Mary Tooth, 28 October 1841, MARC: MAM Fl. 14/N/89.

11

Holding Tightly to the "Promise of the Father"

*Phoebe Palmer and the Legacy of the Fletchers of Madeley
in Mid-Nineteenth-Century Methodism*

Harold E. Raser

WHEN PHOEBE PALMER (1807–74), accompanied by her physician husband, Walter, stepped off the train at Madeley, Shropshire, in mid-January 1862, Mrs. Palmer was one of the most widely recognized and admired religious figures in the English-speaking world. At the time, the Palmers were just past the midway point of what would turn out to be a four-year evangelistic tour of the British Isles.[1] The Palmers, American Methodists, had traveled to Britain in the flush of a religious awakening that had stirred North America between 1857 and 1859. This North American awakening, which was widely reported by the religious press in Britain, eventually sent some of its embers eastward, and these were fanned into flame throughout the British Isles by various groups of Evangelical Protestants, resulting in a parallel religious awakening in much of Ireland, Scotland, Wales, and England.[2] The Palmers hoped to assist in the British awakening.

1. See Phoebe Palmer, *Four Years in the Old World; Comprising the Travels, Incidents, and Evangelistic Labors of Dr. and Mrs. Palmer in England, Ireland, Scotland, and Wales* (New York: Foster & Palmer, 1866).

2. See Kathryn Teresa Long, *The Revival of 1857–1858: Interpreting an American*

Phoebe Palmer was at the very apogee of a more than three-decades-long career as an itinerant revivalist, an author of best-selling religious books, and a fervent Christian humanitarian when she visited England. Having begun in relative obscurity as an "activist" Methodist in the city of New York, Palmer had quickly ascended ever-larger stages. In 1843 she published the first of nearly twenty books she would write.[3] An itinerant "preaching" ministry had been launched in 1840, and this would eventually take her thousands of miles across the United States and Canada (as well as to the British Isles) by steamship, carriage, and train; she spoke and taught in churches, camp meetings, religious colleges and seminaries, and public auditoriums. Palmer also invested substantial time and energy in a variety of significant and highly visible charitable and humanitarian works serving the poor and needy. In addition she developed a lively correspondence with hundreds of spiritual seekers in various parts of the world, providing them with regular religious counsel and advice by post. Much of Palmer's work took place within the context of Methodism (she was a member of the American Methodist Episcopal Church from childhood, and her father, English-born, had joined a Methodist society in England while still a youth), but she frequently worked outside the boundaries of Methodism as well, extending her influence widely throughout English-speaking Protestantism.[4]

Thus, in 1862 Palmer arrived in Madeley as a "religious celebrity" from America, an object of great affection and respect, but also of considerable curiosity, and at least a little hostility. She was an American, a Methodist, a "revivalist," and a "woman preacher." She was also a zealous promoter of the doctrine of Christian Perfection, a central part of the Methodist heritage, but a feature always liable to provoke controversy and misunderstanding. Palmer and her husband had already

---

Religious Awakening (Oxford: Oxford University Press, 1998). On the British awakening and its connections to the American revival see Richard Carwardine, *Transatlantic Revivalism: Popular Evangelicalism in Britain and America, 1790–1865* (Greenwood, CT: Greenwood Press, 1978) 159–97.

3. See Palmer, *The Way of Holiness, with Notes by the Way* (New York: Piercy & Reed, 1843).

4. See Richard Wheatley, *The Life and Letters of Mrs. Phoebe Palmer* (New York: Palmer & Hughes, 1876); Charles E. White, *The Beauty of Holiness: Phoebe Palmer as Theologian, Revivalist, Feminist, and Humanitarian* (Grand Rapids: Francis Asbury, 1986); Harold E. Raser, *Phoebe Palmer, Her Life and Thought* (Lewiston, NY: Edwin Mellen, 1987).

held meetings from Scotland to the Isle of Wight and had briefly visited Ireland as well.

The Palmers did not travel to Madeley, however, for the purpose of holding religious meetings, even though they were in the midst of a lengthy evangelistic tour. Instead, their visit to Madeley was to be a brief tourist stop on their way to a long-planned engagement in Wales. Phoebe especially did not want to pass up an opportunity to visit the place associated with one of her most revered mentors, John Fletcher (1729–85). "Who could pass within twenty miles of its [Madeley] locality," she wrote, "without feeling an irresistible desire to tread the ground, and survey the scenes, where the sainted Fletcher exercised his ministry of about twenty-five years, wrote his inimitable 'Checks,' and in so many memorable ways glorified God?"[5]

Throughout her life, Palmer considered John Fletcher, vicar of Madeley, to be one of the leading lights of early Methodism. She also held Fletcher's wife, Mary (née Bosanquet; 1739–1815), in high esteem. So did she revere Hester Ann Roe Rogers (1756–94), an acquaintance of the Fletchers and an influential "popularizer" within Methodism of many of John Fletcher's distinctive theological ideas.[6] Having already visited many places in Britain connected with the history of early Methodism, the Palmers now intended to visit ground hallowed by the Fletchers. In fact, the Palmers' quick "tourist stop" at Madeley turned into something much more, but we shall consider this later.

The main purpose of this essay is to explore the role that Phoebe Palmer played in transmitting to mid-nineteenth-century Methodism (and beyond) significant elements of the legacy of John and Mary Fletcher. The essay argues and seeks to demonstrate that through her extensive evangelistic travels, many publications, and correspondence ministry of religious counsel, Palmer disseminated a theological vision that in several of its particulars owed more to the Fletchers than to anyone else in the Wesleyan tradition.

In *The Holiness Revival of the Nineteenth Century*, Melvin Dieter claimed that the American holiness movement (which had significant influence far beyond the United States, and which was shaped by Phoebe Palmer more than any other person) resulted from a blending of "the

---

5. Palmer, *Four Years in the Old World*, 516.

6. See Raser, *Phoebe Palmer*, 245–54.

American mind, prevailing revivalism, and Wesleyan Perfectionism."[7] Dieter is surely correct on the whole, but his statement also needs a slight qualification. The statement might better read that, the American holiness movement resulted from a blending of "the American mind, prevailing revivalism, and Wesleyan Perfectionism as held and taught by John Fletcher and propagated by several influential popularizers of Fletcher's thought." Palmer, I would suggest, was the "master chef" behind this creative and potent "blend."

"THE PROMISE OF THE FATHER"

Fletcher has been called by some "the Theologian of Methodism" because he was the first to articulate a comprehensive "Wesleyan" theological position, especially in his *Checks to Antinomianism* (1771–75).[8] Undergirding his theological structure is a concept or doctrine of "dispensations."

Fletcher was convinced that God's self-revelation in history is "progressive" and unfolds in stages (i.e., successive "dispensations"). Each dispensation brings a fuller revelation of God's nature and purposes and is significantly superior to the one that preceded it. The successive "dispensations" are the dispensation of the "Father," that of the "Son," and that of the "Holy Spirit" (which was inaugurated at Pentecost, as described in the Acts of the Apostles). It is only the last that brings the "perfect Gospel of Christ" and that fulfills the "Promise of the Father."[9]

The "Promise of the Father" is that which was foretold and described by the Hebrew prophet Joel (Joel 2:28–29) and declared by the Apostle Peter to be fulfilled on the Day of Pentecost: "In the last days it will be, God declares, that I will pour out my Spirit upon all flesh, and

7. Melvin E. Dieter, *The Holiness Revival of the Nineteenth Century* (Metuchen, NJ: Scarecrow, 1980) 3.

8. See *The Works of the Rev. John Fletcher*, 4 vols. (New York: Carlton & Phillips, 1854) vols. 1–2. For helpful, though somewhat differing, analyses of Fletcher's theological work see Patrick Streiff, *Reluctant Saint? A Theological Biography of Fletcher of Madeley* (Peterborough: Epworth, 2001); Laurence W. Wood, *The Meaning of Pentecost in Early Methodism: Rediscovering John Fletcher as John Wesley's Vindicator and Designated Successor* (Lanham, MD: Scarecrow, 2002); Peter S. Forsaith, ed. *"Unexampled Labours": Letters of the Revd John Fletcher of Madeley to Leaders in the Evangelical Revival* (Peterborough: Epworth, 2008).

9. *Works of John Fletcher*, 2:259ff.

your sons and your daughters shall prophesy, and your young men shall see visions, and your old men shall dream dreams. Even upon my slaves, both men and women, in those days I will pour out my Spirit; and they shall prophesy" (Acts 2:17–18). This clearly has both corporate and individual implications. That is, the "Promise of the Father" refers to both an individual experience of the divine presence and a new corporate reality, both of which result from a "pouring out" of the Spirit of God upon all humanity in the "last days" (i.e., the final stage of God's unfolding self-revelation). For the individual Christian believer the "Promise of the Father" brings the possibility of "full sanctification" (cf. the Wesleyan concepts of Christian Perfection and Perfect Love). For the Church it brings into being a radically new order of things; it overturns, or at least undermines, conventional gender, social, and cultural boundaries. In the dispensation of the "Holy Spirit," in which the "Promise of the Father" is fulfilled and the "full Gospel" of Christ revealed, God's Spirit, the divine presence, comes upon and empowers all: young and old, women and men, Israelites (i.e., "Chosen People") and their slaves (presumably non-Israelites) for the worship and service of God in the world. God's Spirit is active everywhere and in all persons who receive the Spirit, and human gender, social, and cultural distinctions are transcended by a divine "leveling" order made possible by the Spirit "outpoured."[10]

Clearly, John Fletcher's doctrine of dispensations has numerous important ramifications. A major one is that it could be used to justify and legitimate numerous "novelties" and innovations associated with the early Methodist movement. These would include such things as a "connexion" of religious societies outside the approved structures of the established Church, lay exhorters, and most pertinent for this essay, female exhorters and itinerant ministers. Of course, it is well known that Fletcher's wife, Mary Bosanquet Fletcher, carried on an active ministry of what can only be called "preaching" before she was married, during her marriage to Fletcher (1781–85) (one historian has declared: "John and Mary Fletcher functioned, for all practical purposes, as co-pastors of his parish throughout the course of their brief marriage"), and for nearly thirty years after her husband's death.[11]

10. See Wood, *Pentecost in Early Methodism*, 113–19.

11. Paul Wesley Chilcote, *John Wesley and the Women Preachers of Early Methodism* (Metuchen, NJ: Scarecrow, 1991) 184. Also see Henry Moore, *The Life of Mrs. Mary Fletcher: Consort and Relict of the Rev. John Fletcher, Vicar of Madeley, Salop; Compiled*

Significantly, Phoebe Palmer had published one of her most important books just prior to departing the United States for Britain. The book's title was *Promise of the Father*, and its subtitle was, *A Neglected Speciality of the Last Days Addressed to the Clergy and Laity of all Christian Communities.*[12] The book's foundation is Fletcher's doctrine of dispensations and his interpretation of the Day of Pentecost, although Palmer nowhere in the book gives credit to Fletcher for this idea. She did, however, include ten pages on the work of Mary Fletcher, as a prime example of how God empowers women for public ministry in the "dispensation of the Holy Spirit," thus fulfilling the "Promise of the Father."[13]

Palmer developed several distinct lines of argument in the book for the right of women to publicly minister in the Church, but the central thread throughout is the "argument from Pentecost," which was based on Fletcher's doctrine of dispensations.[14] According to Palmer, the present age is the "dispensation of the Spirit," which was inaugurated at Pentecost with "signs and wonders," the chief of these being the power to "prophesy," which Palmer understands to mean to "herald the glad tidings [of Jesus] to others" or to proclaim "to every creature . . . the love of God to [humanity] through Christ Jesus."[15] On the Day of Pentecost this power was given to all Christian believers that were present, both women and men. In fact, this gift of power and its extension to females as well as males is "a marked speciality [*sic*] of the Christian [i.e. Holy Spirit's] dispensation."[16]

However, the Church of Palmer's day had deviated from the "Pentecostal" pattern and as a result was spiritually enfeebled and under the condemnation of God. Palmer wrote that, "The attitude of the [contemporary] church in relation to this matter is most grievous in the sight of her Lord, who has purchased the whole human family unto himself, and would fain have every possible agency employed in preaching the gospel to every creature."[17] Since the model of Pentecost is normative

From Her Journal and Other Authentic Documents (New York: Soule & Mason, 1831).

12. Palmer, *Promise of the Father; or, A Neglected Speciality of the Last Days Addressed to the Clergy and Laity of all Christian Communities* (Boston: Degen, 1859).

13. Ibid., 100–109.

14. See Raser, *Phoebe Palmer*, 199–210, for a detailed analysis of the book.

15. Palmer, *Promise of the Father*, 37.

16. Ibid., 14, 22–23. In the book Palmer equates "preaching" with "prophesying."

17. Ibid., 70.

for the entire "dispensation of the Spirit," Palmer asks, "If the Spirit of prophecy fell upon God's daughters, alike as upon his sons in that day, and they spoke in the midst of that assembled multitude, as the Spirit gave utterance, on what authority do the [leaders] of the churches restrain the use of that gift now?"[18]

Palmer's *Promise of the Father* thus put forth clear theological justification for "women preaching," and more broadly, for the full participation of laypersons in the ministry of the Church. The case she made was grounded in Fletcher's doctrine of dispensations and his interpretation of Pentecost. Palmer's book became extremely influential in many religious circles. Most receptive were the numerous "holiness" associations, bands, and missions that began to form first in the United States, and then elsewhere, beginning in the late 1860s, as part of a "holiness movement" which was inspired largely by the work of Palmer. Some of these groups developed into independent "holiness churches" or "denominations," and most endorsed the public ministry of women.[19]

"BAPTISM WITH THE HOLY GHOST"

Palmer also embraced the "Pentecostal" language that accompanied Fletcher's focus on the biblical account of the Day of Pentecost as the culminating event in the fulfillment of the "Promise of the Father" and the inauguration of the "full" and "perfect" revelation of God in the world. Especially significant is Palmer's adoption of Fletcher's practice of speaking of entire sanctification as a "baptism with the Holy Spirit," and his teaching that individual human experience of God parallels the successive "dispensations" of divine activity in history so that every individual Christian believer needs to experience the "fullness of the Spirit" (i.e., a "personal Pentecost") in order to embrace the "perfect gospel of Christ." During the most influential years of Palmer's career, these were both central elements of her teaching.

Palmer did not always echo John Fletcher's "Pentecostal" images and vocabulary; early in her public career these were scarce. Instead, prior to the middle to late 1850s Palmer generally taught that Christian

18. Ibid.

19. See Donald W. Dayton, *Discovering an Evangelical Heritage* (New York: Harper & Row, 1976) 86–112.

believers are required to "be holy" as God "is holy." This required individual Christian believers to make an "entire consecration" of themselves to God (in her early parlance, to "lay all on the altar") together with an appropriating act of faith in the promise of God to "make holy" whatever is so consecrated. The life of an "entirely consecrated" believer would then be made "holy" by the power of God, free from conscious sinning and fully dedicated to God and God's purposes.[20] This is a reasonably conventional nineteenth-century Wesleyan Methodist view of "entire sanctification" or "Christian perfection."

However, for reasons that are not entirely clear, Palmer began during the 1850s to use "Pentecostal" images and language more frequently to refer to "full sanctification" and to the work of God in the world generally.[21] This is vividly illustrated by comparing her earlier writings with her later books. Beginning with *Incidental Illustrations of the Economy of Salvation, Its Doctrines and Duties* (1855), then *Promise of the Father* (1859), and finally *Four Years in the Old World* (1866), one can trace a growing preference for the language of Pentecost and the book of Acts in referring to spiritual matters. In *Four Years in the Old World* the transformation is virtually complete: this book is filled with references to and descriptions of religious meetings characterized by "extraordinary effusions of the Holy Spirit," "manifestations of divine power," "Pentecostal blessings and Pentecostal power," and professing Christians, including numerous clergymen, receiving "the full baptism of the Spirit," "the full baptism of the Holy Ghost," or being "filled with the Spirit." Describing a meeting in Newcastle-upon-Tyne, Palmer wrote: "A local preacher was the first to hasten to the communion-rail, and was the first to receive 'the tongue of fire.' Would that you could have heard his clear, unequivocal testimony, as with a holy boldness, which perhaps scarcely was more than equaled on the day when the holy flame first descended on the

---

20. See Palmer, *The Way of Holiness*; *Entire Devotion to God: a Present to a Christian Friend* (New York: Piercy & Reed, 1845); *Faith and Its Effects: Fragments from My Portfolio* (New York: Published for the Author, 1848).

21. For discussion of this see Dieter, "Wesleyan-Holiness Aspects of Pentecostal Origins: As Mediated through the Nineteenth-Century Holiness Revival," in Vinson Synan, ed., *Aspects of Pentecostal-Charismatic Origins* (Plainfield, NJ: Logos, 1975) 55–80; Timothy L. Smith, "The Doctrine of the Sanctifying Spirit: Charles G. Finney's Synthesis of Wesleyan and Covenant Theology," *Wesleyan Theological Journal* 13 (1978) 92–113; Donald W. Dayton, *Theological Roots of Pentecostalism* (Grand Rapids: Zondervan, 1987).

Pentecostal morn, he spake as the Spirit gave utterance . . . as in the early days of the Spirit's dispensation, Pentecostal blessings bring Pentecostal power. Surely there was One in our midst who 'baptizeth' with the Holy Ghost and with fire."[22]

By adopting "Pentecostal vocabulary," Palmer threw her weight as one of the premier revivalists of the nineteenth century not only behind Fletcher's "dispensational theology" but also his distinctive way of articulating the Methodist doctrine of "Christian perfection" in terms of the Day of Pentecost, equating "full sanctification" (John Wesley generally favored the terms "Christian perfection" or "perfect love") with being "filled with the Holy Spirit" as described in the book of Acts. Fletcher's ideas were of course already a part of the developing Wesleyan "tradition," and were in fact particularly prominent in the published journals of several widely read eighteenth-century and early nineteenth-century Methodist lay men and women like Hester Ann Roe Rogers and William Carvosso (1750–1834), both of whom Palmer read and greatly admired.[23] However, Fletcher's ideas vied with those of others, notably Wesley himself, whose *Plain Account of Christian Perfection* is essentially devoid of "Pentecostal" images and references to the Day of Pentecost and its accompanying phenomena. Palmer's endorsement of Fletcher's language tipped the balance in Fletcher's direction and made "Pentecostal language" and ideas normative, especially for those associated with the "holiness movement" after the American Civil War, a movement that grew to a great extent out of Palmer's propagation of "Christian holiness" or "entire sanctification."

This decisive turn toward the "Pentecostal" rhetoric of Fletcher within Methodism (and beyond) in the mid-nineteenth century had profound consequences. Among these were: a growing fascination with the Holy Spirit and the work of the Holy Spirit in the church;[24] a marked tendency to view "full sanctification" as an instantaneous

---

22. Palmer, *Four Years in the Old World*, 96–97.

23. See Hester Ann Rogers, *An Account of the Experiences of Hester Ann Rogers* (New York: Lane & Scott, 1850); Rogers, *The Life of Faith Exemplified; or, Extracts from the Journal of Mrs. Hester Ann Rogers* (New York: Carlton & Porter, 1861); Benjamin Carvosso, ed. *Life of William Carvosso, Sixty Years a Class Leader* (Cincinnati: Jennings & Pye, n.d [first edition 1835]).

24. See for example George Moberly, *The Administration of the Holy Spirit in the Body of Christ: Eight Lectures Preached Before the University of Oxford in the Year 1868* (Oxford: Parker, 1868).

"event" delivering spiritual perfection in a moment of extraordinary divine "blessing"; a tendency to give special preference to the book of Acts in theological reflection about the Church; a tendency to emphasize the importance of manifestations of extraordinary divine power (i.e., miracles) in the Church, a characteristic of the book of Acts;[25] and a tendency to focus on the "evidence" of the "baptism with the Holy Spirit."[26] These emphases became widely dispersed throughout English-speaking Protestantism in the second half of the nineteenth century. In some places they coalesced to provide a coherent theological foundation for the emergence of "Pentecostal" Christianity, perhaps the most significant development in the Church in the twentieth century. Fletcher, largely through the influence of Palmer in the nineteenth century (although neither Fletcher nor Palmer was ever a "Pentecostal") was a major progenitor of this movement.

FAITH FOR A VICTORIAN CHURCH

In addition to the doctrine of dispensations, especially as it pertained to ministry by women in the Church, and a theological "rhetoric" of "Pentecostal" themes and images, Palmer also transmitted to mid-nineteenth-century Methodism, and beyond, a concept of "faith" borrowed from Fletcher which was especially well suited to a "Victorian church."

25. This subtly shifted the emphasis within the Wesleyan tradition away from understanding "Christian perfection" or "full sanctification" as primarily removing sin and bestowing "perfect love" for God and humanity to understanding the "baptism with the Holy Spirit" as primarily providing extraordinary divine *power* to believers to enable them to "witness," "prophesy," perform miracles, and in other ways persuasively bring persons to Christian faith. In time this preoccupation with power and "signs and wonders" would play a prominent role in the emergence of modern Pentecostalism.

26. "Evidence" of "holiness" or divine grace generally, was always an important issue for Wesleyans who taught that authentic Christianity required personal "holiness." Wesleyanism produced myriad "rules," guidelines, and the like to nurture, and measure, one's possession of divine grace. Phoebe Palmer was especially impressed by the descriptions of the boldness with which ordinary believers witnessed to Christ after being "baptized with the Holy Spirit" and began to teach that the primary evidence of "Spirit baptism" is boldness in "speaking for Christ" and zeal in spreading the Gospel. Others, however, found more compelling and incontrovertible "evidence" of "Spirit baptism" in things like "speaking in other tongues." This latter understanding of evidence became a foundational part of modern Pentecostalism.

I have argued this at some length elsewhere, so will only give a brief summary here.[27]

As compared to John Wesley, Fletcher developed and taught a concept of faith that is more "rational" and gives a greater role to assent to intellectual propositions. For Wesley "faith" is "both a supernatural 'evidence' of God and the things of God, a kind of spiritual 'light' exhibited to the soul, and a supernatural 'sight' or perception thereof." By "supernatural" Wesley meant that this "sight" or faculty of spiritual "perception" did not arise naturally from fallen human nature; it resulted instead from God graciously awakening otherwise moribund human spiritual capacities in order to rouse human beings and draw them to God. Thus, faith is for Wesley a "supernatural faculty" given to the seeker after God, and also a "conviction" concerning the things of God which arises from the exercise of that faculty. Faith is first of all given, and "experienced," and only then "exercised" by a seeker after God to primarily "trust in" and rely upon God for "salvation."[28]

Fletcher introduced some quite different ideas about faith into the Wesleyan tradition, or at least promoted a stream of thinking that was already present but that Wesley himself moved away from in his mature years. Over time Fletcher's ideas tended to overshadow those of Wesley, contributing to the eventual "dethronement of John Wesley's heart religion" within Methodism.[29] Whereas Wesley had described faith as a divine gift, a supernatural faculty given so that one might apprehend "divine things" and be able to "trust" in Christ, Fletcher saw faith as more of an act of the human will. He tended to describe it as a strenuous believing in propositions, or divine "promises" given in the Bible. To a "Mr. Vaughan" he wrote concerning full sanctification: "To aim aright at this liberty of the children of God requires a continual acting of faith—of a naked faith in a naked promise or declaration . . . By a naked faith in a naked promise, I do not mean a bare assent that God is faithful, and that such a promise in the book of God may be fulfilled in me; but a bold, hearty, steady venturing of my soul, body, and spirit upon the truth of

27. See Raser, *Phoebe Palmer*, 230–41.

28. Albert C. Outler, ed. *John Wesley* (New York: Oxford University Press, 1964) 275–76

29. See Randy L. Maddox, "A Change of Affections: The Development, Dynamics, and Dethronement of John Wesley's Heart Religion," in Richard B. Steele, ed., *"Heart Religion" in the Methodist Tradition and Related Movements* (Lanham, MD: Scarecrow, 2001) 3–31.

the promise."[30] In this connection Fletcher took some important steps toward stressing free will at the expense of grace. This was due partly to the fact that much of his thought was forged in the heat of controversy with Calvinists who emphasized absolute divine sovereignty, predestination, irresistible grace, and the perseverance of the elect. Fletcher thus tended to state his own "Arminian" outlook (which he shared with Wesley) in the strongest possible terms. As a result, it can be argued that Fletcher actually initiated the movement in Methodism from "free grace to free will" that Robert Chiles traced back to Richard Watson.[31] This emphasis simplified the "way of salvation," making it possible for Christians to think of the work of God and the "works" of human beings as divided into discrete categories, but intersecting in predictable ways on the basis of specific contractual "conditions," clearly established by God. This tendency can be traced within Methodism at a formal theological level from Fletcher, through Adam Clark (1762–1832), to Richard Watson (1781–1833), and beyond. It can also be found at the level of popular Methodist biography from Fletcher through Hester Ann Roe Rogers, William Carvosso, and others, down to Palmer in the nineteenth century.[32]

William Carvosso presents a striking example from the tradition of popular Methodist biography. A legendary figure among early Methodists, Carvosso carried on a wide-ranging itinerant ministry throughout Cornwall as a "lay evangelist" for many years. Palmer read the *Life* of Carvosso when she was a young adult and ever after considered him one of the greatest pioneers of Methodism. In his understanding of faith, Carvosso was clearly guided by Fletcher and Hester Ann Rogers, although he added to them some touches of his own. While Palmer never credited Carvosso, Rogers, or Fletcher for her own views on faith, she was immensely indebted to all of them.[33]

30. Joseph Benson, *The Life of the Rev. John W. De La Flechere* (New York: The Methodist Book Concern, n.d.) 80.

31. Robert E. Chiles, *Theological Transition in American Methodism, 1790–1935* (Nashville: Abingdon, 1965) 144–83.

32. For the formal theological tradition see Adam Clarke, *Christian Theology* (New York: Mason & Lane, 1840 [first edition 1835]); Richard Watson, *Theological Institutes: or, A View of the Evidences, Doctrines, Morals, and Institutions of Christianity*, 2 vols. (New York: Lane & Scott, 1834). For popular biography see Rogers, *Experiences of Hester Ann Rogers*; Rogers, *Life of Faith Exemplified*; Carvosso, *Life*.

33. This is especially obvious on nearly every page of Palmer, *Faith and Its Effects*.

The faith that God requires of human beings is reasonable, according to Carvosso, and rests upon "objective" grounds, that is, the Word, or promises of God recorded in the Bible. "Faith is an act of reason, and believing is a kind of knowing" based upon the "testimony of Him whom we believe," declared Carvosso.[34] A seeker who credited Carvosso with helping him grasp the nature of faith noted that "his remarks on the nature of [faith] were clear and forcible in an extraordinary degree, commending themselves to my reason."[35]

The faith that Carvosso commended is a "naked faith," a belief that stands bare upon the word of God, with nothing else to sustain it. Carvosso quoted with approval Fletcher's comments on "naked faith" (i.e., independent of all feeling or sensibility) in a "naked promise" and often applied these to his own experience. In an unusually intense bout with temptation, Carvosso found that "naked faith was my only defense; the only weapon with which I could maintain the fight."[36] Near the end of his life, he observed, "After fifty-six years spent in the service of God, I find I have nothing to keep my soul in motion but faith."[37]

Palmer found the understanding of faith articulated by Fletcher, and transmitted through popular Methodist biography, to perfectly fit both her own personal religious experience and that of her large receptive mid-nineteenth-century audience. For Palmer herself, grasping Fletcher's idea of "naked faith" finally resolved a lengthy spiritual quest for Christian Perfection, or full sanctification, which consumed more than a decade of her early adult life. Guided by her older sister, Sarah Worrall Lankford (1806–96), who had herself found spiritual satisfaction by applying principles derived from Fletcher that she found in the *Life* of Hester Ann Rogers, Palmer testified that she finally attained "entire sanctification" in 1837. Professing and guiding others into this state would become the all-consuming passion for Palmer for most of the rest of her life.[38]

34. Carvosso, *Life*, 154. This directly parallels Phoebe Palmer's insistence that faith is one's "reasonable obligation," and her repeated statement that belief in divine promises for salvation "is hardly of faith, but rather of knowledge; it is so easy." See Palmer, *Faith and Its Effects*, 343, and elsewhere.

35. Carvosso, *Life*, 8.

36. Ibid., 246–48, 136.

37. Ibid., 230.

38. For Sarah Worrall Lankford, see John A. Roche, *The Life of Mrs. Sarah A. Lankford Palmer* (New York: Hughes, 1898). For an account of Palmer's quest for full

Palmer's concept of faith, borrowed from Fletcher and his Methodist "popularizers," found a receptive audience throughout North America and the British Isles in the mid nineteenth-century (although Palmer was not without her detractors). Faith as "naked" believing in "naked" (visible, stark, and definite) "promises," essentially embracing a truth based on clear evidence or assenting to the stipulations of a definite "contract," was an idea that was readily grasped by and highly appealing to the Victorian Age.[39] This was so even among Methodists whose eighteenth- and early nineteenth-century heritage of spirituality made a large place for the affections, heightened emotions, and other subjective phenomena including visions, dreams, "impressions," and even physical prostrations when experiencing the divine presence.[40] By the middle of the nineteenth-century Methodists in both Britain and the United States were well on their way to taming the affections and carefully controlling their "enthusiastic" impulses. They desired "order" and predictability in their religion. Victorian Methodists tended to prefer "consecrated respectability" and "sanctified gentility" to "a boiling hot religion," and a concept of faith that made God a trustworthy, predictable business partner who conscientiously kept his word and fulfilled his obligations was preferable to an inscrutable sovereign deity that acted in unpredictable ways and fell upon persons with sometimes terrifying power.[41]

sanctification see Palmer, *The Way of Holiness*, 1–69. For analysis of Palmer's quest see Raser, *Phoebe Palmer*, 43–48.

39. For some analysis of the social context and implications of Palmer's ministry in the "Victorian" era see Kathryn Teresa Long, "Consecrated Respectability: Phoebe Palmer and the Refinement of American Methodism," in Nathan O. Hatch and John H. Wigger, eds., *Methodism and the Shaping of American Culture*, (Nashville: Kingswood, 2001) 281–307.

40. Helpful analyses of the role of "feeling" in early Methodism and its displacement as Methodism developed include Steele, ed., *"Heart Religion"*; David Hempton, *Methodism: Empire of the Spirit* (New Haven: Yale University Press, 2005) 32–54; Hempton, "Methodist Growth in Transatlantic Perspective, ca. 1770–1850," in Hatch and Wigger, eds., *Methodism and the Shaping of American Culture*, 41–85; Wigger, *Taking Heaven by Storm: Methodism and the Rise of Popular Christianity in America* (Urbana: University of Illinois Press, 1998).

41. "Consecrated respectability" and "sanctified gentility" are terms used by Long, "Consecrated Respectability," 281–307. "A Boiling Hot Religion" is used by Wigger to describe early nineteenth-century Methodism in *Taking Heaven by Storm*, 104–24.

CONCLUSION

What about Phoebe and Walter Palmer's brief "tourist stop" at Madeley to see the sites associated with the lives of John and Mary Fletcher? Phoebe wrote in *Four Years in the Old World*, "We did not come expecting to enter upon any duty."[42] However, it turned out that the Palmers had a sizeable group of admirers in and around Madeley, who had actually been praying that they might be divinely led to minister in the community. One of these was the vicar of Madeley at the time of their visit, whom Phoebe described as "a clergyman of evangelical, fervent piety"; she judged that she had "met with few in any region [of Britain] of more manifest zeal, or more in love with the spirit of his eminent predecessor of a century since."[43] The vicar had read Palmer's *The Way of Holiness, Faith, and Its Effects*, and *Promise of the Father*.[44]

These admirers prevailed upon the Palmers to delay their planned travel to Wales and to conduct meetings in Methodist chapels in Madeley and its environs. Phoebe and Walter stayed in the area for three weeks, ministering in three different parts of the Methodist "circuit": Madeley Village, Madeley Wood, and Dawley. Phoebe reported that Methodists, members of the Church of England, and others "densely filled" the chapels night after night and that "many are unable to get in, as it is crowded before the time of service."[45] She reported attendees coming from as far away as Birmingham and Banbury.

Following the conclusion of the services and their departure from Madeley, the Palmers received word that as a result of their meetings, over nine hundred new believers had been added to Madeley Circuit, four hundred to adjoining Wellington Circuit, and that revival had even begun to spill over into neighboring communities that the Palmers had not visited.[46] These were fairly typical results for almost

42. Palmer, *Four Years in the Old World*, 516.

43. Ibid., 520. Palmer also reported that this vicar regularly held weekly "revival prayer-meetings" and "class" meetings "quite in the Methodist fashion," 526. This vicar, although not named by Palmer, was Edward Yate, who served the parish from 1859 to 1908. A memorial plaque honoring Yate adorns a wall of the present parish church in Madeley.

44. Ibid., 528.

45. Ibid., 530.

46. Ibid., 530–34.

everywhere they went, even when their meetings were hastily arranged with no advance publicity.

This dénouement to Phoebe and Walter Palmer's brief stopover in Madeley, Shropshire, in January 1862 provides a fitting conclusion for this essay. The noted female revivalist changed her plans and for three weeks publicly declared the gospel of Christ, convinced that this was "the order of God."[47] This ministry of an American Methodist woman, whose message was deeply influenced in important ways by John Fletcher, the celebrated eighteenth-century "Vicar of Madeley," found an enthusiastic response from crowds of nineteenth-century British Methodists, Anglicans, and others. Some sought pardon for their sins while others sought full sanctification through "baptism with the Holy Spirit" under Palmer's guidance. What can only be described as a religious revival or awakening resulted, in which "All classes [of persons]" were visited by the Holy Spirit of God.[48] According to Palmer, and Fletcher before her, this could only be understood as a convincing fulfillment of the "Promise of the Father."

47. Ibid., 517.
48. Ibid., 534.

12

John Fletcher as the Theologian of Early American Methodism

Laurence W. Wood

R ANDY MADDOX HAS NOTED that Fletcher was considered a supplementary authority to Wesley in early American Methodism but that the two were viewed as equal authorities on Methodist doctrine in the first course of study for Methodist elders in the Baltimore Conference in 1817, which became a model for other conferences.[1] John Fletcher's significance for American Methodism is reflected in a motion which Francis Ward, assistant secretary of the 1808 General Conference, proposed on Tuesday, May 24, 1808: "that it shall be considered as the sentiment of this Conference, that Mr. Wesley's Notes on the New Testament, his four first volumes of Sermons, and *Mr. Fletcher's Checks* [italics mine], in their general tenor, contain the principal doctrines of Methodism, and a good explanation of our articles of religion; and that this sentiment be recorded on our Journal without being incorporated in the Discipline."[2]

Richard Heitzenrater and Thomas Oden have debated why this motion was voted down with instructions that it be stricken from

---

1. Randy Maddox, "Respected Founder/Neglected Guide: The Role of Wesley in American Methodist Theology," *Methodist History* 37:2 (1999) 75.

2. Cited by Richard P. Heitzenrater, *Mirror and Memory* (Nashville: Kingswood, 1989) 197.

the Journal. Oden has suggested that one reason was that it included "Fletcher's *Checks*" which would have been "an intrusive *innovation*."[3] Heitzenrater believes this indicates that the Articles of Religion alone constitute the doctrinal standards of Methodism.[4] Another explanation could be that *The Doctrines and Discipline of the Methodist Episcopal Church* already included Wesley's and Fletcher's writings as doctrinal standards. It specifically instructed Methodist preachers in an adapted version of the Large Minutes: "Let all the preachers carefully read over Mr. Wesley's and Mr. Fletcher's tracts."[5] Fletcher's *Checks to Antinomianism* were also cited in the adapted version of Wesley's Large Minutes as having "so fully handled" and "completely considered" Methodist belief on the subject of antinomianism.[6]

This first book of discipline said the purpose of the Articles of Religion was to show that Methodists believe what all Protestants believe, but moved beyond to show what was distinctively Methodist. Thomas Coke and Francis Asbury, in a preface requested by the General Conference, wrote:

> We wish to see this little publication [*Doctrines and Discipline*] in the house of every Methodist, and the more so as it contains our plan of Christian education, and the articles of religion, maintained, more or less, in part or in the whole, by every reformed church in the world. We would likewise declare our real sentiments on the scripture doctrine of election and reprobation; on the infallible, unconditional perseverance of all who ever have believed, or ever shall; and on the doctrine of Christian perfection. Far from wishing you to be ignorant of any of our doctrines, or any part of our discipline, we desire you to read, mark, learn, and inwardly digest the whole.[7]

3. Thomas C. Oden, *Doctrinal Standards in the Wesleyan Tradition* (Grand Rapids: Francis Asbury, 1988) 202.

4. Richard P. Heitzenrater, *Mirror and Memory*, 197–98. See also Richard P. Heitzenrater, "At Full Liberty: Doctrinal Standards in Early American Methodism," *Quarterly Review* 5 (1985) 15–19.

5. Thomas Coke and Francis Asbury, *The Doctrines and Discipline of the Methodist Episcopal Church in America, with explanatory notes*, 10th ed. (Philadelphia: Tuckniss, 1798) iv. Original date of publication was Nov. 16, 1792 in Baltimore by Thomas Coke and Francis Asbury, 59.

6. Ibid., 187.

7. Ibid., iv.

Notice that these instructions in the preface to the discipline state that "the whole" of the discipline represents "our real sentiments," so it can be seen that the Articles form only a part of the doctrinal standards, and there is no explicit or implicit indication that they were the only standards.

Since the conference had just approved the Restrictive Rule forbidding the addition of any standard,[8] and Wesley and Fletcher were already referenced within the *Doctrines and Discipline* as implicit standards, the Ward motion probably failed because it was unnecessary and confusing. Nathan Bangs reported that the 1784 Conference "adopted" the Articles of Religion, then immediately "adopted"[9] Wesley's *Large Minutes*, which specifically required Methodist preachers to read both Wesley and Fletcher.[10] The Articles were an expression of their agreement with the larger Christian tradition, but the writings of Wesley and Fletcher provided the distinctive beliefs of Methodists. In order to make it clear that Methodists were to take the "whole" of the *Doctrines and Discipline* as specified, the book of discipline further stipulated: "A Methodist preacher is to mind every point, great and small, in the Methodist discipline!"[11] Hence the doctrinal standards of the Methodist Episcopal Church were not merely the Articles of Religion, nor were Fletcher's *Checks* "an intrusion." On the contrary, the authority of Wesley and Fletcher was implied in *Doctrines and Discipline* and further in the claim: "A few good writers in one church are quite sufficient, especially in ours, which has already been honored with a Wesley and a Fletcher."[12]

FLETCHER'S *CHECKS* AS A DOCTRINAL STANDARD

Thomas Coke's *A Series of Letters Addressed to the Methodist Connection* in 1810 engaged in an extended discussion of Fletcher's idea of dispensations, endorsing it and arguing that it "coincides" with Wesley's view.[13] He particularly noted that Fletcher's *Checks* were "acknowledged

8. Heitzenrater, *Mirror and Memory*, 197–98. Cf. Richard P. Heitzenrater, "At Full Liberty," 15–19.

9. Nathan Bangs, *A History of the Methodist Episcopal Church* (New York: Lane & Tippett, 1845) 1:175.

10. Ibid., 1:192.

11. *The Doctrines and Discipline of the Methodist Episcopal Church*, 59.

12. Ibid., 89

13. Thomas Coke, *A Series of Letters Addressed to the Methodist Connection*

and disseminated by Wesley" and officially "recognized by the [British] Methodist Conference."[14] If the 1784 Christmas Conference of the Methodist Episcopal Church also endorsed Fletcher's writings as a doctrinal standard, it was Francis Asbury who introduced and promoted them (as a young man he knew and heard Fletcher preach even before he knew John Wesley).[15] In a letter (December 31, 1801) to the Methodist book agent, Ezekiel Cooper, Asbury instructed him to publish the writings of Fletcher and Wesley,[16] even placing Fletcher's name before Wesley's.

The first collected edition of Fletcher's writings was begun in 1788 when Wesley was still alive and completed in 1795, was printed by Paramore (who Wesley's will specified be retained as printers),[17] and was the basis of the first American edition.[18] This was printed in Philadelphia between 1791 and 1796 for the Methodist Episcopal Church.[19]

The Last Check (Philadelphia, 1796) was reprinted in the same year as an abridged edition titled *Christian Perfection, An Extract from John Fletcher*, for the Methodist Episcopal Church in which a dominant motif was that Pentecost and "the baptism of the Holy Ghost" are the means for attaining Christian perfection.[20] The editor of this abridged edition assured readers that Wesley and Fletcher represented the same point of view. It had eight reprints for the Methodist Episcopal Church between 1837 and 1875, and was widely cited by Methodist writers throughout the nineteenth century.

Even before Wesley's complete *Works* were published in 1826, there were thirteen American imprints of Fletcher's various writings, including five reprints of his *Works*. Fletcher's *Checks to Antinomianism* were

---

(London: A. Paris, 1810) 72, 97, 147–157.

14. Coke, *Letters*, 190.

15. *Journal and Letters of Francis Asbury*, ed. J. M. Potter, Elmer T. Clark, and J. S. Payton (Nashville: Abingdon, 1958) 1:124 (July 24, 1774).

16. Asbury, *Journal*, 3:232.

17. Wesley, *The Works of the Rev. John Wesley*, ed. Thomas Jackson, 3rd ed., 14 vols. (London: Mason, 1829–31) 4:500, "Mr. Wesley's Last Will and Testament."

18. Wesley, *Works* (Jackson) 4:500, "Mr. Wesley's Last Will and Testament." See *National Union Catalogue*, 175:232–40, for a list of Fletcher's published writings.

19. Joseph Crukshank vols. 1 and 2, 1791, vol. 3, 1792; Parry Hall vol. 4, 1793; Henry Tuckniss vol. 5, 1794, vol. 6, 1796.

20. *Christian Perfection, Being an Extract from the Rev. John Fletcher's Treatise on That Subject* (New York: Mason & Lane, 1937 edition) 25 passim.

reprinted for the Methodist Episcopal Church eight different times, and his *Works* twenty-two times, in the nineteenth century. Joseph Benson's biography (1804),[21] extending Wesley's 1786 Short Account, ran to seventeen American editions, including sixteen thousand copies of the 1837 New York edition. *The Portrait of St. Paul* was reprinted nine times. There were at least 174 different printings of John Fletcher's various books in the nineteenth century.[22]

This remarkably large number of reprints of his writings shows that his doctrinal views formed the thinking of American Methodism from its inception. Abel Stevens, a nineteenth-century Methodist historian, claimed that Fletcher's writings "control the opinions of the largest and most effective body of evangelical clergymen of the earth . . . They have been more influential in the denomination than Wesley's own controversial writings on the subject."[23]

In "An Address of the Editors," published in *The* [American] *Methodist Magazine* in 1823,[24] Fletcher's writings are referenced as the authoritative doctrinal standard. In 1828, an editorial comment found in *The Christian Advocate* noted: "I consider Mr. Wesley and Mr. Fletcher as standing foremost, perhaps, in the Christian world, as faithful interpreters of the mind and will of God to man, as revealed in the Scriptures of truth" and added a further comment about Fletcher's *Checks*: "Oh what, an invaluable work!" This editorial particularly cited from Fletcher's treatise, *Christian Perfection*, to refute critics.[25]

MARY BOSANQUET FLETCHER'S DIARIES

The Life of Mary Fletcher was compiled by Wesley's assistant, Henry Moore,[26] and became a prominent piece of devotional literature published fifteen times in America from 1817 to 1850, with three further editions, the last in 1883 by Thomas O. Summer (Southern Methodist

21. Joseph Benson, *The Life of the Rev. John W. de la Flechere* (London: Wesleyan Conference Office, 1805) 3.

22. *National Union Catalogue*, 175:232–40.

23. Abel Stevens, *The History of the Religious Movement of the Eighteenth Century, Called Methodism* (London: Watson, 1864) 2:55.

24. *The Methodist Magazine* 6 (January–February 1823) 9, 65.

25. *Christian Advocate and Journal* 2:29 (New York, July 11, 1828) 73.

26. Henry Moore, *Life of Mary Fletcher* (New York: Hunt & Eaton, 1817).

Publishing House). Mary Bosanquet also frequently used the language of the baptism with the Spirit as a functional equivalent for perfection in her diaries and in her preaching. Considering her special relationship to Wesley, it is most likely she felt his approval of this theme. For example, in his sermon on "The General Spread of the Gospel," Wesley expected the Methodist movement to spread until there would be a "grand Pentecost" when the whole world would be filled with righteousness.[27] Wesley explained the basis for this hope in the gift of perfect love (Deut 30:3–6) was the day of Pentecost.[28]

After John Fletcher's death, Mary Fletcher "preached" with Wesley on occasions.[29] In an exhortation possibly given after Wesley's sermon on "The General Spread of the Gospel," she spoke about Wesley's expectation of a coming global Pentecost. "We often talk of the time when *righteousness is to overspread the earth*, but this millennium must overspread our own hearts, if we would see the face of God with joy." This millennium, she said, must begin with a personal Pentecost and with a personal entrance into the "spiritual Canaan [of perfect love], that *baptism of the Spirit*, to which every believer is expressly called."[30]

BISHOP ASBURY'S INDEBTEDNESS TO FLETCHER

Francis Asbury and Thomas Coke became the first Methodist Episcopal bishops in America; both were deeply indebted to Fletcher. Asbury was inspired by Fletcher's biography: "In reading Mr. Benson's excellent Life

---

27. Albert C. Outler, ed. *Sermons II*, The Bicentennial Edition of the Works of John Wesley (Nashville: Abingdon, 1985) 2:494–98, "The General Spread of the Gospel."

28. Ibid., 2:498–99, "The General Spread of the Gospel."

29 Cf. Wesley, *Works* (Jackson) 4:362, (journal entry, March 8, 10, and 12, 1787) where Wesley records on three separate occasions that they ministered together. Wesley noted in his journal entry for March 12: "In the evening we had a love feast, at which Mrs. Fletcher simply declared her present experience" and "her words were as fire conveying both light and heat to the hearts of all that heard her." Wesley also noted her effective "manner of speaking." On another occasion, Wesley advised Mary Fletcher to minister beyond Madeley and to travel to other places like London and Yorkshire, requesting that they should arrange their schedules to "be in those places at the same time." Wesley, *Works* (Jackson) 12:408–9 (letter to Mary Fletcher, Dec. 9, 1786).

30. *Life of Mary Fletcher*, 398.

of Fletcher, my soul was brought into God, deeply into love. This has sweetened the toils of between 4 and 5000 miles travelling."[31]

Asbury considered Fletcher to be Wesley's virtual equal as the source of Methodist belief.[32] For example, writing to Joseph Benson, Asbury referred to "our dear John the divine of London, and John the divine of Madeley."[33] He asked Wesley (after Fletcher's death) to provide him with copies of Fletcher's writings to help spread Methodism in America.[34] He gave away Fletcher's *Works* to help others understand Methodist doctrine and recommended Fletcher's writings for clarification of holiness.[35]

Responding to a Methodist critic, Asbury wrote in his *Journal*: "But Mr. Fletcher . . . has fully answered all his witty arguments" and instructed one of his bishops in Ohio to read Wesley and especially Fletcher.[36] In writing about Hervey's idea of imputed righteousness, Asbury stated: "But providence has brought forth that eminent man, Mr. John Fletcher, to manage this subject . . . ; his arguments are incontestable."[37] He recorded that he gave a copy of Fletcher's *Checks* to a minister of another denomination so that he could "view the whole plan of Methodism" and mentioned a critic who spoke "against Mr. Wesley and Mr. Fletcher."[38] Elsewhere in his journal, Asbury referred to a writer "against Mr. Wesley, Mr. Fletcher, Doctor Coke, and poor *me*."[39] Throughout the Methodist world, Fletcher was seen as an authorized interpreter of Wesley's theology.

In 1796, Asbury read Fletcher's *Portrait of St. Paul*[40] which explained his doctrine of dispensations and highlighted the baptism with the Holy Spirit as the agent of full sanctification. Asbury gave a copy of this to a

---

31. "Extract of a Letter from the Rev. Francis Asbury, to Mr. Zachary Myles, Baltimore," *The Methodist Magazine*, volume 10, a continuation of the *Arminian Magazine*, volume 36, London edition (July 1813) 557.

32. Asbury, *Journal*, 1:728.

33. Ibid., 3:546.

34. Ibid., 3:26 (September 3, 1780).

35. Ibid., 1:300.

36. Ibid., 3:414.

37. Ibid., 1:287.

38. Ibid., 1:300, 654.

39. Ibid., 1:746.

40. Ibid., 2:92.

Dutch Reformed Church minister who wanted to be informed about Methodism, noting: "I gave him a book of our discipline, and recommended to his attention the Portrait of St. Paul by John Fletcher." Asbury later exclaimed: "O that all ministers would read it, and labor to impress it upon their hearts, and show a likeness in their lives and labors."[41] This work became a textbook for all American Methodist ministers in the beginning of the nineteenth century.[42] It continued to be published and read throughout the nineteenth century.

BISHOP ASBURY AND HIS PREACHERS AFFIRMED PENTECOSTAL PERFECTION

One distinctive feature of Fletcher's writings was to make Wesley's developing views on perfection consistent. Fletcher was aware that his interpretation carried nuances that expanded Wesley's initial ideas; his specific contribution was to pentecostalize (to coin a word) Wesley's theology of perfection, which became a prominent theme in American Methodism.

On September 24, 1778, Asbury described his own religious experience of sanctification in these Pentecost terms: "My soul at present is filled with his Holy Spirit; I have a glorious prospect of a boundless ocean of love, and immense degrees of holiness opening to my view; and now renew my covenant with the Lord, that I may glorify him with my body and spirit, which are his . . . I am blessed with the sweet gales of God's love."[43] A preacher who received his license in 1793 wrote that he could experience and defend the doctrine of full sanctification because he had read Fletcher's treatise on *Christian Perfection*. Asbury responded that it was important to profess perfection: "I think we ought modestly to tell what we feel to the fullest. For two years past, amidst innumerable toils, I have enjoyed almost inexpressible sensations." Asbury then follows this personal profession with a report of the widespread revival of holiness: "Our *Pentecost* is come, in some places for sanctification."[44]

41. Ibid., 2:572 (June 12, 1808).

42. Tyerman, *Wesley's Designated Successor* (New York: Phillips & Hunt, 1883) 456.

43. Asbury, *Journal*, 1:281 (September 23, 1778). Sept. 24 is given as the date in the text.

44. Francis Asbury to Henry Smith, July 20, 1806, in *Recollections and Reflections of an Old Itinerant*. A series of letters originally published in the *Christian Advocate and*

Writing to Freeborn Garrettson, February 18, 1792, Asbury showed that being "baptized in God" means being freed from the "remains of sin."[45] Asbury learned this Pentecostal nomenclature from Fletcher and devotional literature inspired by Fletcher, such as the autobiography of Hester Ann Rogers that he had printed in New York in 1804 and that was reprinted numerous times throughout the nineteenth century.[46] Her personal testimony of being baptized with the Holy Spirit was attached to Coke's published funeral sermon: "Lord, make this the moment of my full salvation! Baptize me now with the Holy Ghost, and the fire of pure love. Now, cleanse the thoughts of my heart, let me perfectly love thee."[47] Abel Stevens referred to her testimony as "exemplary . . . of the Methodistic teachings respecting Christian Perfection."[48]

Henry Boehm was Asbury's traveling companion and assistant. He heard Asbury preach more than fifteen hundred times and reported that Fletcher was "a great favorite" among these early Methodists, including the United Brethren.[49] He referred to Fletcher as the pattern of holiness for the Methodists.[50] Boehm also used Pentecostal nomenclature.[51] He reported that Bishop Asbury referred to camp meetings as "our harvest seasons."[52] In a camp meeting in the Dover Circuit in Pennsylvania, he recorded in his diary for July 1806 that Governor Bassett of Pennsylvania testified to being sanctified. He "was full of faith and the Holy Ghost. He

---

Journal and the *Western Christian Advocate,* by Henry Smith and George Peck (New York: Lane & Tippett, 1848) 7, 30, 52, 112–25.

45. Ibid., 3:111.

46. Ibid., 3:304; *National Union Catalogue,* 501:180–83.

47. *Life and Correspondence of Mrs. Hester Ann Rogers* (Nashville: Publishing House of the Methodist Episcopal Church, South, 1870) 300.

48. Stevens, *The History of the Religious Movement of the Eighteenth Century Called Methodism,* 3:101.

49. Henry Boehm, *Reminiscences, Historical and Biographical* (New York: Carlton & Porter, 1866) 440, 383. Henry Boehm was the son of Martin Boehm, who with Philip William Otterbein were the first bishops of the United Brethren in Christ, elected in 1800. A. W. Drury, *History of the Church of the United Brethren in Christ* (Dayton, Ohio: Otterbein, 1924) 185. Steven O'Malley has informed me that Fletcher was also influential among the Evangelicals. See Raymond Albright, *A History of the Evangelical Church* (Harrisburg, PA: Evangelical, 1942) 209.

50. Ibid., 143.

51. Ibid., 108, 131, 136, 151.

52. Boehm, *Reminiscences, Historical and Biographical,* 147.

obtained a wonderful baptism [of the Holy Spirit], and gave his testimony before listening thousands."[53]

John Bangs, ordained by Bishop Asbury in 1815,[54] reported that an "itinerating minister" explained to him in 1804 that "it was my privilege not only to be justified by faith, but to have a clean heart, which blessing God gave me by the baptism of the Holy Ghost . . . I have held on my way, and grown stronger and stronger, and now enjoy the blessing of perfect love."[55]

In 1804, Nathan Bangs was elected by the General Conference as the Methodist "book agent," becoming the first editor of the *Methodist Magazine* in America. He authored the first official history of American Methodism in 1838 which recorded the conversion, full sanctification, and call to preach of many of the early Methodist preachers. One was Joseph Everett who was converted under Asbury's preaching, "and by consulting the able and luminous writings of Wesley and Fletcher he was led to a new view of the plan of redemption and the way of salvation by faith in Christ."[56] Another early Methodist preacher was John Wilson, who after a time of spiritual mediocrity "in 1795 . . . received a new baptism of the Holy Spirit, and was led on step by step, from a class leader to a local preacher, until in 1797 he entered the traveling ministry."[57] He particularly promoted the doctrine of holiness of heart and life.[58] Bangs' history of early Methodism reveals that holiness was a theme of great importance of early Methodist preaching in 1799 and that it was explicitly connected with the phrase "the baptism with the Holy Spirit."[59]

Bangs reported on a great holiness revival that swept through Maryland, Delaware, Pennsylvania, Vermont, Connecticut, and New Hampshire, noting "that most of the preachers had received a new baptism of the Holy Spirit—like that which had been showered upon Calvin Wooster, and others in Canada, the preceding year [1799]; and wherever they went they carried the holy fire with them, and God wrought

53. Ibid., 151.

54. John Bangs, *Auto-Biography of John Bangs* (New York, 1846) 37, 43. John Bangs was the younger brother of Nathan Bangs.

55. Ibid., 19.

56. Bangs, *A History of the Methodist Episcopal Church*, 2:286.

57. Ibid., 2:288.

58. Ibid., 2:288–89.

59. Ibid., 2:75.

wonders by their instrumentality."[60] Bangs himself frequently used the phrase "baptism with the Holy Ghost" for entire sanctification, as seen in a series of letters which he wrote to a friend.[61]

THE PREVALENCE OF THE FLETCHERS' PENTECOSTAL NOMENCLATURE IN EARLY AMERICAN METHODISM

The early Methodist preachers who profoundly influenced American Methodism, such as Thomas Coke, Adam Clarke, Nathan Bangs, and Richard Watson, specifically linked the "baptism with the Spirit" and entire sanctification.[62] The early Methodist devotional literature used in America highlighted "the baptism with the Holy Spirit" as the meaning of entire sanctification, including Henry Moore's biography of Mary Fletcher (1817) and Adam Clarke's biography of Mary Cooper (1814), along with the diaries of Hester Ann Rogers.

The writings of preachers who used explicitly this Pentecostal terminology show how pervasive Fletcher's influence was in early American Methodism. Joseph Pilmore and Richard Boardman were Wesley's first two preachers for America, leaving England on August 21, 1769.[63] The Pentecostal motif is found in Pilmore's journal, as he preached sermons on the text, "And they were baptized with the Holy Ghost and fire."[64] On June 3, 1770, he wrote: "In the evening, I declared to a very large and attentive audience, 'He shall Baptize you with the Holy Ghost and with fire' (Matt 3:11) and had good reason to believe God fulfilled the promis[e] to many of the hearers by the comforts of his heavenly love." [65] Frank Bateman Stanger, the late president of Asbury Theological Seminary,

---

60. Ibid., 2:101.

61. Nathan Bangs, *The Necessity, Nature, and Fruits, of Sanctification: In a Series of Letters to a Friend* (New York: Phillips & Hunt, 1851) 135.

62. See Laurence W. Wood, *The Meaning of Pentecost in Early Methodism* (Lanham, MD: Scarecrow, 2002) chaps. 12–13.

63. John Wesley, *The Methodist Societies: History, Nature, and Design*, ed. Rupert E. Davies, The Bicentennial Edition of *The Works of John Wesley* (Nashville: Abingdon, 1989) 9:490–91, "Short History of People Called Methodists."

64. *The Journal of Joseph Pilmore, Methodist Itinerant, for the Years August 1, 1769, to January 2, 1774* (Philadelphia: Message, 1969) 46, 81, 156.

65. Ibid., 46. The phrase "the comforts of his heavenly love" was commonly used in early Methodism for Christian perfection—the essence of which is "heavenly love."

commented: "Pilmore gave his personal endorsement to this Wesleyan doctrine of Christian perfection. Frequently, he preached upon themes relating to the soul's experience of receiving the baptism of the Holy Spirit and the purity of heart and the holiness of life which resulted."[66] Pilmore was a friend of Fletcher, and they visited together[67] (most likely between 1768 and 1769) just prior to the open conflict with the Calvinist Methodists at Trefeca College over the meaning of the baptism with the Spirit and perfection. This would have been a likely talking point with them. Fletcher and Pilmore also at least once preached on the same day at Wesley's annual conference.[68]

Hannah Syng Bunting valued the spiritual help that Pilmore gave to her family. In 1822 she sought for "sanctifying grace" after reading Fletcher's *Essay on Truth*.[69] She specifically defined entire sanctification as being "filled with the Spirit" and being "more deeply baptized into the spirit of Christ." On January 1, 1826, she received "perfect peace that passeth understanding." She wrote of her need for a renewal of sanctifying grace as a "fuller baptism of the Holy Spirit."

She not only knew Joseph Pilmore, but also heard Wilbur Fisk preach.[70] He professed full sanctification after hearing Timothy Merritt preach on the baptism with the Spirit.[71] The network of Pilmore, Miss Bunting, Fisk, and Merritt shows the influence of Fletcher's writings in early American Methodism. Another indication is found in the *Memoirs of Mrs. Mary Cooper*, edited and published by Adam Clarke in 1814 and reprinted in New York in 1832, which illustrate how a new convert to Methodism was introduced to Pentecostal perfection. In 1809, she heard Clarke and Coke preach, and soon afterwards she heard Henry Moore and Joseph Benson. The Methodist doctrine of holiness especially caught her attention. During the sacrament of the Lord's Supper, she prayed for "the gift of the Holy Spirit" for "entire sanctification." On December 29,

66. Frank Bateman Stanger, "The Life and Ministry of the Rev. Joseph Pilmore," PhD diss., Temple University, 1942, 273–74.

67. Benson, *Life of John W. de la Flechere*, 170. See Frank Stanger, "Biographical Sketch of Joseph Pilmore," in *The Journal of Joseph Pilmore*, 236.

68. Cf. Tyerman, *Wesley's Designated Successor*, 543.

69. *Memoir, Diary, and Letters of Miss Hannah Syng Bunting of Philadelphia*, compiled by Timothy Merritt (New York: Mason & Lane, 1833) 1:50–51.

70. Ibid., 1:50–51, 63, 93, 84, 180, 106, 163.

71. Joseph Holdich, *The Life of Wilbur Fisk* (New York: Harper, 1842) 72.

1809, she came to a point of accepting "the indwelling of the Spirit." The pursuit of the Spirit's "indwelling" and "baptism" became central concerns of her spiritual life. On January 24, 1810, she wrote: "I wish more powerfully to feel the necessity of constantly seeking the influence of the Holy Spirit, to renovate my nature, to baptize me afresh . . . If He has been, and is manifested to my soul, sin will be destroyed." Shortly before her death, Mary Cooper wrote this prayer in her diary on March 11, 1812: "O Lord, I will renew my dedication to Thy service. Baptize me afresh with Thy Holy Spirit, and sanctify *bodily affliction*. O may it be the *one* desire of my soul, to gain more and more of the Divine image, and to be increasing in holiness and meetness for the eternal world!"[72]

The widespread influence of Fletcher's Pentecostal theology is revealed in American issues of *The Methodist Magazine*. Mrs. Elizabeth Keagey of Pennsylvania in 1811 was "filled with the Spirit and . . . made perfect in love" as a result of becoming a Methodist and hearing her minister preach on this theme.[73] The *Magazine* in 1822 reported that Miss Eliza Higgins was "perfected in love," through "the blessed Comforter [who will] descend, that sweet messenger of rest, and make his continual abode in your heart."[74] A sermon on Christian perfection in the same issue quoted John Fletcher and identified the giving of the Holy Spirit on the day of Pentecost with entire sanctification.[75]

The Methodist Magazine and Quarterly Review (1831) included an extensive review of Fletcher's *Portrait of St. Paul*: "After the Holy Scriptures, and, in subordination to these, the works of Mr. John Wesley, the writings of John Fletcher are held next in estimation, we believe, by the whole body of Wesleyan Methodists throughout the world."[76] The *Portrait* represented Fletcher's most mature thoughts and highlighted the baptism with the Holy Spirit, which was noted in the review.[77]

---

72. *Memoirs of Mrs. Mary Cooper who departed this life, June 22, 1812, in the twenty-sixth year of her age, extracted from her diary and epistolary correspondence*, by Adam Clark (New York: Waugh & Mason, 1832) 52ff., 93, 97, 105, 115, 223.

73. *The Methodist Magazine* 6 (New York edition, 1823) 258.

74. "Memoir of Miss Eliza Higgins," *The Methodist Magazine* 5 (New York edition, July, 1822) 259.

75. R. Treffry, "A Sermon on Christian Perfection," *The Methodist Magazine* 5 (New York edition, March–April, 1822) 124–26.

76. *The Methodist Magazine and Quarterly Review* 13 (January 1831) 104.

77. Ibid., 110–11.

In 1832, *Twenty-Eight Sermons on Doctrinal and Practical Subjects* was published "contributed by different ministers of the Methodist Episcopal Church" including such Methodist authors as Wilbur Fisk, Nathan Bangs, and Richard Watson. One sermon, "The Nature and Importance of Growing in Grace," by Aaron Lummus, affirmed that "on the day of Pentecost, the disciples . . . were *all filled with the Holy Ghost,* Acts ii.4. They were therefore emptied of sin, were wholly sanctified."[78]

The British *Wesleyan Methodist Magazine* in 1837 reported on a holiness revival in New York. It specifically linked "the baptism with the Spirit" with holiness.[79] In 1842, George Peck, author of *The Scripture Doctrine of Christian Perfection* and the American editor of *The Methodist Magazine,* quoted extensively from Fletcher to show that Christian perfection means "the pure love of God, shed abroad in the hearts of established believers by the Holy Ghost, which is abundantly given them under the fulness of the Christian dispensation."[80] Peck encouraged believers to seek their own personalized Pentecost: "For this baptism of the Spirit we must pray in secret." In *The Methodist Quarterly Review* (1841), the editor reviewed Wesley's *A Plain Account of Christian Perfection* to remind Methodists of his teaching, followed by an emphasis on John Fletcher's writings, calling attention to Fletcher's emphasis on the Holy Spirit. "But [Christian perfection] is especially indicated [in Fletcher's writings] as the work of the Holy Spirit by being denominated the *baptism of the Holy Ghost, sanctification of the Spirit.*[81]

Further excerpts from the American Methodist Magazine show the influence of John and Mary Fletcher whose idea of Pentecostal perfection was widely embraced in early American Methodism. In the first issue of *The Methodist Magazine* in America (1818), the "Memoir of Miss Millward," reported that she "was very conversant with the writings of the Rev. Mr. Wesley and Mr. Fletcher, and highly esteemed them." Her dying words were: "I shall see Mr. Wesley, Mr. Fletcher, St. Paul,

---

78. *Twenty Eight Sermons on Doctrinal and Practical Subjects,* contributed by different ministers of the Methodist Episcopal Church (Boston: Strong, 1832) 317.

79. "Revival of Religion in New York," *The Wesleyan Methodist Magazine* 16 (May 1837) 371–72.

80. George Peck, *The Scripture Doctrine of Christian Perfection* (New York: Carlton & Porter, 1842) 49.

81. Ibid., 149–50, 151.

Abraham, Isaac, and Jacob, and all the Prophets, and Martyrs."[82] In the same issue appeared "A Short Account of a Camp-Meeting Held at Cow-Harbour; Long Island," when "some of the preachers were baptized afresh with the Holy Ghost and fire; and their cup run over with love to God."[83] "This doctrine" of Christian perfection "was never greater than at the present time," and "the incomparable writings of Messrs. Wesley and Fletcher" were credited with this success. The article further reported that "this doctrine every Methodist minister professes to believe."[84] In the 1821 issue appeared the "Memoir of Mr. Stephen Butler" who came to see the "necessity of perfect holiness" through reading Fletcher's Last Check. "He continued to seek earnestly for the full renewal of his soul in righteousness, and rested not until, by faith in the purifying blood, and receiving a larger measure of the Spirit of Christ, he laid hold on the promise of a full deliverance from all sin."[85] In 1822 the "Memoir of the Late Mr. R. Bealey" was printed whose life was an "example" and who subsequently "received his deeper 'baptism of the Spirit.'"[86] In 1826, a reference is made to one who "received a fresh baptism of the Holy Spirit" and became a local preacher.[87] In 1827 a report of "a glorious revival of religion" was given where "many aged members . . . of the society are receiving a deeper baptism of the Holy Ghost, and power to believe to the entire sanctification of their souls."[88]

In 1823, *The Methodist Magazine* urged its readers: "Read Fletcher then, but don't forget Wesley . . . On the doctrine of Repentance, Justification, and Sanctification, you can find no authors who have illustrated those subjects with greater clearness and accuracy, than Wesley

82. "Memoir of Miss Millward," *The Methodist Magazine* 1 (New York edition, March 1818) 65–66.

83. "A Short Account of a camp-meeting held at Cow-Harbour, Long Island, which commenced August 11, 1818," *The Methodist Magazine* 1 (New York edition, September 1818) 358.

84. "The Perfecting of the Saints, the Grand Object of the Gospel Ministry," *The Methodist Magazine* 6 (New York edition, September 1819) 344.

85. "Memoir of Mr. Stephen Butler," *The Methodist Magazine* 4 (New York edition, May 1821) 169.

86. "Memoir of the Late Mr. R. Bealey," *The Methodist Magazine* 5 (New York edition, October, 1822) 371.

87. "Memoir of Mr. John Kidger," *The Methodist Magazine* 9:6 (New York edition, June 1826) 211.

88. "Religious and Missionary Intelligence," *The Methodist Magazine* 10:4 (New York edition, April 1827) 183.

and Fletcher."[89] In 1827 it noted "that all Methodist preachers ought to be well read in the writings of Messrs. Wesley and Fletcher" and in 1830: "But let them take our phrase, 'Christian perfection,' with the explanation given of it by Wesley and Fletcher."[90] *The Methodist Magazine and Quarterly Review* in 1833 carried an extensive review of Fletcher's Works, including references to the baptism with the Spirit.[91]

CONCLUSION

John Fletcher's writings functioned as a doctrinal standard of early American Methodism. Along with Wesley, he was listed as a normative source of Methodist doctrine in the first book of discipline of the Methodist Episcopal Church in 1784. As stated by the editor of the Methodist Magazine and Quarterly Review in 1832, Methodism was guided "first and principally of the Bible, and next after it of the standard works of Methodism—those of Wesley and Fletcher in particular."[92] Mary Fletcher's biography and diaries produced by Henry Moore were widely read and were a major source of devotional inspiration. From the very beginning, American Methodism embraced John Fletcher's theology of Pentecostal perfection and was inspired by the numerous reprints of Mary Fletcher's diaries to expect a personal Pentecost. Others who were influenced to embrace Pentecostal perfection by the Fletchers were Hester Ann Rogers and Mary Cooper, whose diaries were imprinted deeply into the minds of American Methodists.

89. "Importance of Study for a Minister of the Gospel," *The Methodist Magazine* 6 (New York edition, January 1823) 33.

90. "Pastoral Duties: A Charge," *The Methodist Magazine* 10:11 (New York edition, September 1827) 378. "A Farther Review of the Christian Spectator's Strictures on Doctor Adam Clarke's Discourses," *The Methodist Magazine and Quarterly Review* 12, n.s. 1:4 (October 1830) 450.

91. *The Methodist Magazine and Quarterly Review* 15:4, n.s. 4:4 (October 1833) 406–50.

92. John Emory, A review of "Wesley's *Works*," *The Methodist Magazine and Quarterly Review* 14.2, new series 3.2 (April 1832) 130.

13

The Long Fletcher Incumbency

A Personal View of the Context and Continuity[1]

Peter S. Forsaith

IT HAS BEEN JUST thirty years since I submitted my original dissertation on John Fletcher.[2] At that time I may have been the only person working biographically on him: certainly it seemed so. Barrie Trinder had already highlighted Fletcher's local context in the emerging "Industrial Revolution" in east Shropshire[3]—and had used Fletcher's surviving correspondence. There were those who were interested in him theologically.[4] Away in Switzerland a promising young scholar named Patrick Streiff was thinking about his doctoral subject.[5] No one

1. I want to acknowledge my gratitude to Dr. John Walsh for his inspiration and support especially in the preparation of this paper.

2. Peter S. Forsaith, *The Eagle and the Dove, John Fletcher: Vicar of Madeley: towards a new assessment,* final year diss., Wesley College, Bristol, 1979.

3. Barrie Trinder, *The Industrial Revolution in Shropshire,* 3rd ed. (Chichester: Phillimore, [1973], 2000).

4. Such as Timothy L. Smith, "How John Fletcher became the Theologian of Wesleyan Perfectionism 1770–1776," *Wesleyan Theological Journal* 15 (1980) 68–87.

5. Patrick Streiff, *Jean Guillaume de la Fléchère, John William Fletcher, 1729-1785; Ein Beitrag zur Geschichte des Methodismus* (Frankfurt: Lang, 1984); *Reluctant Saint? A Theological Biography of Fletcher of Madeley* (Peterborough: Epworth, 2001).

had given much thought to Mary Fletcher or her circle. A meeting at the Nazarene Theological College, Manchester, in 2006, hosted by Dr. Herbert McGonigle, demonstrated the breadth of studies emerging and provided the original impetus and base for the "Religion, Gender, Industry" conference.[6]

I think it would then have been beyond my dreams that one day such a conference might have taken place. My dissertation was subtitled "Towards a new assessment," and over the years Fletcher has been—and continues to be—reassessed in the light of emerging evidence about him, about his personal background, religious, educational, and social influences, evangelical networks, and parochial engagement. I hope I have played some part in that. What I could hardly have foreseen then was just how much interest Mary Fletcher and the people and issues around Madeley parish would start to generate among historians. Gareth Lloyd's patient cataloguing of the Fletcher-Tooth papers has played a considerable part in this growth of scholarship.[7] In 1979, many mainstream historians paid scant attention to eighteenth-century religion—unless to marginalize it. This too has changed.[8]

My purpose, however, is more prospective than retrospective. The conference has been evidence of the fruits of much time and many avenues of research. I want to concentrate on proposing that John Fletcher specifically, although in the wider context of place and people, can be seen as a kind of case study, or cameo, of some critical themes and concerns of historians who focus on English church life in the extended eighteenth century. To put it another way, I have a sense that many of the ley-lines of historical enquiry around religion in Georgian and early Victorian Britain run through Madeley and the Fletchers.

Such a suggestion reflects a wider historical attitude to the locale. Klingender, in *Art and the Industrial Revolution*, noted that "Coalbrookdale . . . became, as it were, the test place for studying the new

6. Neither Dr. Herbert McGonigle nor Bishop Patrick Streiff were able to be present at the conference.

7. In the Methodist Archive and Research Centre, John Rylands University Library of Manchester (MARC).

8. E.g., John Walsh et al., eds., *The Church of England c. 1689–c. 1833* (Cambridge: Cambridge University Press, 1993); J. C. D. Clark, *English Society, 1660–1832: Religion, Ideology and Politics during the Ancient Régime*, 2nd ed. (Cambridge: Cambridge University Press, 2000).

relationship between men and nature created by large-scale industry."[9] I shall start to explore my proposition by illustrating it with biographical examples from John Fletcher. Later I will address the question of Fletcher's biographers but would observe that they have not always found it easy to deal with their subject chronologically. I say that with at least an element of personal experience. More than with most individuals, I suspect, a thematic approach presents itself more readily, perhaps because aspects of Fletcher's life do not always seem readily connected. But let us at least start at the beginning.

Patrick Streiff's research uncovered some significant elements of Fletcher's early years—as any childhood, a time which was enormously influential but which, partly through Fletcher's own reticence, and partly because Switzerland was geographically and culturally distant for British authors, had hitherto eluded biographers. Streiff was able to identify details of the de la Fléchère family and Jean's educational background, including his taking just one year of a general course at Geneva University, rather than (as had generally been presumed) theological studies before dropping out to join the military. He apparently never gained his degree.[10]

In addressing the religious and political situation in Switzerland, Streiff made a significant connection between Fletcher and his maternal uncle, Theodore Crinsoz "de Bionens," a dissident minister. This is not wholly straightforward in that no direct interchange can be traced. Yet de Bionens' residence in Nyon, Fletcher's hometown, from 1732 (when Fletcher was three), his religious interests such as millenarianism, his theological writings and works of charity, including schooling for poor children, so corresponded with Fletcher's they are too close to be ignored.

However, early influences went beyond the personal and avuncular. Streiff analyzed the politico-religious tensions in Switzerland, between the hard-line orthodoxy of Bern and the Pays de Vaud, or Waadtland (which includes Nyon) and the progressive rational thinking gaining ground in nearby Geneva—to which school and university Fletcher's parents sent him. The interface between these European currents can be understood as shaping much of Fletcher's later attitudes and theological writings.

---

9. F. D. Klingender, *Art and the Industrial Revolution* (London: Paladin, 1972).

10. Streiff, *Reluctant Saint*, 3–17.

As well as the intellectual setting, Streiff identified personal paradoxes: perhaps the first biographical study to challenge the habitual hagiographic obeisance. Alongside Fletcher's "driving Methodism," his perennial concern for divine approbation, sits also a resigned passivity of "still mysticism," about which John Wesley was critical of both his own brother and Fletcher.[11] Streiff also examined Fletcher's relationship to Methodism—a broader "Methodism" than Wesley's "connexion"—and identified tensions between Fletcher and John Wesley, again something of a first. He particularly noted Wesley's failure to understand and accept Fletcher's vocation to Madeley and Fletcher's rejection of Wesley's request to be named his "designated successor." But we are jumping ahead of ourselves.

Professor Reginald Ward has explored links between continental, British, and American evangelical movements, giving much of his attention to Germanic roots in Pietism.[12] Fletcher's Swiss origins can help to extend that discussion to other European aspects, towards France and Switzerland, and identifying the strands of religious life and thought which spread in the late seventeenth and eighteenth centuries. Just as Streiff has filled in early detail about Fletcher's childhood and youth, my own work has looked at his first years in England, specifically his links with émigré francophone communities in London.[13]

He crossed the Channel armed with a letter of introduction to a French minister in London, Jean des Champs, who seems to have shaped Fletcher's early years in England. It was among broadly Huguenot groups in London that Fletcher socialized, learned English, studied "divinity," secured employment, and developed his religious life. I now date his arrival in London to 1749,[14] possibly 1750, earlier than previously thought,

11. John Wesley to Miss Sarah Wesley, Sept. 26, 1788, in John Telford, ed., *The Letters of John Wesley* (London: Epworth, 1931) 8:93.

12. See W. R. Ward, *The Protestant Evangelical Awakening* (Cambridge: Cambridge University Press, 1992).

13. See Forsaith, "The Correspondence of the Revd. John Fletcher," unpubl. PhD thesis, Oxford Brookes University, 2003, 297–311; and "A dearer country: the Frenchness of the Rev Jean de la Fléchère of Madeley, a Methodist Church of England Vicar," in Randolph Vigne and Charles Littleton, eds., *From Strangers to Citizens: The Integration of Immigrant Communities in Britain, Ireland and Colonial America, 1550–1750* (London: The Huguenot Society of Great Britain and Ireland/Brighton: Sussex Academic Press, 2001) 519–526.

14. See Peter S. Forsaith, *"Unexampled Labours": Letters of the Revd John Fletcher to leaders in the Evangelical Revival* (Peterborough: Epworth, 2008) 11 and 300 n. 184.

and his involvement with Wesley's Methodists to later—probably from 1753.[15] Through the 1750s Fletcher lived the elite life of a gentleman-tutor in the wealthy, landed, political Hill family.[16] Winters were spent in town, at the Hills' London home in Cleveland Court, St. James, and summers at Tern Hall, Shropshire, with its spacious grounds. While in some ways the lifestyle offended his sensitivities, he was not entirely uncomfortable in it. Barbara Coulton has contributed valuable research about Fletcher's life with the Hill family.[17]

The Huguenot influence, I have posited, goes further than is immediately obvious. While it undoubtedly shaped his socialization, it possibly also impacted upon his doctrinal understandings and ecclesiology. In August 1775 Fletcher wrote to John Wesley outlining a suggested scheme for a "Methodist Church of England."[18] What became of the letter, if it was ever sent, is unknown. It was intended for Wesley's conference about to meet in Leeds, but there is nothing of it in the Minutes or Wesley's papers. But where did Fletcher get such ideas? My suggestion is that he derived these from the Huguenots who had secured accommodation as a distinct ecclesial body under the jurisdiction of the Bishop of London. A question which has received little attention is the relationship between Huguenots and early Methodism: did the one step into the shoes of the other? What about those of Huguenot background who were caught up with Methodism—among them James Rouquet, William Lefevre, John Valton, and, of course, Mary Bosanquet.[19] The Perronets, like Fletcher, were Swiss rather than Huguenot, but from similar roots.

To summarize, Fletcher can represent a pan-European influence in English religious life. There is also a hint that Methodism did touch

---

15. Streiff, *Reluctant Saint*, 32.

16. See Sir Lewis Namier, *The Structure of Politics at the Accession of George III* (London: Macmillan, 1957) for connections between Shropshire Whigs and evangelicals.

17. Barbara Coulton, "Tutor to the Hills: The Early Career of John Fletcher," *Proceedings of the Wesley Historical Society* XLVII/3 (1989) 94–103; also, Coulton *A Shropshire Squire: Noel Hill, first Lord Berwick 1745-1789* (Shrewsbury: Swan Hill, 1989) and "Tern Hall and the Hill Family 1700–75," *Transactions of the Shropshire Archaeological Society* LXVI (1989) 97–105.

18. John Fletcher to John Wesley, August 1, 1775, in Forsaith, *Unexampled Labours*, 324–30.

19. See G. E. Milburn, "Early Methodism and the Huguenots," *Proceedings of the Wesley Historical Society* xlv/3 (Dec. 1985) 69–79.

some elite sectors of society. In London in the late 1750s, Fletcher was closely involved with Lady Huntingdon's evangelical and aristocratic circle.[20] So perhaps where Fletcher himself most personifies an issue is at the blurred and jagged edges of what constituted "Methodist" or "Evangelical." How did those issues relate to the "Old Ship," the national Church of England, boundaries which are further complicated by the leading personalities involved, in particular the Wesleys and George Whitefield who sat more loosely to ecclesiastical structures and canon law? As papers to this conference indicated, this is a disparate area where definitions and distinctions are considerably debatable.

It was into the national Church that Fletcher was ordained deacon and priest in March 1757, though lacking either degree or naturalization, which might be taken as indicating either the laxity or flexibility of the Georgian church.[21] Whether it was Mr. Hill's encouragement or the Wesleys' remains unclear: however, for his title he became curate of a Hill family living, Madeley parish. Here he was briefly permitted to preach, an experience which fired a consuming and enduring vocation. Victorian denominational historians—Luke Tyerman in particular—saw Madeley parish as a quiet rural benefice where Fletcher "had abundance of leisure for reading and study" which he would have lacked in a Methodist itinerancy.[22] How far from reality! Madeley parish was possibly one of the most demanding in the kingdom: neither the largest nor the most populous, but with a burgeoning inward migration, the social problems of early industrialism and concomitant theological and ethical issues posed by the new industries. It was against these challenges that Fletcher hammered out his pastoral practice and doctrinal frameworks: checks, for instance, are a mechanical device to restrict lateral movement, not an absolute stop.

The conduct of everyday parish life in the eighteenth-century English church remains a matter for continuing investigation. Hard evidence of what passed from day to day and parish to parish is not

20. "We boast some rich ones whom the Gospel sways / And one who wears a coronet and prays . . ." (William Cowper: "Truth").

21. See William R. Davies, "John Fletcher's Georgian Ordinations and Madeley Curacy," *Proceedings of the Wesley Historical Society* xxxvi/3 (1968) 139–42.

22. Luke Tyerman, *Wesley's Designated Successor* (London: Hodder and Stoughton, 1882) 57.

always readily recoverable, although William Jacob[23] has latterly explored something of this. Fletcher's practice can be reconstructed with harder evidence than some: a pattern of systematic house-to-house (and also workplace) visitation was modeled on Berridge and Baxter.[24] This became supplemented by locally based classes which in turn fed into the life and liturgy of the parish church, although Fletcher found himself in probable breach of the Conventicle Act in this approach to church extension.[25] This pattern was, of course, inherited, perpetuated, and developed by Mary Fletcher and her associates. Here, Fletcher and Madeley can provide useful insights into the wider picture.

I have recently suggested that Fletcher's dogmatic position was not simply the result of wide reading and abstract theologizing but was significantly influenced by his parochial experience.[26] This may be seen in two particular aspects. First, that Fletcher's emphasis on moral aspects of Christianity—the working out of faith—was weighted particularly through his recognition of the social issues around early industrialism in the parish. This is evident in his 1772 *Appeal to Matter of Fact and Common Sense* in which his vivid descriptions of the dangerous conditions in the pits and ironworks, although dramatized, give some of the best accounts of the reality of early industrial life—and death.

> To go no farther than this populous parish: with what hardships and dangers do our indigent neighbours earn their bread! See those who ransack the bowels of the earth to get the black mineral we burn . . . In these low and dreary vaults, all the elements seem combined against them. Destructive damps, and clouds of noxious dust, infect the air they breathe. Sometimes water incessantly distils on their naked bodies; or, bursting upon them in streams, drowns them, and deluges their work. At other times, pieces of detached rocks crush them to death, or the earth breaking in upon them buries them alive. And frequently sulphureous vapours, kindled in an instant by the light of their candles,

23. W. M. Jacob, *The Clerical Profession in the Long Eighteenth Century 1680–1840* (Oxford: Oxford University Press, 2007) 144–70, 203–35.

24. See D. Bruce Hindmarsh, *John Newton and the English Evangelical Tradition* (Grand Rapids: Eerdmans, 2001) 203.

25. The Conventicle Acts (from 1664) forbade meetings in private houses of more than five people for worship, other than that prescribed in the Book of Common Prayer. These were variously interpreted and enforced.

26. Peter Forsaith, "A Dreadful Phenomenon at the Birches," unpublished paper presented to the Ecclesiastical History Society conference, Galway, July 2008.

form subterranean thunder and lightning. What a dreadful phenomenon![27]

This extrapolates moral lessons and was aimed at "the principal inhabitants" of his parish rather than "the inferior class" of his parishioners, since they "do not choose to partake with them of my evening instructions."[28]

In the second place, his proto-romantic view of the created order also came from local influences, seen in his 1773 published sermon *A Dreadful Phenomenon at the Birches*[29] following a landslip on the northern boundary of the parish.

> Some fields and a road and a grove have been workd up by a mighty slip or earthquake, which blockd up the turnpike road & Severn then very full make the water fly back the wonder of Jordan has been repeated: fields have walked rocks have been rent, a valey sank raised into a little hill, and fields sunk into valeys the great river sunk 2 yards downward till it work'd another chanel by carrying off some rich meadowland. I suppose you will see an account of it, in the papers. The earthquake just graz'd my parish, and demolish'd the bridge that parts it from the next. No lives are lost.[30]

Here he spoke of the world God had made, its beauty and wonder, but how humanity had defiled it. With his later poem *Grace et Nature*,[31] some roots of evangelical romanticism can be identified.

To return to the earlier question of the breadth of the "evangelical revival" (for want of a better term), two letters show something of Fletcher's position as broader than Mr. Wesley's "connexion." Over recent years, one can detect the drawing of some battle lines around the personality and achievements of John Wesley. Was he, on the one hand, a flawed personality who drove an energetic and unscrupulous empire-building project, or was he, on the other hand, a great man of God to be ranked with the Reformers, whose unstinting commitment to his mission

27. John Fletcher, *An Appeal to Matter of Fact and Common Sense*, 21st ed. (London: Wesleyan Conference Office, [1772] n.d.) 36–37.

28. Fletcher, *Appeal*, 2.

29. J. Fletcher, *A Dreadful Phenomenon Described and Improved* (Shrewsbury: Eddowes, 1773).

30. John Fletcher to John or Charles Wesley, May 30, 1773 (the addressee is unclear), in Forsaith, *Unexampled Labours*, 308.

31. John Fletcher, *La Grace et la Nature, Poème*, 2nd ed. (Londre: R. Hindmarsh, 1785).

founded a global denomination? Mr. Wesley's elusiveness continues to offer material for scholars to debate. Was he new enlightened man or old religious fanatic? Or something of both—a "Reasonable Enthusiast"?[32] I sense that as revisionist accounts of Wesley's contemporaries or aspects of Methodism's history continue to emerge this will become more of an issue. Curiously, David Hempton, in his seminal *Methodism: Empire of the Spirit*, while he ponders and analyzes the emergence of Methodism from the flotsam and jetsam of the 1730s to a significant global denomination in 150 years,[33] hardly challenges the centrality or dominance of John Wesley.

Yet recent treatments of other evangelicals, such as Gareth Lloyd's study of Charles Wesley,[34] cast John in a poor light. Both his personal conduct (especially towards his brother) and public integrity are called into question. Recent biographers of Lady Huntingdon raise similar concerns.[35] My own position has long been to challenge John Wesley's claims to his being Fletcher's intimate companion and colleague as well as representing Fletcher as his loyal acolyte.[36] While I do not retreat from that position, I do think that the Wesley-Fletcher relationship might be more nuanced in ongoing discussions of Wesley-centrism.

In the first place, the tensions between them were focused on Fletcher's parochial ministry: hiding his light under a bushel, according to Wesley, while Fletcher talked of the snail in its shell. John Wesley opposed Fletcher going to Madeley; Fletcher's reply to Wesley's (now lost) letter is one of the most strongly worded Fletcher wrote. Why this letter, in the Methodist Archive and History Center at Drew University, has not surfaced in scholarly work hitherto is uncertain.

---

32. See Richard P. Heitzenrater, *The Elusive Mr. Wesley*, 2 vols. (Nashville: Abingdon, 1984); Henry D. Rack, *Reasonable Enthusiast: John Wesley and the Rise of Methodism* (London: Epworth, 1989); and see also Kenneth G. C. Newport and Ted Campbell, eds., *Charles Wesley: Life, Literature and Legacy* (Peterborough: Epworth, 2007).

33. David Hempton, *Methodism: Empire of the Spirit* (New Haven: Yale University Press, 2005) 3.

34. Gareth Lloyd, *Charles Wesley and the Struggle for Methodist Identity* (Oxford: Oxford University Press, 2007).

35. Edwin Welch, *Spiritual Pilgrim: A Reassessment of the Life of the Countess of Huntingdon* (Cardiff: University of Wales Press, 1995); Boyd Schlenther, *Queen of the Methodists* (Bishop Auckland: Durham Academic Press, 1997).

36. Peter S. Forsaith, "Wesley's Designated Successor," *Proceedings of the Wesley Historical Society* xlvii/3 (Dec. 1979) 69–74.

Tern Octr. the 27th. 1760

Revd. & dear Sir

. . . You have taught me after Xt. that who soever loveth Father, Brother, &C, more that Xt. is not worthy of him,[37] I may then consistently with the sincere love & respect I bear to you follow the divine will in a manner that seems to cross that love & respect. You bid me "see the Snare of the Devil"[38] I can not see it, what appears to you a snare seems to me a door providentialy open'd . . .

[he continued]

And as to "prefering things temporal to things eternal"[39] I am so far from doing it, in accepting the Church of Madeley, that if I was inclined to make godliness a gain, I could easier save 20 out of the 40£ you have offerd me,[40] than make both ends meet in living at Madeley upon 70 - To say nothing of my having declined the offer of other livings, 3 or four times better, in a worldly view,

[and concludes]

. . . as my acting at present in a different line from You Sir will not hinder me to tending to the center, & endeavour at least to follow you as you follow the Lord. I hope also it will not impair the affection you have so long shewd to your unworthy Servant

Sir
J. Fletcher[41]

But matters did not end with an exchange of letters. John Wesley continued to scheme to lever Fletcher from Madeley for the following quarter-century. Fundamentally he seems to have objected to what he perceived as Fletcher's choice of a life of solitude over against the busy round of an itinerant preacher. As early as 1760 he was "laying a . . . plot" that Samuel Furly become Fletcher's curate[42] with the implication that

37. Matt 10:37.

38. See 1 Tim 3:7; 2 Tim 2:26. Fletcher burned much of his correspondence in 1776, which may account for the lack of many inward letters; see John Fletcher to Lady Huntingdon, May 28, 1777, in Forsaith, *Unexampled Labours*, 341.

39. 2 Cor 4:18; cf. Col 3:2.

40. See John Fletcher to Charles Wesley, Sept. 4, 1759, in Forsaith, *Unexampled Labours*, 74.

41. John Fletcher to John Wesley, Oct 27, 1760, in Forsaith, *Unexampled Labours*, 115–17.

42. John Wesley to Samuel Furly, Dec 9, 1760, in Telford, ed., *Letters*, 8:118.

Fletcher would be released for a wider sphere of work. More startling was his proposal to Fletcher the following year apparently to head the connexion:

> Your brother has done me the goodness to write to me very recently the extract from his letter is: "You are not fit to be alone you will do and receive much better among us, come and if you do not want to be my equal I will be below you" & C. In my last I mentioned to him that I was prepared to quit my benefice without repugnance should providence give me the signal, far from feeling myself attached here by particular views: but I make a distinction between his obliging invitation and the ordering of providence: I don't care to leave my post before I have been relieved by the sentry: I came passively, I will go in the same way.[43]

John Wesley seems to have misinterpreted Fletcher's inbuilt reticence and self-doubt for a mistaken calling. In 1773 Wesley suggested Fletcher accept nomination as his "successor," which Fletcher refused, repeating his sentiments half-humorously three years later: "but your recommending me to the societies as one who might succeed you (should the Lord call you hence before me) is a step to which I could by no means consent: It would make me take my horse, and gallop away."[44]

In 1781, following Fletcher's return from convalescence in Switzerland, Wesley listed Fletcher on his "stations" for London whereon Fletcher wrote to his wife-to-be: "The noise has spread that I am going to leave M–y; owing to the Minutes."[45] Whatever agreement Wesley may have thought he had with Fletcher, with whom he (and Coke and four other senior preachers) had conferred daily at the Leeds conference, it did not include Fletcher reneging on his commitment to his parish. Even after Fletcher's death Wesley suggested that his widow would fare better based in London, a suggestion she declined.[46]

John Wesley and Fletcher were temperamentally very different. Wesley found his environment most naturally in company, leadership, and busyness. For Fletcher, solitude, submissiveness, and quiet formed

---

43. John Fletcher to Charles Wesley, Aug 19, 1761, in Forsaith, *Unexampled Labours*, 134.

44. John Fletcher to John Wesley, Jan. 9, 1776, in Forsaith, *Unexampled Labours*, 335.

45. John Fletcher to Mary Bosanquet, Sept 2, 1781, (MARC, MAW Fl Box 36.3).

46. John Wesley to Mary Fletcher, Dec. 9, 1786, in Telford, *Letters*, 7:356.

his keel. Whatever doubts he may have vocalized about his calling, his actual commitment to his parish never wavered. For Wesley the world was his parish, for Fletcher his parish was his world, as Bishop Nuelsen put it on the bicentenary of Fletcher's birth.[47]

This contrasts with Fletcher's relationship with Charles Wesley, the "man born for friendship." They enjoyed what seems to have been a relationship of mutual trust and intimacy, Fletcher at one point writing that he could not conceive of a heaven without Charles Wesley there.[48] This, incidentally, does raise a curtain on the nature of some deep friendships between evangelicals: it was not just women who could be confidently confidential. Jeremy Gregory has discussed the identity of "Homo Religiosus" in eighteenth-century England as straddling a contrast between Continental (and Catholic) effeminacy and English muscular Protestantism,[49] although I am not sure how far Fletcher's friendship with Charles Wesley fits that analysis, nor others between Evangelical clergy and gentry more broadly.

The second area of tension subsists around John Wesley's 1786 *Short Account of the life and death of Mr Fletcher* for which Charles Wesley apparently promised an Elegy which never appeared.[50] Nor did other of Fletcher's friends provide Wesley with material he requested. I remain unrepentant in my criticism of Wesley's *Short Account*. I consider that it is unbalanced and inaccurate, in parts downright misleading. John Wesley's claim that he and Fletcher were "of one heart and soul"[51] and that they shared a long preaching journey at the least cannot be substantiated (which even Tyerman suspected),[52] and can most charitably be attributed to octogenarian amnesia.

---

47. "Für Wesley war die Welt sein Kirchspiel, für Fletcher war sein Kirchspiel seine Welt," in J. L. Nuelsen, *Der erste Schweizerische Methodist* (Zurich: Vereinsbuchandlung, 1929) 11.

48. John Fletcher to Charles Wesley, Nov. 15, 1759, in Forsaith, *Unexampled Labours*, 91.

49. Jeremy Gregory, "*Homo Religiosus*: Masculinity and Religion in the Long Eighteenth Century," in Tim Hitchcock and Michele Cohen, eds., *English Masculinities 1660-1800* (London: Longman, 1999) 85–110.

50. See Telford, *Letters*, 7:324, 356.

51. John Wesley, *A Short Account of the Life and Death of the Rev. John Fletcher* (London: Paramore, 1786) iii.

52. Tyerman, *Wesley's Designated Successor*, 354.

Fletcher's ministry in Madeley was relegated to just four pages—Wesley stated that he went there "according to his desire,"[53] inferring no providential direction. And Charles Wesley, who was Fletcher's closest friend besides his wife and the wealthy Bristol wine and sugar merchant, James Ireland, goes unmentioned. For these reasons alone, Wesley's *Short Account* is suspect. Its propagandist tenor sets it alongside other of Wesley's work: it is not so easy to dismiss it as Wesley in his anecdotage.

Yet the *Short Account* has shaped most understandings of Fletcher since and depicts Fletcher as Wesley's bulldog, in Henry Rack's phrase.[54] So Fletcher came to be seen as a progenitor of Wesleyan Methodism, the archetypal exemplar of Wesley's "Christian perfection" and his "Designated Successor," an image further promulgated in Benson's and Tyerman's lives and which probably governed Horne's editing of Fletcher's letters.[55]

The other influence on shaping the Fletcher legend, it has to be said, was his widow, who cultivated his memory, distributed mementos of her late husband, and continued his work. Hence my title "the long Fletcher incumbency"—the ministry of his memory was perpetuated long, long after his death. Maybe it is still so? Mary Fletcher interpreted their happy relationship as the blissful norm for his life, although it occupied less than the final four years, when his health was not at its best and his personality softened by age, tribulation, illness—and marriage. She depicted the man she had known and loved, which contributed to the legend of the "perfect man" and model husband. The idealized hagiography is in some ways a gendered creation.[56]

Fletcher's letters (as I have explored) tell a fuller story. They tell of uncertainty, of misunderstandings, of relationships, possibly betrothals, which seemingly ran into the sand. The happily married Fletcher was not the angst-ridden Fletcher he had sometimes been (as might also be said for Mary Bosanquet/Fletcher, or Abiah Darby), a man thoroughly cynical of marriage who seems to have chosen celibacy or, to see it from another side, became wedded to his parish.

---

53. Wesley, *Short Account*, 40.

54. Rack, *Reasonable Enthusiast*, 457.

55. Joseph Benson, *The Life of the Rev. John W. de la Flechere* (London, 1806); Tyerman, *Wesley's Designated Successor*; Melvill Horne, ed., *Posthumous Pieces* (London, 1791).

56. In Benson, *Life*, 339–54.

Wesley's omission of any account of the depth of friendship which subsisted between Fletcher and Charles Wesley might be thought puzzling. Perhaps, as Gareth Lloyd suggests, relationships between the Wesley brothers had so deteriorated by the 1780s that John Wesley was either unaware of their close friendship or preferred to ignore it.[57] Fletcher's letters to Charles are frank and personal; the few return letters which survive show that the relationship was reciprocal. Together, for instance, they shared a profound commitment to the Church of England and, in their different ways, fought to keep Methodism within the national church.

The constructed Fletcher narrative, its locus and context, has thus been distorted by biography, further magnified by erroneous published sources, then in turn taken up by historians (in default of other available sources), and needs to be remodeled. The recent internal reordering of St. Michael's parish church, Madeley, could serve as a parable. I suggest that Fletcher is better viewed in the ranks of Evangelical clergy, although in many ways he fits no template easily. The revisionist task is set within a wider revisionist agenda around the "Revival," which in part needs to set the record straight about Wesley and his "Methodism."

However, if my position is critical of John Wesley, I want to recognize that the reality may be that there are two sides to the question. I see Wesley biographically as the distorter of Fletcher's image, as the usurper of his brother Charles' claim to deep friendship. But that may not be the case seen through a wider historical lens, and theologians may want to take strong exception. Might it be put that they brought out the best in each other? Although emphatically Arminian, Fletcher was strongly nonpartisan, so while he supported Wesley it was not an exclusive adherence. To put it slightly differently, while Fletcher stood by Wesley doctrinally, that was not the whole of his doctrinal compass, but neither would he renege on his loyalty even when Wesley seemed to want to fence him in.

Wesley, on the other hand, habitually exercised domination over his preachers and people, which captivated some while alienating others. He might have said "he who is not for me is against me;" Fletcher (and this is also true of Mary Fletcher) would not be awed. They would remain their own people, following their calling. A cynic might suggest that they were too well regarded for Wesley to alienate, but I think

57. Lloyd, *Charles Wesley*, 214–17.

the evidence suggests that Wesley was not always too bothered in that direction. He distanced himself from George Whitefield and Lady Huntingdon fairly decisively. Did he sense that otherworldliness in Fletcher which so many sensed (and which defies cold dissection) but which he could not but respect.

I might suggest that it was integrated paradoxes in Fletcher's life which made him appear saintly: the belligerent soldier who championed peace, the elite gentleman who embraced simplicity and poverty, the unbookish scholar, the confirmed bachelor yet contented husband. But I am not a psychologist and would not want to overstress this Jungian approach.

Another light on Fletcher which shows his place on the wider map appears in two letters which survive of late 1774. At the height of the Calvinistic Controversy, when Fletcher was taken up defending Wesley's Arminianism, he wrote to Lord Dartmouth, who on the eve of the American Revolution was Secretary to the Colonies:

> Madeley 19th. Sept 1774
>
> My Lord
> As soon as I had the honour of your letter I wrote to Mr. Ireland and an American friend to inform them of your gracious intentions. I expected to hear from Mr. Ireland, that I might join his thanks to mine, but finding that he has been gone to France for some time, I can no longer differ acknowledging the receit of your letter, and humbly thanking you for the contents . . .
> . . . While your Lordship tries to restore harmony between the English and the Americans; in my little way I try (a no less difficult task!) to reconcile heated Augustine with heated Pelagius; and I go as far, in upon the arminian scheme, to meet the Calvinists as reason and scripture allow me. I shall take the liberty to transmit privately to your Lordship a copy of my plan of reconciliation when it is finished, in hope that you might relax your mind from state-labours by perusing it. If it should appear to do in general justice to reason and scripture, might not a hint from you, My Lord, to Mr. Newton (or Mr. Venn) make him draw up a plan of reconciliation also, with a design to come as near the anticalvinists as reason and conscience will let him. Should he hit upon a more reasonable and scriptural method, it would be I think, the joy of my heart to adopt it, and recommend it to others. Tho' bigots will not be reconciled, yet judicious and candid persons may; and some private hints from your Lordship

might do more towards so desirable an event, than polemical tracts, which too often embarass instead of clearing the question. I beg your Lordship would forgive my taking so much of your time: but precious as I am conscious it is, I must intrude upon one moment more to assure you, My Lord, that I am

> Your Lordship's
> grateful and obedient
> tho' unworthy Servant
>
> J. Fletcher[58]

Note that Fletcher was consulting, not with either Wesley, but with James Ireland, and an "American friend," presumably the extrovert Captain Thomas Webb, whom Fletcher had married to Grace Gilbert (Melvill Horne's aunt) in Shropshire the previous year.

This tantalizing letter raises several issues. First, the suggestion is that Lord Dartmouth had offered Fletcher patronage, and by inference, an appointment in America. Another letter, surviving in the same archive, is from the Methodist preacher Thomas Rankin, in Philadelphia, to Lord Dartmouth that December. He had seen "a few lines that your Lordship had wrote to Mr. Fletcher in which you mention Captain Webb . . . " and later in the letter refers to "a worthy good man in your eye, whom you thought would make an acceptable Bishop for America . . . But I am ready to think, that our political troubles must first Subside before your Lordship will be instrumental of making such an happy Era, to take place in this land."[59]

Had Lord Dartmouth, on the eve of the American Revolution, offered Fletcher a senior church position in America—even Episcopal? Does this relate to what John Wesley recorded two years later, that, through Lord Dartmouth, Fletcher was offered (but declined) preferment?[60] An enticing prospect for speculation, but history by contrafactuals, while tempting, is to be firmly resisted. Yet the intriguing question remains: What were Lord Dartmouth's "gracious inten-

---

58. John Fletcher to Lord Dartmouth, Sept. 19, 1774, (Staffordshire County Record Office, Dartmouth papers, D(W) 1778 V697 Box 2). Used with the kind permission of the Earl of Dartmouth.

59. Thomas Rankin to Lord Dartmouth, Dec. 29, 1774, (Staffordshire CRO, Dartmouth papers, D(W) 1778/11/104). Used with the kind permission of the Earl of Dartmouth.

60. Wesley, *Short Account*, 15.

tions," which might have extended the transatlantic influence Fletcher later exercised through his writings?

Fletcher was also clear on another matter: that there was an essential unity across the Evangelical Revival, and one which was being destroyed by the polemical quarrels which he so loathed. The image of "early Methodism" conjured by Wesley's literature, his letters and journal (that "misleading document" as I heard Henry Rack describe it recently), depicts a network of societies, classes, bands, all "in connexion" with him, whereas there was in reality a wider but less organized network of clergy and parishes sympathetic to evangelicalism. Calvinistic and Arminian clergy were active in their parishes: some were known for who they were (John Berridge, John Newton, Henry Venn, Samuel Walker),[61] others merged with the scenery more subtly.

Fletcher was more concerned to make peace than to perpetuate the conflict and was, as was said after his death, too great a man to bear the name of any sect.[62] While firmly loyal to the Wesleys, doctrinally and connexionally, he cast his networks much wider. He was an Evangelical who was instrumental in running a regional clergy society across diocesan boundaries (Lichfield, Worcester, and Hereford).[63] His relations with such clergy also transcended dogmatic, polemical territory, and he always maintained his links with sympathetically minded local colleagues, even inviting his polemical opponent Richard Hill (a layman) to Madeley to preach "to cement love."[64] There is ample scope for continuing study of Arminian-Evangelical clergy and their networks, for a broader analysis of "Methodism."

Over the years I have been studying Fletcher I have become accustomed to seeing, in my mind and imagination, historical events and people, not from a metropolitan perspective nor from that of Mr. Wesley's saddle or chaise, but from East Shropshire. What was it like to be located in this "howling wilderness,"[65] largely out of the way of the

---

61. See Donald M. Lewis, ed. *The Blackwell Dictionary of Evangelical Biography 1730–1860* (Oxford: Blackwell, 1995); L. E. Elliott-Binns, *The Early Evangelicals: A Religious and Social Study* (London: Lutterworth, 1953).

62. James Ireland to Mary Fletcher, Nov. 6, 1785, (MARC, Fl4/1/14).

63. Peter S. Forsaith, "An Eighteenth Century Worcester Association," in Wesley Historical Society West Midlands Branch *Silver Jubilee Miscellany 1965–1990* (Warwick, 1990).

64. John Fletcher to James Ireland, c. 1781 (MARC, MAW Fl/3.3).

65. John Fletcher to Lady Huntingdon, Jan. 6, 1761, in Tyerman, *Wesley's Designated Successor*, 62.

world? There is more space for locally based accounts of church life; the hegemonic national picture is not always the main narrative.[66]

My final conclusions will be very brief, and perhaps help to stimulate discussion. How are we to continue to work on reassessment? By careful reference to the sources. In Fletcher's case I would argue that his letters represent the central primary source for study of his life. He kept no journal, his published writings were in the most part edited fairly significantly, and secondary narratives are unreliable. The use of original sources has challenged—and will continue to challenge—received understandings of the Fletchers, their circles, and their parish. Fidelity to those sources, and preparedness to overwrite even long-held narratives or assumptions will be a central facet of continuing research.

Yet for the East Shropshire coalfield area we also have particularly rich material sources: the evidence of industrial archaeology and other local studies which provide nondocumentary insights into the place and people which have been. These too are sources to be given due weight and to which historians owe as much relentless fidelity as to, say, Fletcher's letters in French. So not only are there multiple sources, but the imperative of a multidisciplinary approach.

This conference has brought together historians ecclesiastical, industrial, and general, theologians, academics, and others. In any field scholars from different disciplines need to be talking together and learning from each other. Certainly, that must be true around the Fletchers, and the success of this conference will be measured by how we continue to talk and learn and—I hope—together find in the Fletchers of Madeley and their context that crossroads of issues which speaks to a wider audience.

66. A point made by David Hempton, *Methodism: Empire of the Spirit*, 78ff.

Contributors

Carol Blessing is Professor of Literature, Point Loma Nazarene University, USA.

Peter S. Forsaith is Research Fellow at The Oxford Centre for Methodism and Church History, Oxford Brookes University, UK.

William Gibson is Professor of Ecclesiastical History and Director of The Oxford Centre for Methodism and Church History, Oxford Brookes University, UK.

Jeremy Gregory is Professor of the History of Christianity, The University of Manchester, UK.

Geordan Hammond is Lecturer in Church History and Wesley Studies, Nazarene Theological College and Director of the Manchester Wesley Research Centre, UK.

John H. Lenton is Honorary Librarian, Wesley Historical Society, UK.

Peter James Lineham is Associate Professor of History and Regional Director for the College of Humanities and Social Sciences, Massey University Albany Campus, New Zealand.

Kenneth M. Loyer is Pastor of Otterbein United Methodist Church of Spry and Adjunct Lecturer, United Theological Seminary, USA.

Brett C. McInelly is Associate Professor of British Literature, Brigham Young University, USA.

Harold E. Raser is Professor of the History of Christianity, Nazarene Theological Seminary, USA.

Barrie Trinder is a writer, lecturer, and consultant on industrial archaeology and social history, UK.

David R. Wilson is Adjunct Professor of Theology, George Fox University, USA.

Eryn M. White is Senior Lecturer in the Department of History and Welsh History, Aberystwyth University, UK.

Laurence W. Wood is Frank Paul Morris Professor of Theology and Wesley Studies, Asbury Theological Seminary, USA.

Index